New York   Jan. 15—**Departure**

S0-BBM-848

Bermuda

Feb. 1

Clipperton Rock

EQUATOR

Fernando de Noronha

EQUATOR

Cape St. Roque

Galapagos Isls.

Feb. 15

April 15

San Felix Isl.

San Ambrosio Isl.

Rio
de Janeiro

Sala-y-Gomez

Juan Fernandez Isls.

Valparaiso

Montevideo   March 1

River Plate

April 1

March 15

0° South Pacific

50° South Atlantic

Magellan
Strait

Falkland Isls.

Staten Isl.

Cape St. John

Diego Ramirez

Le Marie Strait

Cape Horn

LONGBOAT TO HAWAII

Clipper Hornet, starboard bow view at sea. From a painting by Frank Vining Smith. Seamen's Bank for Savings, New York

LONGBOAT TO HAWAII

*An Account
of the Voyage
of the Clipper Ship
HORNET of New York
Bound for San Francisco
in 1866*

As Recorded in the Journals of

CAPTAIN JOSIAH A. MITCHELL, Master

HENRY FERGUSON, Passenger

SAMUEL FERGUSON, Passenger

Together with Observations on the Burning of the
Vessel at Sea and the Subsequent Miraculous Preservation
of Fifteen Persons During a 43-Day, 4,000-Mile Voyage
to Hawaii in the Ship's Longboat, as Prepared by a
Newspaper Reporter Writing under the Pen Name of

MARK TWAIN

Assembled and Edited
and with a Foreword and Afterword by

ALEXANDER CROSBY BROWN

CORNELL MARITIME PRESS, INC.

Cambridge   Maryland

Copyright © 1974 by Alexander Crosby Brown

All Rights Reserved

Library of Congress Cataloging in Publication Data

Brown, Alexander Crosby, 1905-   comp.
    Longboat to Hawaii.

    Bibliography: p.
    Includes index.
    1. Hornet (Clipper-ship) 2. Shipwrecks.
3. Voyages to the Pacific coast. I. Title.
G530.H82B76   910'.45   74-22317
ISBN 0—87033—201-5

Printed and Bound in the United States of America

Vignette from BALLOU'S PICTORIAL, Oct. 6, 1855

Jacket illustration, "Clipper Ship Hornet . . . on fire," *from a print after the painting by Charles Rosner, 1941. Courtesy the Mariners Museum, Newport News, Virginia.*

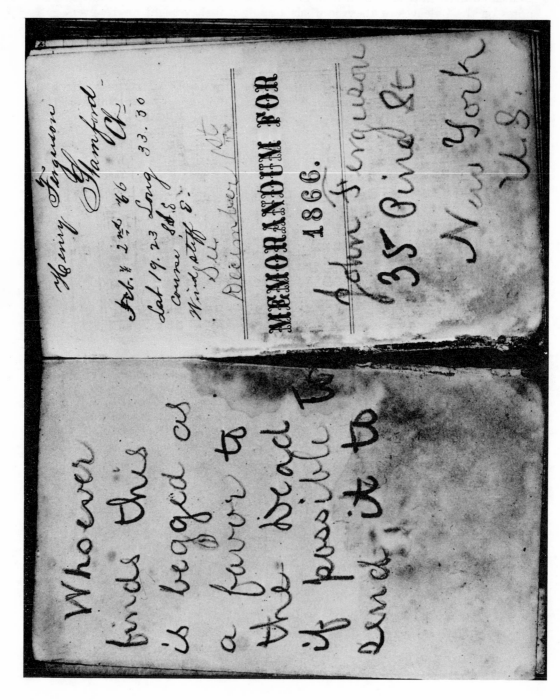

Henry Ferguson
Stamford Ct

Feb. 4 1865 46
Lat 19. 23 Long 33. 30
course SSS
Wind stiff E.

December 1st
Sid.

MEMORANDUM FOR
1866.

John Ferguson
35 Pine St
New York
U.S.

Whoever
finds this
is begged as
a favor to
the dead
if possible to
send it to

Note on the flyleaf of Henry Ferguson's journal.   Actual Size

TABLE OF CONTENTS

Coleman's California Line sailing card. State Street Trust Co., Boston.

FOREWORD

On January 15, 1866, the American clipper ship *Hornet* left her home port of New York on a routine voyage to San Francisco via Cape Horn. She carried a full cargo which included principally cases of candles and barreled kerosene oil. Also loaded were 400 tons of Pacific Railroad iron and three steam engines. Although at this time the *Hornet* was fifteen years old, she was still a fine, well found and smartly manned vessel, equal to any in this, the heyday of sail in the United States Merchant Marine. There were thirty-one people on board the clipper including the ship's ordinary complement of officers and crew, and two passengers, brothers from Stamford, Connecticut.

The *Hornet* made an exceptionally fine passage around the dreaded cape of storms and nothing of particular note occurred until the morning of May 3, with the greater part of the voyage safely accomplished and the ship ghosting along in almost flat calm near the equator, a thousand miles or so west of the Galapagos Islands. On that fatal day, the mate went below to draw some varnish from a cask carrying an open light. The varnish accidentally spilled and immediately ignited, flaring up through the open booby hatch and setting on fire sails suspended from yards above. Within seconds, the flames spread ravenously, aloft and alow, so sealing the ship's doom and making it imperative for her company to take to the boats without a moment's delay.

Over the years there have been many and varied reasons why men have deliberately embarked upon ocean voyages in small, open boats. But, for those undertaken in desperate haste in the wake of disaster, none, not even that of the famous *Bounty*'s launch, can match the voyage which then ensued for the men in the *Hornet*'s longboat. Though two of the three boats launched from the clipper were never heard from again, the seaworthy 21-foot longboat with fifteen men on board made an incredible passage of four thousand miles to Hawaii, her crew subsisting for six desperate weeks on rations which would be considered short for even a voyage of ten days.

Their salvation was due in very considerable part to the seamanly skills and resourcefulness of Captain Josiah Angier Mitchell, a remarkable "Down East" shipmaster in the finest tradition, and to the courage and faith of his two passengers — 19-year-old Henry Ferguson, a student at Trinity College of the class of 1868, and his 28-year-old brother Samuel, a 1857 Trinity graduate. Samuel was going to California with his younger brother for company hoping the climate would improve his weak lungs for he was suffering from consumption.

For nineteen days the *Hornet*'s three boats kept together with the longboat towing the quarter boats as they struggled to escape the clutch of the doldrums. The captain then reluctantly concluded that each boat would fare better on its own and stand a greater chance of being picked up sailing independently. What little food then remaining was divided and they went their separate ways.

Captain Mitchell sought to reach some islands, then designated the American Group — indicated on the charts as doubtful and bitterly proven non-existent when the longboat later sailed right over their assumed position. But hope never left the starving men and they continued on their westerly course hoping at length to reach the "Sandwich Islands," as Hawaii was then called. Finally, after enduring incredible hardship including a threat of mutiny on the part of a few then mentally deranged sailors, the fifteen men — mere skeletons of their former selves — landed at a little settlement named Laupahoehoe on the rock-bound windward side of the island of Hawaii. Friendly natives recognized their plight and swam out to guide the longboat to a safe haven and the 43-day ordeal was over. Even Captain Bligh's voyage — he had navigated the *Bounty* launch 3,600 miles from a point in mid-Pacific to the East Indies island of Timor — could hardly equal the performance of Captain Mitchell's craft. In 1789, Bligh and eighteen loyal members of the *Bounty*'s crew had been turned adrift in a 23-foot open launch by mutineers. But they managed to reach safety at the Dutch island haven after sailing from May 3 to June 14 with a short pause at an islet of the Great Barrier Reef on the way.

From the beginning of the *Hornet's* voyage, both Captain Mitchell and the two passengers kept pocket-size journals — simple, ingenuous documents they turned out — in which they were recording for their own and later, hopefully, their families' pleasure each day's events as they occurred. Providentially, they managed to save these little notebooks to take with them into the longboat, shielding them from the weather, and they continued faithfully to record as much as their strengths would permit right through to the end. As remarkable accounts as have ever been written resulted and reading them today makes one feel vividly a part of their lives and inheritor of their incredible courage.

When the voyage commenced on leaving New York, both brothers stated that they liked Captain Mitchell immediately and he, too, felt that his passengers would make good quarter-deck company to have on board the ship. From the initial entries we learn that on January 15, 1866, the *Hornet's* lines were cast off and the clipper started down the harbor in tow of the paddlewheel steam tug *Wm. Fletcher*. The weather was foul. In a blizzard ensuing, some of the crew working in the rigging became badly frostbitten.

Happily, the *Hornet* soon gained more decent weather on entering the Gulf Stream and the brothers settled down to a routine of pleasurable activity — reading, studying, observing things around and about the ship, learning navigation from the captain and the mates, learning the ways of the ship in the midst of the sea. Card games in the cabin were the rule after supper, so wiling away long evenings. Saturday nights brought out the grog and the traditional toast "to wives and sweethearts" — a good custom, Samuel observed. Thus passed the time on a passage expected to be in the neighborhood of four months duration.

The voyage was routine business for the captain, though. His diary is generally brief and cryptic, concerned principally with the weather and the business of the ship, though he did observe that one Sunday was a "home-thinking day". But for the Fergusons, it was a unique adventure, chronicled sometimes in prose of almost lyric quality. On one occasion Samuel noted that "the brisk breeze made everything lovely and the waves danced about as if they were having a real good time." And, on another he observed, "sunsets are our nightly treats and beautiful they are, too — always varied and always different." Henry commented on "the most lovely green clouds I ever saw against a golden background." And so it was, with wonder and awe, they recorded the first flying fish to come aboard, their first sight of the Southern Cross, their first wandering albatross.

February 11 came along and that night Sam's twenty-eighth birthday was observed by toasting him with a glass of Madeira. Henry's turn came with his nineteenth birthday on April 18. They opened a bottle of sherry to celebrate, but Henry confessed continuing concern for Sam's cough. Meanwhile, the homemade gingersnaps they'd brought with them were still crisp and tasty — Captain Mitchell thought them delicious.

The captain, too, had a birthday during the trip — his fifty-fourth. There was no celebration, though, for by then the *Hornet* was gone and they had already been more than five weeks in the longboat. "Still permitted to live and write," the captain recorded, however, adding, "This is my birthday. God grant it may be to me a new birth day for my soul . . . Nothing to eat, sucking rags and leather, hoping to be preserved to reach the [Hawaiian] islands, which may God in His great mercy grant. We have been spared so long, 40 days to-day, that we dare think we may arrive."

What courage!

Only two days later, Henry was to write: "Most lovely rainbow last evening . . . It is a good sign. Saw new moon. God has spared us wonderfully to see it."

And the next day they saw the land!

Mark Twain was in Honolulu at the time the electrifying message was received announcing the longboat's safe arrival at Laupahoehoe. A fledgling newspaper correspondent, 31-year-old Samuel Langhorne Clemens had only recently begun to use his later famous alias. At the time, he was touring the Hawaiian Islands on a roving assignment and recording his impressions in a series of "letters" he had been commissioned to prepare for the *Sacramento* [California] *Daily Union*.

Though laid up with saddle boils following an enterprising horseback excursion, Clemens had himself taken to the hospital where the first contingent of the *Hornet's* people had been brought from Hilo. There he was able to interview them and take down the testimony of the Third Mate and several seamen. Then, apparently being more enterprising than other Honolulu correspondents, he sat up all night writing up the story for his newspaper. The very next morning, his manuscript was tossed on board the packet schooner *Milton Badger* which had already cast off her lines as she started out for the States. And it so became the first full account of this remarkable event to reach the mainland.

Mark Twain followed his famous scoop — for journals all over the country avidly copied the *Sacramento Union's* account — with a more leisurely prepared article based on the journals kept by Captain Mitchell and the Ferguson brothers. Since the writer accompanied them on the same ship back to San Francisco, the bark *Smyrniote*, he had plenty of time to copy out what parts from all three narratives that took his fancy. "Literary gold," he subsequently characterized them. From all this, plus the material obtained during his first interview, eventuated a dramatic story which he sold to *Harper's New Monthly Magazine*, then one of America's most influential eastern journals.

In later years, Mark Twain recognized this contribution as the first giant step of his subsequently meteoric career in letters — a fact acknowledged thirty years later when he rewrote the *Harper's* article for *Century Magazine*, entitling it "My Début as a Literary Person."

In the ensuing text, we present not only full transcriptions of all three journals themselves, but also Mark Twain's running commentary as taken from his articles. Rather than present each journal separately from beginning to end, we have elected here to print all three daily entries on the same page, adding Mark Twain's notes for that particular day as well. Expectedly, this triplicates the record of identical events by three separate writers, but it gives the reader the chance to compare their different viewpoints as they wrote them.

Captain Mitchell is terse and to the point, as one would expect of a ship master. Yet as their pitiful supplies diminished, he recorded drawing more and more strength from the Lord and He sustained him to the end. Young Henry Ferguson, exuberant and keen, shows the vision of a young man — a boy really — embarked on the greatest adventure of his life. Samuel Ferguson, incurably ill and well aware of it, is determined to make the best of everything, writing often with depth and feeling and rarely complaining.

Herein every attempt has been made to use the diarists' exact words — a task reasonably easy in the beginning when their authors composed them neatly in ink and at leisure in the comforts of the ship's cabin — more difficult when subsequently written in pencil in the always tossing, often spume-drenched open boat. In all cases a propensity of the writers to abbreviate has been checked. The average reader would be slowed down while he tried to figure out what was meant by such a passage as "Brg in Co." And so we have spelled out in full "brig in company" and other abbreviated entries. We have also brought some of the spelling in line with present day usage. Henry's journal gives bonito in at least three different spellings — none correct. Captain Mitchell recorded the old fashioned Honolula.

Except for these amendations which go unmarked, the customary convention of including added or explanatory matter within square brackets has been followed. Another departure from the originals is that although all three diarists noted the ship's position at the head of each daily entry, since they generally agreed, we have included the position only once, as Captain Mitchell recorded it.

With the exception of occasional brief footnotes expressly credited to Mark Twain (as taken from comments in his printed *Harper's* and *Century* articles), all other footnotes have been supplied by this editor. We have tried not to go overboard, supplying only such additional information as seemed interesting or clarifying. But in this age of motor propelled small craft, we felt it necessary to explain at least what the diarists meant by an "ash breeze." Few people walk, let alone row, any more!

The lion's share of the long, difficult and frequently tedious task of transcribing the journals to prepare a typescript was undertaken — albeit somewhat reluctantly — by my wife, then Miss Shirley Baysden of the staff of The Mariners Museum of Newport News,

Virginia. A series of checks and double checks, with revised drafts then being typed out as required, eventually reduced the copy to the near-perfect version that follows, as typed for printing by Mrs. Lillenas Ward for Multi-Print of Hampton, Virginia.

My most profound gratitude goes to the owners of the original manuscripts at the time I needed to consult them: Mr. Samuel Ferguson [II] of Hartford, Connecticut, for the journal of his father, Henry Ferguson; Mr. Henry L. Ferguson of Fishers Island, New York, for the journal of his uncle, Samuel Ferguson; and Mrs. C.L. Tilden of Alameda, California, and Mrs. Chester Hudson Hatch of Auburn, California, for the journal of their ancestor, Captain Mitchell.

These generous people consented to part with their treasured documents long enough to forward them to me at The Mariners Museum for copying. Accordingly, photostats were promptly made at the blueprint laboratory of the Newport News Shipbuilding and Dry Dock Company under the direction of Mr. Andrew Hull, the originals being promptly returned. These photostat copies were deposited in the Library of The Mariners Museum, then presided over by Miss Cerinda W. Evans.

The journal owners also consented to the publication of the documents if undertaken unspectacularly as a public service. This has now been accomplished, so enabling the accounts to be shared in their original form by a wider audience and making it possible for more people to learn of this epic chapter in the story of man's conquest of the seas.

Similarly, Messrs. Harper and Brothers (now Harper and Row), publishers, holders of copyrights for most of Mark Twain's writings, granted me permission to use such of his material here as pertained to the *Hornet*. And the California State Library kindly supplied a photostat copy of Mark Twain's famous newspaper "scoop" in the July 19, 1866 issue of the Sacramento *Daily Union*.

Undertaking the preliminary work a number of years ago, as a project of the Mariners Museum of Newport News, Virginia, was enthusiastically endorsed by the museum's then president and board chairman, Homer L. Ferguson. But delays ensued and, compounded by the advent of World War II and my departure on active duty in the United States Naval Reserve, it was subsequently decided that other hands should undertake the publication.

Many persons have helped me along the way. It would be impossible to cite them all, but the following made significant contributions of advice and encouragement: James Norman Hall, famous co-author of the *Bounty* books; Miss Marian Mitchell, Captain Mitchell's well-traveled granddaughter; Lincoln Colcord, beloved "Sage of Searsport," more knowledgeable than any on the subject of the American Merchant Marine under sail; Miss Marjorie Dent Candee, an editor of *The Lookout*, published by the Seaman's Church Institute of New York; Lawrence W. Jenkins, director of the Peabody Museum of Salem, Massachusetts; John L. Lochhead, librarian of the Mariners Museum; and editors and publishers Edward H. Dodd, Jr., my former class- and shipmate; Robert E. Farlow; Basil Davenport and, latterly, Miss Regina Ryan and Mrs. Iris M. Wiley.

Dr. George J. Ryan professor of ancient languages at the College of William and Mary in Virginia, kindly undertook the translation of three entries appearing in the journals which scholarly young Henry Ferguson, to amuse himself, had written in school-boy Greek!

Particularly I appreciate the encouragement of the following old and fast friends: Frank O. Braynard of the South Street Seaport Museum and a maritime historian of note; Professor John Haskell Kemble of Pomona College, Claremont, California, for his unflagging enthusiasm for the project; and Frank R. Hannah, owner of the Multi-Print Company of Hampton, who is largely responsible for the production of this handsome, well-printed volume. Photographer Bill Radcliffe was of great help with the illustrations.

Thomas McCance, my ever trusted right bower, and his good wife Elizabeth Ferguson McCance, have had firm faith in the task from the very beginning. Betty McCance's keen interest stems from the fact that she is the granddaughter of the diarist Henry Ferguson, he whose faith never faltered during the long and harrowing ordeal of the *Hornet's* longboat.

Newport News, Virginia   ALEXANDER CROSBY BROWN

PART I—THE SHIP

Clipper Hornet, starboard beam view at sea. Captain Benson's painting presented to Seamen's Church Institute, New York

THE SHIP

HORNET, by Octavius T. Howe, M.D., and Frederick C. Matthews *

Extreme clipper ship, built by Westervelt & Mackay, at New York, and launched June 20, 1851. 207' x 40' x 22'; 1426 tons. She was very sharp, had a flush deck and was one of the finest modeled and best constructed vessels afloat. Chamberlain & Phelps of New York were her owners.

Her maiden passage was 155 days from New York to San Francisco and being made in the face of extreme difficulties, was no criterion of what her sail abilities were. She made nine passages, subsequently, from eastern ports to San Francisco, averaging 121 5/9 days; shortest, 106, 111 and 113 days; longest, 131 and 135 days. On the fastest run she was 19 days from New York to the line and 18 days from the equator to the bar off San Francisco. On two other occasions she had the excellent runs of 19 days and 18 days from the equator in the Pacific to anchorage in San Francisco Bay. In 1854 she was ten days between the two 50's and in 1855 had 17 days from off Cape St. Roque to 50° South. On her passage of 124 days in 1863 she made the excellent run of 56 days from 50° South in the Atlantic and 41 days from 50° South in the Pacific, to San Francisco. On some of her homeward passages she also did most excellent work. San Francisco to Panama in 33 days, anchor to anchor, in 1852; in 1853, San Francisco to Callao in 34 days, having made Pt. St. Elena, Gulf of Guayaquil, when 21 days and 22 hours out. This is the record passage to Callao by the eastern route and within two days of record by the western course. In 1857 she was only 47 days from Calcutta to the Cape of Good Hope; in 1859, 88 days from San Francisco to New York and the following year, 96 days over the same course. In 1861 her passage from New York to Bristol, England, was 14 days and 20 hours and in 1865, 58 days from Tome, Chile, to New York.

On her first run she left New York, Aug. 21, 1851, deeply laden, drawing 20 feet and 6 inches. On deck she had two boilers with stacks, totaling 49 tons weight, for the steamer *Senator*,[1] and these had to be thrown overboard during a severe gale in which the ship was laboring hard. Except for one good day of 318 miles, she had no change; gales, light winds and calms prevailing throughout. In addition to this, Captain Lawrence was sick and on arrival out the mate and steward were under arrest. She was 73 days to the Horn, off which she was 17 days; thence 36 days to the equator and 26 days from there to port. Sailed from San Francisco, Mar. 1st, with 300 passengers for Panama and made the run in 33 days; thence about 90 days to Hong Kong and 117 days from Whampoa to New York.

On her second voyage, the *Hornet* left New York, Apr. 26, 1853, and two days later the *Flying Cloud*[2] sailed, both for San Francisco. The *Hornet* had a very poor start, as on Apr. 29th the *Cloud* had caught up with and passed her, being about 12 miles in the lead; this lead was slowly increased in the Atlantic and in rounding the Horn an additional five days was gained, the *Cloud* being seven days ahead at the crossing of 50° South, in the Pacific. The *Hornet* gained two days thence to the line, crossing in 113° West, after which Captain Knapp made practically a direct course to destination, thereby recovering not only her handicap but actually arriving off San Francisco Bar one day ahead of the *Cloud*. Cressy, in the *Cloud*, crossed the line three degrees to the eastward, going out to longitude 140° 43', and as far north as latitude 38° 30', thereby covering a much greater distance. Both ships arrived in San Francisco harbor, Aug. 12th, the *Hornet*, 45 minutes ahead; she had been off port one whole day in the fog. The *Hornet's* passage, 106 days; best day, 281 miles; *Flying Cloud's* passage, 104 days, best day, 316 miles. Off the Horn, the *Hornet* saw the clippers, *Eclipse*[3] and *John Land*[4] and led them into San Francisco, 5 days and 14 days, respectively. Continuing this voyage the *Hornet* was 34 days to Callao and from there went to Philadelphia, arriving Apr. 9, 1854.

* *AMERICAN CLIPPER SHIPS, 1833 - 1858. Salem, Massachusetts: Marine Research Society, Publication No. 13, 1926. (Vol. I, pp. 268-272.)*

THE BOSTON-BUILT CLIPPER SHIP "FLYING CLOUD," LOADING AT HER WHARF IN NEW YORK.

Woodcut of Flying Cloud *at New York. Gleason's Pictorial July 26, 1851*

The third voyage was made under Captain Benson and was 126 days from Philadelphia to San Francisco, with 1½ days calms off the Horn and five days calms north of the line in the Pacific. Had skysails set for 91 days on the passage. Returned to New York via Mazatlan, Mexico. Captain Benson again took the *Hornet* out to San Francisco, being 113 days from New York, but was close to the California coast on the 107th day, then having six days of calms. Went to Calcutta in 69 days and was thence 102 days to New York; crossed to London and thence to Calcutta; passed the Lizard, Jan. 12, 1857, and was 97 days thence to destination. Sailed from Calcutta, June 28, 1857, and on the 47th day was off the Cape of Good Hope.

On her fifth passage to San Francisco, the *Hornet* arrived out, May 28, 1859, Captain Mitchell in command, in 128 days from Boston. The *Flying Childers*[5] reached port the same day, in 117 days from the same port. The *Hornet* returned to New York, direct, in 87 days. The following year she reached San Francisco, Sept. 4th, in 135 days from New York. Had light winds and calms nearly all the passage except 12 days of severe gales off the Plate and 15 days of heavy weather off the Horn. Returned to New York, direct, in 96 days; passed the Horn, 47 days out. From New York she crossed to Bristol, England, in 14 days and 20 hours and returned in 27 days, in ballast. On the outward passage had a hurricane

- 16 -

of 20 hours in which she had bulwarks stove, decks cleared and cabin filled. On the return had much fog and generally light and baffling winds. She then loaded for San Francisco and was 131 days on the passage; then went to Valparaiso in the fine time of 42 days; thence to Iquique and Pisagua and arrived at Philadelphia, July 23, 1862; reached New York, Aug. 4th, two days from Philadelphia, with nitrate of soda, part of her inward cargo. Again loaded for San Francisco and arrived out Feb. 17, 1863, in 124 days. Was 30 days to the line; 38 days thence to 50° South, in gales and calms; in a pampero, had bulwarks stove, lost sails and had jibs washed from the booms; was 15 days between the 50's, 21 days to the equator and 20 days to port. From San Francisco took a wheat cargo to Liverpool, in 120 days; loaded coal for New York and was 32 days crossing over, the final 20 days being nearly a calm. Arrived at New York, Oct. 3, 1863.

In December 1863, the *Hornet*, Captain Harding, and the *Star Of The Union*,[6] Captain Reed, were loading at New York for San Francisco. The two captains bet $500 each that their respective ships would arrive out in 120 days or less. Both lost as the *Star* reached port Apr. 1st, in 121 days, while the *Hornet* was at the Heads, but not at anchor, on her 120th day. The *Hornet* had been 23 days to the line; 53 days to 50° South; 18 days rounding the Horn; 103 days to the equator and 18 days thence to port. She returned to New York, direct, in 101 days. Went back to San Francisco, in 111 days; thence to Valparaiso; thence to Tome where a cargo of wool was loaded and the passage to New York was made in 58 days.

At New York, Capt. Josiah A. Mitchell again took command of the *Hornet* and after loading a full cargo, including 45 barrels and 2000 cases of oil and 6195 boxes of candles, she sailed Jan. 11, 1866, for San Francisco. Light winds were experienced from the start, the line being crossed 30 days out; on May 2nd they were on the equator, in the Pacific, 111 days out. The following morning, at 7 o'clock the mate went below to draw some varnish, when his lantern caused an explosion, the flames from which shot up through the open hatch and ignited the crossjack, which was hanging clewed up. The fire spread and in a short time the whole ship was in flames and all hands were obliged to leave the ship in haste. Captain Mitchell took two passengers, the third mate and eleven men in the long boat; the first mate and eight of the crew were in one quarter boat and the second officer and six men in the other quarter boat. At 8 o'clock the masts went over the side and at 5 A.M., May 4th, the ship went down. The position was latitude 2° North, longitude 112° 30′ West, being 1250 miles south of Cape St. Lucas and about 2500 miles southeast of the Island of Hawaii. The three boats kept together for 19 days before separating, at which time they divided what few remaining stores were left and then parted on different courses. The captain's boat reached Laupahoehoe, Island of Hawaii, on June 15th, two natives swimming out through the surf and assisting in the rescue. All the 15 were in a pitiable condition after being in the boat 43 days, being practically starving; latterly had been reduced to eating scraped boot leather and an occasional flying fish which blundered into the boat. The consul at Hilo[7] promptly relieved Captain Mitchell of the care of his men.

Nothing was ever heard of the fate of the two quarter boats, containing the first and second mates and fourteen members of the crew. The *Hornet* and cargo were insured for $400,000.

---

1   The wooden hull paddle steamer SENATOR, 219 feet long, was built in New York in 1847 for use on the New England coast. She soon joined the ranks of boats sailing around Cape Horn to California during the Gold Rush, proving a bonanza to her enterprising owners on arrival. The SENATOR served continuously on the West Coast until 1870 and was ultimately dismantled in Australia in 1882.

2   The FLYING CLOUD was the most famous of all American clipper ships. Built by Donald McKay at East Boston, Massachusetts, in 1851, this "extreme clipper" measured 1,782 tons and was 229 feet long by 40.8 feet beam by 21.6 feet deep. She made two record runs from New York to San Francisco of only 89 days — in 1851 and again in 1854. Her famous race over this course with the HORNET in 1853 ended in 105 days. (Particulars on the FLYING CLOUD and other clipper ships cited in this section are taken from Carl C. Cutler's authoritative GREYHOUNDS OF THE SEA, New York, 1930.)

3 The ECLIPSE had a short life. This clipper was built in 1850 by Jabez Williams of Williamsburg, New York and measured 1222 tons, 194.10 feet long by 36.8 by 21.6. She was lost in 1853.

4 The JOHN LAND was a clipper ship built by E. and H. O. Briggs of South Boston, Massachusetts, in 1853. Tonnage and dimensions were 1054 tons by 176 feet long by 36 beam by 22 deep. She was abandoned at sea on March 25, 1864.

5 Samuel Hall of East Boston, Massachusetts, built the clipper FLYING CHILDERS in 1852. Tonnage and dimensions were 1125 tons by 183.9 by 36.4 by 22.6.

6 The STAR OF THE UNION was a clipper built in 1852 by J. O. Curtis at Medford, Massachusetts. 1057 tons by 200 feet long by 35 beam by 21.6 deep.

7 Captain J. Worth.

American Clipper Ship, woodcut from Ballou's Pictorial, 1855.

PART II—OUTWARD BOUND
TO THE CAPE

*Newspaper advertisement from New York
Shipping and Commercial, Jan. 10, 1866.
Captain Mitchell relieved Captain Harding just
before the* Hornet *sailed even though Harding's
name continued to run in the ad.*

Crew list of the American Clipper Ship *Hornet* leaving New York, January 15, 1866.

Josiah A. Mitchell, Master*
Samuel F. Hardy, Mate
John H. Parr, 2nd. Mate
John S. Thomas, 3rd. Mate*

Samuel Ferguson, Passenger*
Henry Ferguson, Passenger*

B. Lawson, Carpenter
Joseph A. Washington, Cook
Henry Chisling, Steward

Henry Morris, Seaman*
Joseph Williams, Seaman*
Peter Smith, Seaman*
C. H. Kaartman, Seaman*
Antonio Possene, Seaman*

John Ferris, Seaman*
Thomas J. Tate, Seaman*
James Cox, Seaman*
John Campbell, Seaman*
Frederick Clough, Seaman*
Neil Turner, Seaman*
William Laing, Seaman
George Whitworth, Seaman
William Linten, Seaman
Joseph Frank, Seaman
Joseph Collagan, Seaman
Charles Beale, Seaman
Joachim Betinke, Seaman
John Noldt, Seaman
A. J. Andersen, Seaman
James A. Mathson, Seaman
Peter Paulson, Seaman

Total 31

Saved in longboat (15)

- 20 -

Extracts from Captain Mitchell's Journal:

January 2.
Telegram from New York, also letter from Capt. Prince Harding, to come on immediately.

January 3.
Busy all day getting ready to leave, settling up, and packing trunk.

January 4.
Left home at 6 A.M. for Yarmouth. Train for Boston.

January 5.
Arrived in New York at 6 A.M. Breakfast at Howard House. Called on Capt. Harding and looked about generally. Agreed to go in *Hornet* and commenced duty.

January 6.
Crew on board all paid up for today.

January 7.
Came on board to tea and remained on board. Very cold day.

January 8.
Cold intense, very little done in way of business. Bought slops and other things ready for sea. Agreed for wages with Mr. Lawrence, $200 per month.

January 9.
Still cold.

January 10.
Freight comes in slowly. Passed examination and got my certificate.

January 11.
Busy getting ship ready. Cleared ship.

January 12.
Finishing up and getting ready for sea. All on board. Received from Messrs Lawrence, Giles & Co., $25 on account.

January 13.
Unmoored and hauled down the dock ready to go out. Little or no wind and no opportunity of going to sea. Crew got their things all on board and everything ready for Monday morning early. Third mate on board at work.

January 14.
Wrote Wife and Harry* in forenoon. Good N.W. wind blowing, wish I was out.

His son in California.

Extracts from Henry Ferguson's Journal:

January 8.

First had the subject of going to Frisco broached. Felt much in favor of it. Thermometer, 15°. Whewgh! Cold? Oh! No!

January 9.

Decided to go and went to Hartford to transact necessary business.

January 13.

Left Stamford at 8:30 and came down to New York and went aboard the ship at the time ordered. When we got down there we found that the pilot was afraid of ice and that we would not start till Monday morning. So we went round town and then went up to Aunt's where we dined and slept.

January 14.

Spent today in New York at Uncle E's. . . . After tea at about 7:30 came down to ship. Took car to Astor House and walked the rest of the way. When down at the ship there was nobody round and some time before we got aboard. Father and Uncle E. came on board for a little while and then left and went back. Very comfortably situated and we think we will get along very well. We like the Captain and Mate, what we have seen of them, very well. Tow-boats are to come six o'clock tomorrow and we will haul out about 7:30 or 8.

MONDAY, JANUARY 1, 1866 — SUNDAY, JANUARY 14.

Extracts from Samuel Ferguson's Journal:

January 11.

Father, uncles, and friends generally have been very kind in fixing us out with all sorts of things to make us comfortable. My list of stores is as follows: 2 boxes, 4 doz. pints cider; 1 box, 2 doz. P.E.I. ale; 6 boxes, 4 doz. quarts ale; 4 doz. qts., 4 doz. pts. claret; ½ barrel apples in paper; 1 box, 2 doz. 3 lb. cans peaches; 1 box, 1 doz. wine (8) and brandy (4) 1 box, 1 doz. whiskey (10) and sherry (2); 1 box (Snow) oysters, fresh and pickled; 1 box (E.F.) oysters pickled; 1 keg tamarinds; 1 basket lemons; 1 box Valentine; 1 tin box ginger snaps (M & G); 1 tin box French gingersnaps; S.F. trunk and bag; H.F. trunk and bag and shawl.

January 12.

At Stamford. Received telegram from Father saying that 12 noon Saturday fixed for hauling out. Made a few hurried calls, during which found B.'s card in blind(?). Returned home and spent remainder of the afternoon with Mr. and Mrs. B. Spent evening at home writing and talking. Last night at home probably for a long time. May we all again assemble in as good or better health.

January 13.

Father and J.Day breakfasted at 6:30, all down to breakfast together. Henry and I go to New York by the 8:30 train. Went to see aunts, said goodbye and I then called at Miss Snow's and saw Mr. and Mrs. Bull and Miss Andrias and Mrs. D. They were out, left farewells; thence to office, thence to ship to find that the pilot was afraid of ice starting at this time and wished to wait till Monday, so was ordered aboard by 7 A.M. on that day. Went back to office, thence to aunts. Mr. L.H. Holmes called in the afternoon and had a chat about Nevada. Spent the evening in chatty conversation not determining when to go aboard till we saw the weather of tomorrow. Took $100 gold and $100 silver in case of need and to keep us going in San Francisco until further need.

January 14.
Spent the day with 20th. 56 party. Father staying down. He, Henry, and I went to hear Mr. Eaton, a recommendation. Was disappointed in hearing him preach; liked his reading much and general bearing though. Visited Dr. Bigart, only saw Mrs. Returned to dinner by way of St. Georges and found Miss Dunford and nephew had come to dinner - she a mighty staid old maid, he a rather go ahead sort of a fellow, but number-one-ish. Henry and I went to Trinity Chapel, in the evening C.P. Holmes called. At 7:45 started with Father and Uncle E. for the ship, thinking it better to go aboard tonight than wait till 5:30 A.M. Monday found the ship as she was on Saturday, but the steps hauled up on ship along side the wharf. Crawled up ship's ladder and went aboard and got the Second Mate with lantern and got steps let down. Father, Uncle E. and Henry came aboard *Hornet*. Father and Uncle E. sat awhile in the cabin and at about 9:15 said goodbye, Father intending to come down early on Monday morning. Turned in at 10:30 about and slept comfortably the night, though outside was very cold and windy. Talked with and like Captain Mitchell very well, think we will have a first rate time with him.

MONDAY, JANUARY 15

Lat. 40° 25′ N. Long. 74° 01′ W.

Captain Mitchell's Journal:

Left the dock at 7:30 A.M. Crew came off at 9 A.M. Towed down. At 12, passed Sandy Hook. At 12:30, discharged pilot and steamer. 2 P.M. Highlands. N. by W., 18 miles. Wind N.E. Steered S.E. At 6 headed off S.S.E. At 8, S. by E. Fresh wind S.E. by S. Hard gale from S.E., snow and rain. At 7 A.M., 16th., wore ship. Wind hauling to S. and S.W. Very bad night.

Henry Ferguson's Journal:

Left the wharf at 7½ A.M. with the tug *Wm. Fletcher**. Hauled out to Bedloe's Island and waited for the men who came at about 9 o'clock. Went then down the bay and rounded the Hook about noon. Shipped the pilot when about 5 miles outside and have been sailing on course S.E. by E. with a N.E. wind. Sent letters off by pilot. Wind went down somewhat toward evening. Very good grub. Sunk the land at about 1½ P.M. In afternoon unpacked library. Makes quite a show. Captain and pilot both predict snow storm with North-easter.

* *The WILLIAM FLETCHER was a wood hull side sheel steam tug of 204 tons. She was built in 1864 at Keyport, New Jersey, and long used as a New York harbor tug.*

Sidewheel steam tug Wm. Fletcher *towed the* Hornet *out of New York Harbor, Jan. 15, 1866. From a James Bard painting.*
Courtesy Mariners Museum

Samuel Ferguson's Journal:

12 M. passed [Sandy] Hook. Pilot aboard very early. Tug came at 6 A.M., hauled out by 7:30, mighty cold and windy. Only 7 of the crew aboard. Towed down to and waited off Ellis Island waiting the rest of the crew. Father kindly sent papers and caps that rascal Fleming neglected to send Saturday. Hoisted jib, staysails, and spanker and were towed to sea. Left tug 3 miles off Sandy Hook. Sent letter to father and girls by Pilot who was taken off soon by *Pilot boat No. 10.* She, rounding up to let her boat go and takes it on again beautifully. Saw steamer *Niagara** headed in, also a ship heavy with ice, also *Pilot boat 12.* Wind light though favorable till evening when we had to head nearly due south, wind having shifted to east-southeast.

Slight motion to ship all afternoon rather increasing towards night. No inconvenience so far. Unpacked books and made Henry's upper berth over Library. Capital soup for dinner; parsnips and potatoes, roast and baked for vegetables.

* *It is impossible to tell with certainty which of two vessels named NIAGARA the journal refers to: the then venerable Cunard Line passenger steamship NIAGARA or the New York and Virginia Steamship Company's new coastwise steamer NIAGARA. Probably the latter is correct, however. The 1848-Scotch-built transatlantic liner measured 1825 tons and was 251 feet long by 38 feet beam. Her employment on the Atlantic ferry terminated this same year of 1866 when she was returned to Glasgow shipbuilders and converted to a sailing ship. The American 1864-built steamer measured 909 tons and was 220 feet long by 36 feet beam by 15 feet deep. She and her sister ship the SARATOGA were built in New York by J.A. Westervelt and Son. This NIAGARA was advertised in the New York HERALD of January 14, 1866 -- the day before the HORNET sailed -- as plying a weekly round trip run between New York, Norfolk, City Point and Richmond leaving New York every Saturday at 3 P.M.*

TUESDAY, JANUARY 16

Lat. 39° 13′ N. Long. 73° 30′ W.

Captain Mitchell's Journal:

Begins heavy gale. At 7 A.M. wore ship. Wind hauls to W. and N.W., blowing hard with very heavy head sea. Ship pitching and rolling very heavy. Men badly frostbitten. Steering S.E. by E.

Henry Ferguson's Journal:

At about 10 last night came up a strong Easterly gale and snowstorm which drove for 6 hours, at one time nearly a foot of snow on the deck. The wind changed in the morning to W. which coming against a head sea made it very rough, so much so as to capsize Sam and myself effectually. Felt pretty miserable most of the day but got on deck in afternoon which made me feel better. Found the pitching was not agreeable. Went to bed early and was not disturbed again though the motion kept me awake. Two of the sailors very badly frostbitten -- one* a gentleman's son, a young fellow who came to sea for pleasure. He says it is his last voyage if he knows himself, rather sickened with it.

* *William Laing.*

Samuel Ferguson's Journal:

Sea increased all last evening till about 10 when a stiff southeast wind set in, which caused a horrid sea. Later it rained and snowed hard, Mate said 6 inches on deck. Captain out all night, had a very hard time getting in sail. Two men badly frostbitten. Ship rolled tremendously, awfully uncomfortable to subscriber who had to brace himself to prevent being split out. Trunk and everything movable, going round, turned out to stop them. About 5 A.M. wind changed to west, changed course to east by south and met old easterly sea which made us pitch like all wrath. Capsized Henry first then me. Was miserable as could be all day. Went on deck about 3:30, felt better, but spilled all pea soup was advised to take. Came down to tea, still rolling and pitching. Tea stayed down about 3 minutes. Went to bed and gave up as a bad job.

Captain said first part of night was very bad, only saved canvas from its being new and if the easterly gale had stood we would have had a bad chance of it. Came to the conclusion that it was pretty rough on beginners. Ordered a cup of tea and some toast at 9 P.M. but was asleep when steward brought it, so made out till morning. Henry also sick.

WEDNESDAY, JANUARY 17

Lat. 37° 51′ N. Long. 69° 10′ W.

Captain Mitchell's Journal:

Fresh gale from N.W. all this day and heavy sea. Latter moderate.

Henry Ferguson's Journal:

Entered the [Gulf] Stream at about 4 A.M. Had a good Westerly breeze all night which took us along well. Our latitude this noon, 37° 50′ N. Longitude, 69° W. Sea a good deal quieter but still she rolls [a good] deal. Both of us are pretty well over seasickness, not having been troubled today. The water this morning was 62° and is the most beautiful blue I ever saw. It is now a fine night, starlight and a tolerable breeze blowing and some sea running. Played cards in evening, euchre and seven-up. (I may as well record here that Sam and I have only missed three meals and now rather like the motion. Monday night capsized us.)

Samuel Ferguson's Journal:

Fine wind still, Westerly. Entered the [Gulf] Stream at 4 A.M. Made good time all day. Nearly all sail set. Still rolling. Observation gives 37° 51′ N. Lat. by 69° W. Long. Did not get up to breakfast but took a cup of tea and some toast about 8 o'clock and about 9 got up and took for first time a little brandy which had the desired effect of settling and strengthening our stomachs. Got on deck and stayed till dinner. Weather pleasant and warm. Were a little particular about soup and so dinner and all went well, felt no bad effects except weak and heady. If we get off with this punishment we will be very fortunate and I am inclined to think we shall. Enjoyed being on deck enormously. Part of the time waves running very high and looked as if they would engulf the ship. Towards night got to feel quite at home with the motion, not minding it any more in the cabin than on deck which is a very pleasant feeling to experience. Steward* an honest sort of a fellow though not a very good man for the place. Captain opened a barrel of apples and had some baked, served for tea, which went well. He told Henry and I to help ourselves when we felt like it as they would only get bad. In the evening we played three-handed euchre and Old Sledge till about 9:30 and went to bed. Ship still rolling considerably. Saw the two men with frost bitten hands, both looked very badly. Froze them getting sail in. Some of the men also had toes bitten, not so bad though.

*   *Henry Chisling*

THURSDAY, JANUARY 18

Lat. 37° 40′ N. Long. 64° 49′ W.

Captain Mitchell's Journal:

First part moderate from south-west. Middle, baffling from north-west to west. Latter, fresh from south-west and cloudy. No observation.

Henry Ferguson's Journal:

We have had a good westerly and south-westerly wind all day and have been making a capital run. Our course is still E.S.E. We are still in the Stream and it is delightfully warm, *sine* overcoat and wore slippers. Clear most of the day, but cloudy at noon so as to prevent observation, so the latitude could not be obtained by observation, but was got out by plane sailing. On deck tonight, saw the new moon and the most beautiful phosphorescence I ever saw. Also there were several shooting stars. Made a good run today, calm sea and fair wind. Our speed this evening is about twelve knots. The wind is getting a little squally and so they furled the royals.

Samuel Ferguson's Journal:

Fine wind, southwest, pretty stiff. On going on deck after breakfast, found all sail set but royals and ship just bowling along. Weather quite warm, no overcoat needed. Was on deck all morning either reading or talking. Just before dinner opened a jar of pickled oysters, which were "hunkey dorey", Henry said. After dinner on deck and admired the sea and color of water. Could get no good observation today. Set the royals and went bowling on until 7 P.M. when, as breeze freshened, took them in. First noticed phosphorescence very bright and beautiful, new moon very fine sight.

Thought how all at home would have enjoyed today's sail. Sea calm, i.e. no swell though some waves which gave some motion to ship. Both of us are beginning to walk with some decency and don't have to hold on to her pitching and rolling, as to its effects on us now, though I have no doubt that the Capes* will fetch us. So far have only missed breakfast and dinner of 16th. and breakfast of 17th.

* *He probably means Cape Horn.*

FRIDAY, JANUARY 19

Lat. 37° 01´ N. Long. 59° 40´ W. Dist. 245

Captain Mitchell's Journal:

Fine breeze all this day from W.S.W. and pleasant weather. Ending at West, warm and fine.

Henry Ferguson's Journal:

Good breeze all day; our day's work from yesterday noon very good indeed being 240 miles in the 24 hours. Beautiful day all along till after sunset it clouded up and at 8 began to rain very hard which slackened the breeze. However, we are still going 5 or 6 knots. Saw today for the first time Mother Cary's Chickens,* which are pretty little birds about the size of a snipe.

Chose the shady side in preference to the sunny today. There is a good deal of wind to forward but no masses of it yet. We are now come about 700 and over miles from Sandy Hook, an average which is very good indeed. The feeling of the air is perfectly delicious and I hope Sam's cough will improve soon.

* *Also called Stormy Petrels. The term "Mother Cary" is a corruption of the Iberian seaman's MATER CARA (Dear Mother), often uttered in prayers to the Virgin Mary during bad weather when the sailors craved divine protection.*

Samuel Ferguson's Journal:

Beautiful fine morning. Got on deck before breakfast to enjoy the view. Get more and more in love with the sea and the color of the water which is different from what I ever saw; very clear but of a beautiful blue, deepening in shade as to the way on. Looked down into it, e.g. we could see to the bottom of the rudder where the color was a very much lighter hue, when three feet either side of it was a dark but clear indigo. Saw today quantities of seaweed which denotes that we were out of the Gulf Stream; also saw Mother Cary's Chickens. Made a good

The Stormy Petrel - woodcut from The World of the Sea, *1882.*

run since noon yesterday: 240 miles. Going on today with everything set but studding sails. Weather perfectly beautiful, warm and pleasant all day in slippers. No one could hardly believe last Monday was so cold. Men getting better though one will probably lose a finger. Latitude today 37° N., Longitude 59° 30′W. Henry went forward and looked down at cutwater. Meal times at 7:30, 12:30 and 5 P.M. Have got now to be really ready for them when the time comes. Don't think much of the cook's pork meats he fixes. Tonight had potatoes and onion salads, but was afraid to try it this time of day. 8 P.M. slowed up and breeze dies to about 5 or 6 knots.

SATURDAY, JANUARY 20

D.R. Lat. 36° 40′N. Long. 56° 00′W.

Captain Mitchell's Journal:

Begins moderate breezes, West to W.S.W. Middle, baffling from W.N.W. to N. moderate and veering from N. to N.E. No observation.

Henry Ferguson's Journal:

Rainy with wind squalls in the early morning, but cleared off and was another beautiful day. The sea was very smooth, hardly a white-cap to be seen, just enough to give us a pleasant motion. Wind next to nothing in morning, but nice breeze all rest of the day. The wind has gone round to east-northeast, and we are hauled very close and heading about S.S.E. We want to reach 40° W. before 30° N. and it is a little doubtful now whether we will do it. For the first time saw the sun sink "into his water bed" as hitherto there have always been clouds in the west at sunset. It looked very queerly and beautifully. Good deal of weed floating by. It is very hard to realize that it is January, the weather is so perfectly charming and delicious. Soon fear it will be too hot for pleasure.

Samuel Ferguson's Journal:

Continued showery during night, cleared up in the morning, wind changed to northeast light. During the day much enjoyed being on deck. Made out this morning to get there before breakfast. Cough not yet gone, seems obstinate though I think yielding. Henry read some Greek today and will find no difficulty with Classics. He wants an instructor in analytics. Most of the day the whole sea was calm, hardly a white cap, though a continued long roll. Did not get a good observation at 12. Captain made out though our latitude: 36° 49′and Longitude 57°. Today we have had to alter our course to south southeast which is considered bad as we want to get to 40° W. Longitude before we get to 30° N. Latitude. Never saw anything like the color of the water. Clear as Long Island water but different. Could see today the rudder to the bottom of it and keel quite distinctly. A good deal of seaweed, mean to catch some and press it. Begin to think it an age since we left home. The time goes very quickly during the day. Opened a can of oysters which were very good. Found some of the cans contained pickled and some preserved, only concluded to wait awhile before making way with the latter. Voted thanks to giver. The custom at sea is always to have a glass of grog on Saturday nights to drink to "Wives and Sweethearts". Aboard the *Hornet* it is, needless to say, this custom, a good custom I might say, is well kept up and in all probability will be observed as long as anything remains to help the observation.

SUNDAY, JANUARY 21

Lat. 36° 30′N. Long. 53° 45′W. Dist. 122

Captain Mitchell's Journal:

Fine weather, wind moderate and hauling to East. Middle part, very moderate wind, E.S.E. At 4 A.M. wind light at S.E. Tacked to E.N.E. Latter part, fresh breeze from South. Ship sharp by the wind, heading E.S.E.

Henry Ferguson's Journal:

Rose and breakfasted at the usual time or rather half an hour later by accident. Another beautiful day and pleasant as beautiful. The wind was about nothing last night, but this morning came out nicely from S.E. and varied between S. and S.E. all day though mostly about South. Sam was favored by luck today twice more than I, having had a sight of a whale and of a Nautilus, neither of which I saw. Read the Psalms, lessons, collect, &c. this morning;

- 29 -

"The Great Headed Sperm Whale" - woodcut from The World of the Sea, *1882.*

no work except necessary changes of sail are done on Sundays and to-day not even that has been needed. It is a day of perfect quiet as distinct as on land and a day of rest for the men who are worked pretty hard all the weekdays. Had turkey for dinner today, the last one we hope for some time as we don't want to touch any more land till May.

Samuel Ferguson's Journal:

Beautiful day, wind southerly but pretty strong. Sails set but stay-, sprit-, and studding sails, hauled close to wind making course east by south. Some parts of day must have gone 12 knots. Make the water boil; sea pretty smooth. Saw today a whale spout; he soon made off, however. Good observation today, Latitude, 36° 30′ Longitude, 53° 34′. Almost becalmed last night. Spent most of the morning on deck, at 11 came down and read Psalms, lessons, and gospel and spent till dinner in stateroom thinking a good deal of all dear ones at home. Hope they have as fine a Sunday. Have not wanted an overcoat for some days, beginning to think such things, superfluous. Have not as yet attacked our stores; meant to have had a bottle of claret today for dinner but was surprised by old time.* This afternoon saw a Portuguese Man-of-war;** hope, however, to get a better view of them. Have got to understand the use of a quadrant pretty well I think. Mean to try tomorrow with the Captain. Mate seems a pretty good sort of fellow but should say that the Third Mate was the best sailor or officer aboard after the Captain. At starting, Captain had a present of two turkeys; said good-bye to number two today.

*He evidently neglected to set his watch to the new time necessitated by changes in the ship's longitude.
**The Portuguese man-of-war is a large oceanic hydrozoan ("jelly fish") with an opalescent air sack rising out of the water by which they are buoyed up and "sail." Their tentacles are very long and of tremendous stinging power.

MONDAY, JANUARY 22

Lat. 36° 18' N. Long. 49° 05' W. Dist. 220

Captain Mitchell's Journal:

Strong south wind and pleasant weather all this day. Ship sharp by the wind on starboard tack. Passed a schooner bound west.

Henry Ferguson's Journal:

Ended our first week out with a very good run of 220 miles which gives us an aggregate of over 1200 miles. Another superb day. This A.M. saw a barkentine about 12 miles off. Captain says she was a Mediterranean fruit vessel. Had a glorious breeze all day but have had to haul too close to do our very best with it. However, we have done very well and have gone slipping through the water. Went up on the 'gallant fo'castle deck and sat, delightful place to see the water and how necely she cuts through. While sitting there, a wave struck the bow and splashed us somewhat filling my ear with water. Have made enough easting to do a little more southing, but as the wind is S. we have to do the best we can and be content with E.S.E. as we have been sailing all day. Horizon nearly cloudless at sunset. Very beautiful appearance of sun extinguishing himself. Opened home gingersnaps, very good indeed, eat the health of the makers.

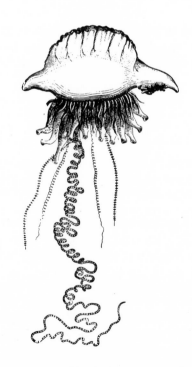

Portuguese Man-of-war - woodcut
from The World of the Sea, *1882.*

Samuel Ferguson's Journal:

Again a beautiful day, wind southwest, pretty fresh. Sailed close, going splendidly. Captain and all hands well satisfied with first week's work which ends at 12. today. Made since noon yesterday, 230 miles. Took latitude today myself and found 36° 18'. Longitude Captain made out to be 49°. This is getting along first rate and is fast pulling the vessel, where she should be to take the Northeast Trades. Last night I dreamed I saw four vessels. About half an hour after breakfast one of the four hove in sight and passed about 12 miles to south of us, probably a Mediterranean fruit trader bound to New York. Got a good splashing today while on the top-gallant forecastle. Ship cuts into sea splendidly and has shown herself a good sailer. Second and Third Mates put 120 days as our passage. If it depends only on ship and we are not becalmed, I think we will do it inside of that. Have been much surprised at the stillness of the ocean; always had an idea that a day's wind from any quarter to raise a big swell and sea. There is, of course, always motion but not very much. The brisk breeze of to-day made everything lovely and the waves danced about as if they were having a real good time, not sullen as sometimes.

TUESDAY, JANUARY 23

Lat. 36° 08' N. Long. 45° 00' W. Dist. 180

Captain Mitchell's Journal:

Begins fresh from south. Middle and latter, moderate and pleasant wind, south. At 9 A.M. spoke an English brig from New York for Constantinople with the crew of the schooner *Ellen Read** on board, taken off wreck.

* *The schooner ELLEN READ of Boston cited here cannot be positively identified. Possibly she might have been either the ELLA REED or the EDWIN REED. According to the 1862 edition of AMERICAN LLOYDS, the ELLA REED, Captain Davis, was a 283 ton bark built in Maine in 1853 and was owned by Bernadon & Bros. of Philadelphia. The EDWIN REED was a 226 ton schooner built in Milford, Delaware in 1855 and was owned by Shaddoch & Jones of Boston. No ELLEN READ appears in the register. A note in the "Marine Disasters" section of the New York HERALD of February 8, 1866 cited the schooner EDWIN REED, from a coal port, then overdue at Boston. "She passed down Vineyard Sound previous to the gale of January 8 and fears are entertained for her safety" the newspaper reported. Possibly it was survivors from this vessel which had been picked up by the unspecified vessel which signaled the HORNET stating that she was bound for Constantinople. Unless she encountered a vessel returning to the United States, it might well be a long time before news of the salvation of the crew would be received back in Boston.*

Henry Ferguson's Journal:

Early this A.M. were hailed by a brig. We finished up letters to send if they came aboard. She proved to be from New York for Constantinople with the ship-wrecked crew of the schooner *Ellen Read*, Boston, aboard. She wanted to know where we were bound and if we had been bound to Europe, to place the unfortunates on board us. She was a Plymouth (England) brig, not very handsome. After breakfast saw another sail going the same way as ourselves, but we overhauled her and passed her by 2 o'clock. She was a bark with very square sails and no royal yards. Wind very slight all day and sea very calm indeed with a long heaving roll. Beautiful day. Saw two "Portuguese men-of-war" this afternoon, pretty little things. Head about S.E. by E. with wind somewhat W. of S. Hoped to send letters but impossible. Beautiful sunset, the most lovely green clouds I ever saw against the golden background.

Samuel Ferguson's Journal:

Another fine day. Steward informed us at 7, there was a brig in sight and signalling us to heave to. Went on deck and found our vessel with a red flag at the peak and U.S. in the rigging. Heaved to, and as she passed, under our stern she hailed and informed us she had the ship-wrecked crew of the *Ellen Reed* aboard and wanted to know where we were bound to. Captain told her and offered provisions, etc., which they declined.

After breakfast, saw another sail on the horizon right ahead. By one P.M. were passed although some distance off, she sailing freer than we. By evening we had sunk her hull. Saw today some more nautili. Henry opened a bottle of whiskey and had some this evening after our usual game of "7-Up" in which the Captain takes a hand. Very light wind today, still going on as well as could be expected. Got our letters ready to put aboard the brig, but as she did not board us, did not send them. This evening wind less, roll more; have made everything snug though. Sailors busy today at making and mending studding sails to be ready for the Trades which we ought soon to feel.

WEDNESDAY, JANUARY 24

Lat. 35° 20′ N. Long. 42° 50′ W. Dist. 100

Captain Mitchell's Journal:

Moderate breezes from south to S.W. all this day. Ending very light with a heavy swell from S.E. Rolling and slatting sails badly. Cut new main topsail brace pennants. Sharp by the wind.

Henry Ferguson's Journal:

Another pleasant day with about as little wind as possible, though still a little. Heavy swell, otherwise very calm, great big rollers that go as easy and lazily as possible. Clouded up in afternoon and looked very much like a thunderstorm, but passed off to the north of us. We have been heading about S.E. by S. all day and have not gone very far. Most splendid deep colored clouds this P.M. about an hour before sunset. Caught some of the drift-weed which floats round so much. Pretty with berries but extremely fishy. Fine night, hardly any wind and rolling considerably. Sailors fixing the studding sails and putting new braces in. Studied all three, Latin, Greek, and Math today, read more than they will have read at college. Wind a couple of points or so West of South. Have had some towel racks and shelves put up in my stateroom. Wonder whether they will think of me tonight at college. I would like to see all the fellows and be with them.

Samuel Ferguson's Journal:

Fine day again, but very light wind and considerable roll, which as the wind lessened seemed to increase towards night. Sailors again busy all day at mending sails. Nothing in sight today but the boundless ocean.

Am deep today in *Uncle Tom's Cabin*.* It is no doubt a splendidly written book though one gets provoked with many of the ideas in it. Our day has got now to be very routine in its way: breakfast at 7:30, reading and study with going on deck till noon at which time we

---

* *Harriet Beecher Stowe's classic, first published in 1852.*

take observation for latitude. Dinner at 12:30, after which we go on deck and lounge about a good while, reading, walking, etc., to 5:30, which is tea time. Ship's bell is unfortunate enough to be cracked. Captain said it was one of the best bells he ever heard, but was one night washed by a sea from its fastening and found in the lee scuppers cracked. Our tea bell is also a melancholy affair, also cracked but I fancy never good for anything.

THURSDAY, JANUARY 25

Lat. 35° 03' N. Long. 41° 34' W.

Captain Mitchell's Journal:

Very moderate and baffling winds from S.E. to S.S.W. and showers of rain all this day with a heavy swell from S.E. Rolling and slatting terribly. Tearing everything all to pieces. Can't do anything on the other tack.

Henry Ferguson's Journal:

Brisker breeze arose today and came out well to the north of west so that we are now heading south. Not much of a wind yet though. Hope it will come up in time. Most beautiful sunset I think I ever saw. I did not think there could be such rich colors though I have seen many very beautiful ones on land. About 7 P.M. there was a little rain squall, but it only lasted a very few minutes. Captain so kind today as to lend me one of his quadrants which he does not use and I think now with three to watch, it will be hard to be mistaken in our observation. It is an old but very good one. I will note here that our breakfast hour is 7½ generally 8, dinner hours 12½, supper 5½. Steward greatest specimen of nigger yet met. Cook decidedly the "greasy old Dark" mentioned in the song. He is one of those very oily looking darkies.*

* *Henry Chisling, steward; Joseph A. Washington, cook.*

Samuel Ferguson's Journal:

This morning early, showery, soon however cleared off fine, wind light. Not much of a run since yesterday noon. This afternoon, wind changed to northwest, so we have our head now due south, which will probably be our course till we strike the Trades. Nothing in sight all day today. Men again busy mending sails and getting ready for the Trades. Still a very heavy old swell which is not convenient. Last night tried three-handed whist and thought it rather a good game, a great relief after euchre and "7-Up" all the time. Had a beautiful sunset this evening, one of the most varied and brilliant I have seen in a long time, more like an October one only without the very bright golden of that month. Have plenty of time to think of all at home and try to fancy at times what you are doing. Our time differs now by about two hours and twenty minutes, but will not increase much more. Captain lent Henry an old, but first rate quadrant which he is to take charge of and practice with daily. The sun at the Equator is only in Zenith a moment, so a number of sights are better than one.

FRIDAY, JANUARY 26

Lat. 32° 30' N. Long. 39° 40' W.

Captain Mitchell's Journal:

Begins very moderate from S.S.W. At 6 P.M. hauls round to N.W. light, gradually veering to N. and increasing. Middle and latter, strong breezes from N. and N.N.W. with occasional showers. Ship dead before the wind. Two vessels in sight standing east.

Henry Ferguson's Journal:

Breeze freshened up into a tolerably stiff Nor'wester which has helped us along nicely although it is a little too fair to make all our sails draw. It has brought up a high sea with it and it is the most beautiful sight to see the great big fellows come up and roll over into white foam. We sat up in the bow for some time and the ship cut the water splendidly and we liked to watch in the big pitches the martingale plough into the waves. A shoal of porpoises came up along side and instead of taking it easy as I have always seen them in the Sound,* they were tearing round skylarking in a great manner. It seemed queer to see them swimming under the waves and then come up to the top in their usual way. Saw two sails, both of which I believe I was the first to see, a brig and a ship, neither with very much sail set and both heading about S.S.E.

* *Long Island Sound*

Samuel Ferguson's Journal:

Wind nearly North, a little showery but only in short light dashes. Henry discovered two vessels, one turned out to be a brig, the other a ship, both going very fast with wind abeam. As we were steering nearly south soon lost sight of them. The sea this morning and day the finest we have yet seen, not angry but giving one the idea of its frolicsomeness, suggesting "let the floods clap their hands" more than anything else. The tremendous waves, for it was lively swell, looked as if they would wholly engulf the ship, but coming up would break, mingling the whites of white foam into that most perfect blue. As far as the eye could see it was mountains of blue rolling up and tipped with white. Must have made a good day's run, though the Captain says the wind is too fair, i.e. too much directly aft, as one set of sails covers the others. Still have fresh meat, though I guess it's about giving out as for dinner we had a piece of boiled corn beef and a fricasse chicken. For vegetables we had today, turnips, beans, potatoes two ways, macaroni, and carrots. Waves 15 to 20 feet from valley to crest.

SATURDAY, JANUARY 27

Lat. 29° 16' N. Long. 37° 00' W. Dist. 240

Captain Mitchell's Journal:

Strong winds, baffling, from N.N.W. to N. and N.N.E. all this day with frequent rain showers. Bent old foresail this day. Pumps attended to carefully.

Henry Ferguson's Journal:

From twelve to four this morning the wind shifted round to abeam and blew very hard which helped us on our course very well, but now it has come around North or Nor'west again and is blowing pretty fresh still. Sea beautiful like it was yesterday: as far as the eye could reach crowds of white caps, while big rollers come up behind and look exactly as if they were coming aboard and then subside under us, coming out ahead again at the bow. From the top of one the valley in between seems pretty deep and I guess that the average of today's and yesterday's were from 18 to 20 ft. Saw one sail today. Think she was a ship, but as she did not stay in sight very long, am not certain. Our course today has been about S. by E. and the day's work from yesterday M to M* today is 240 nautical miles.

* Meridian = Noon.

Samuel Ferguson's Journal:

Real fine wind about the same as yesterday, perhaps a little more westerly, course south by east. Sea running pretty high, white caps all around, still good natured. Saw today a lot of porpoises, they swam and rolled up by the bows for a short time and then disappeared. One ship seen today on our starboard bow, steering southwest, perhaps for some of the Florida ports. Must have made a good run today, though part of the time the mizzen sails monopolized the wind. Walton probably started today, may he have as fine a vacation as we have had. How surprised he will be to hear of Henry's departure with me. Certainly this part of the Atlantic is blessed with fine weather at this time of year. We have not had a single rainy day, nor a stormy one since the Monday we started. Have had a few showers which lasted a few minutes at a time.

Sunsets are our nightly treats and beautiful they are too, always varied and always different from those you see on land.

SUNDAY, JANUARY 28

Lat. 26° 24′ N. Long. 35° 30′ W. Dist. 188

Captain Mitchell's Journal:

Begins fresh from North, dying gradually away. Middle and latter part, moderate from North and fine weather.

Henry Ferguson's Journal:

Wind and sea gone down very much indeed and it has been as lovely a day as one could wish. Nothing of any particular interest has happened today. There is the greatest difference between Sunday and week days here and Sunday is so quiet that it don't seem natural. I never thought that it was observed so well by the sailors. It is a delicious night and our position and the looks of the clouds go far to assure us that we will catch the N.E. Trades soon — tomorrow we hope. We are now in the so-called Horse Latitudes,* but have had a nice breeze

* The region of high pressure on the outer edge of the trades where light and variable winds prevail. The conditions are unlike the doldrums in that the air is fresh and clear and calms are not of long duration. The name is supposed to have originated in the days when sailing vessels in the West India trade lost many horses of their cargoes while becalmed in this area (Gershom Bradford, A GLOSSARY OF SEA TERMS, New York, 1927).

all day. We have had unusual weather ever since we started, the Captain says, for this time of year.

Samuel Ferguson's Journal:

Again another beautiful day. The sea and wind, however, have a good deal subsided. Wind had shifted a little more to the West. Our course remains about the same. After 12, noon changed to a little West of South. Have seen no sail today or anything to break the quiet of the day, which is, as distinctly Sunday aboard ship as on land. The sailors are not required to do any work but what is necessary and during a day like today, in which the wind has been steady, there was really nothing to do. Each watch has, however, about a ten-minute turn at the pumps; the ship making some water while rolling, her upper seams being pretty dry. Read prayers, psalms, lessons, and gospel this morning, also took up study on the Parables. Sunday being a feast day, I opened and got out a bottle of Claret, part of which we drank at dinner and voted thanks of health to the donors. The weather so warm that we begin to talk of a change of underclothing at any rate. We will now soon strike the Trades and are now in the Horse Latitudes.

MONDAY, JANUARY 29

Lat. 24° 30' N. Long. 35° 00' W. Dist. 117

Captain Mitchell's Journal:

Very light from North all this day, ending nearly calm. Changed topsails, fore and aft, upper and lower this day.

Henry Ferguson's Journal:

The breeze was small by degrees and considerably less today as our day's work shows and there is little prospect for better luck tomorrow. We saw this morning several grampuses which were quite near the ship, huge black things that snorted and blew, like a porpoise magnified immensely. The sailors call them blackfish. In the afternoon when in the bow saw several of what the sailors call dolphins,* a pretty fish but no dolphin according to zoologists. Tried to catch some of them but they were too shy to be caught. One made a leap at the hook, but did not condescend to take it into his mouth. They say their changes of color when dying are beautiful. These we saw were about 1½ to 2 ft. long but they sometimes come to 5 ft. or so. Course mainly S. by W., but according to wind.

* *Probably these were not cetaceons (aquatic mammals) but the fish of tropical waters known as dorado.*

Dorado (dolphin) - woodcut view from the Shore Fisheries of Hawaii, *1903.*

The Grampus - woodcut from The Naturalists Library, *1837.*

Samuel Ferguson's Journal:

Fine soft feeling day, changed undershirts and drawers this morning to thinner ones and shall probably soon have to change outer clothing. Our hats and caps now come into use. The sun, however, is very hot from the water as well as from above. Captain's boots too small, I have taken all the lining out of mine and it is yet too tight. They are, however, the right thing in style. Wind today very light North by East, so we are nearing the Trades we hope. Our course has been South by West. Saw today a number of grampuses all blowing like porpoises and headed to windward. This afternoon we saw and tried to catch some dolphin that were swimming about our bows. They seemed very shy. A beautiful shaped fish and different colors in different lights. The most complaining set of men for twenty I ever saw, full half I should say have nothing the matter. One the other day spilled some boiling water on his own foot. The frozen fellows are getting better, though Cox has never been on duty since the Monday we started. Have made over 1000 miles this week, also hope we will do as well next.

TUESDAY, JANUARY 30

Lat. 23° 36' N. Long. 34° 50' W.

Captain Mitchell's Journal:

Begins light airs from North. Middle very light and baffling. From 2 A.M. to 11 A.M. calm. At 11 light breeze from South. Always moderate or calm on the full of the moon about here.

Henry Ferguson's Journal:

Our poorest day yet since we started from New York, A nearly dead calm all day consequently we have been making but little progress. From the middle of last night to 10 or 11 this morning she would not stir at all and our head has been to all points of the compass. The breeze is a little better now and we head S. by W½W. with the wind (what there is of it) from S.E. Most beautiful night. The full moon on the water is lovely and everything is still as possible except just a little ripple on the water and the unceasing heaving which never is quiet. After tea went on deck and sat talking quite a long time. Yesterday and today we have had tea without lights beyond the natural. Rainbow in the N.W. this A.M. Never saw 7 colors so distinct.

Samuel Ferguson's Journal:

This morning showery and calm as was last night. Catspaws for five minutes one way and then another. About noon headed nearly West-southwest. Sea like the Sound* all day. Hardly a ruffle on it, and only a slight motion. Captain grumbles a little for he says we have no business with calms here. He lays it, however, to full moon which he says always brings calm weather with it either 24 hours before or after the full. Have seen no sails for the last two days and begin to think it a good while since we saw anything, though the time has gone very quickly. Took a look today with the Mate at our apples to see how they were keeping and was pleased to see them in good condition, though I found one that was spotted. Saturday Captain brought out a set of dominos; had some good games. We find that three-handed whist the best three-handed game of cards — not dummy. Could see no fish today, either at the bow or elsewhere.

* *Long Island Sound.*

WEDNESDAY, JANUARY 31

Lat. 23° 05' N. Long. 35° 00' W

Captain Mitchell's Journal:

Very baffling winds all day from S.W. to S.E. continually and squally and calms alternately. Regular humbugging wind. Tacking and veering frequently as winds favor.

Henry Ferguson's Journal:

Another day of disappointing wind. There has been a nice breeze all day, but instead of being the N.E. Trade as it ought to be, it persistently stays S.S.E. — just the direction we wish to sail. We are now heading East on the starboard tack and have been so most of the day. Our day's work has been, as the latitude and longitude show, next to nothing. We saw two West India steamers bound North today, but both at a great distance off. Sun set perfectly clear without a single cloud near it. The days are getting much longer and the difference shows itself very plainly. Would like to be in Hartford part of tonight and home the rest. Several rain squalls, but none of any importance.

Samuel Ferguson's Journal:

All morning showery; about 9 A.M. came up a stiff breeze from the Southeast, which has continued all day, much to the Captain's disgust, who says now we ought to be having the Northeast Trades not Southeast. The run yesterday was almost on the back track and today, although we have gone over more space, it is not much better. Saw today two steamers, the first a long way off, the second closer, both bound Northeast, probably West India mail steamers. A year ago, however, we would have tacked ship and chatted. For the last few days we have seen very little seaweed which has been our constant companion since our first Thursday. The sailors are always kept constantly employed and certainly it is no idle life as one might suppose. We have no chance for games aboard on deck, as the main deck is always filled with sails being mended or chaffing gear, etc. Sea today just like the Sound with a stiff Southwest wind as in September. For the past three nights, have sat down to tea without lights. Both days and nights warm.

THURSDAY, FEBRUARY 1

Lat. 22° 25' N. Long. 34° 45' W.

Captain Mitchell's Journal:

First and middle part of this day light breezes from S.S.E. and S. Latter inclining Easterly and ending at S.E. by E. Hard chance this, no Trades yet.

Henry Ferguson's Journal:

Wind better today enabling us to steer nearly south, but yet is not what we expect, the regular N.E. Trade wind. Sea calm of course today, but there is somewhat of a swell. Growing dreadfully hot, but we can generally manage to keep cool while on deck. Saw a brigantine this afternoon, probably a Spaniard or Portugee bound from Rio or some such place. She passed quite near us so that we could observe her very well and she was not a very handsome vessel. We are now heading S. by E. I hope that we may get still more. Saw also today another brigantine on the lee side bound North but a long distance off. Clam soup for dinner today not extra rather heady. Thought of dear Toby apropos to clam heads.

Samuel Ferguson's Journal:

Should be 17 days out, or 18th day. Another fine day; wind, however, light and adverse all morning. Towards evening began to haul to the East so as to allow our course to be laid about South. By 10 P.M., had a stiff East by South breeze which brought considerable sea which we meet, causing us to pitch a good deal. Saw today a Spanish (?) brig going on an opposite course. We passed quite close, not so as to read her name, however. Discovered the other day some disagreeable visitors in my stateroom, so had everything taken on deck today and aired. Thinner clothes are getting to be usable; with the exception of coat, have made no change in outer garments. Am afraid our staterooms and berths will soon seem intolerably hot. Pumped the Mate today about hammock and where to hang it. He told me a good place and said it was feasible. Hope to keep a record of thermometer but it now hangs in sun.

FRIDAY, FEBRUARY 2

Lat. 19° 23' N. Long. 33° 30' W.

Captain Mitchell's Journal:

Begins this day moderate breeze from S.E. by E. Afternoon trades set in fresh from E. by S., and so continue through the day blowing a strong trade with a heavy head sea. Ship braced sharp, heading S. by E., plunging into it fearfully. Ship making a good deal of water. Obliged to shorten sail on account of it.

Flying Fish - woodcut from Fishing in American Waters, *1869.*

Henry Ferguson's Journal:

A rippling breeze all today from the E.S.E. which brought up quite a strong head sea which I grieve to say capsized me again. The horrid pitching was too much for me. However, I did not miss any of my meals and feel nearly straight now. We are going ahead at a tremendous rate and I guess may consider ourselves fairly in the trades though the wind is not as norther-ly as it should be. We saw quite a quantity of flying fish today, the first that we have seen yet. They are queer looking things and look like snipe flying. It is queer to see how far they can fly or rather skim. It is still pretty rough but I guess that the wind will not last very long so stiff.

Samuel Ferguson's Journal:

Almost all the progress made since last observation has been made since 8:30 P.M. last night. Today has been a roarer, the first real hard day's work for the ship. Last night's wind kicked up a pretty big sea nearly ahead and all day today it has blown very fresh so we are pitching heavily and making foam all over and occasionally shipping a sea. Most of the water comes over in spray. We have most all sails set and are going it. Suppose this wind is the Trade though from the wrong place, East-southeast. This is a great relief after the calms of the last two days even if it doesn't come quite from the right quarter. It is impossible to describe the beauty of the sea this afternoon. The ship of course makes her wave in going through the water which, as it winds out astern, would meet the swell and regular waves. At the junction the spray and dash would be thrown up sometimes ten feet or more and, the sun being out, would fall in a splendid rainbow. While watching the above I saw several flights of flying fish, at first sight look like snipe. They fly to windward some three or four hundred feet often.

- 41 -

SATURDAY, FEBRUARY 3

Lat. 15° 56' N. Long. 31° 45' W. Dist. 230

Captain Mitchell's Journal:

Very strong trade all this day and rough water. Wind E. by S. Ship heading (course) S. by E. Leaking a good deal, pumps at work (one) about one fourth of the time to keep her free. Closely attended to.

Henry Ferguson's Journal:

Wind same as yesterday all day blowing pretty hard. We have had all the square sails set except the royals, also the foretopmast staysail and spanker and have been travelling through the water at a great rate. The sea is running pretty high and makes it very rough. The candles every now and then take into their heads to slide. Have not felt sick at all today, only a little unsafe about meal times. The smell of the hash which is a universality is not pleasant to one who don't know but what he feels scary. We saw perfect clouds of flying fish today going in every direction with great swiftness. The 1st. mate gave Sam one of their wings, it is queer when you think it is a fish's. They look a great deal like gigantic devil's darning needles. Made a very good run and have been heading about the same.

Thought much of her whose birthday it is. Long life and happiness to her. Drank her health tonight when we drank Wives and Sweethearts.

Samuel Ferguson's Journal:

Today very much like yesterday, stiff South by East wind with heavy sea making it a trial to weak sailors. Henry all right today, though not very studiously inclined. The motion in cabin very tremendous, dishes and plates rather migratory. On deck most of the day watching the flocks of flying fish, some coming quite near. Hope to find some on deck soon. Our course is the same as it was yesterday and speed from 9 to 10 knots. The sea striking her forward sometimes flies { up} most to the fore- or main-yard, pretty thoroughly wetting all on deck. She leaks somewhat, enough to cause pumping about twenty minutes every watch. The leak is above the copper and Captain thinks just behind the cutwater; means to set the carpenter on it the first calm day. Another week gone, how the time goes and how little do I personally accomplish! I hope, however, to gain in health now to enable me to make up by and by.

SUNDAY, FEBRUARY 4

Lat. 12° 05' N. Long. 29° 50' W. Dist. 240

Captain Mitchell's Journal:

Fresh trades from E. by S. and fine weather all this day. Ship going fast, steering S. by E. Naught to fret about, save the quantity of water coming from the pumps — too much altogether. Home-thinking day.

Henry Ferguson's Journal:

Wind and sea nearly the same as yesterday only having moderated a little. However, there is still enough sea to render it pretty wet occasionally. When in Laing and Cox's room today, it came over in a perfect stream four or five inches deep washing out their place and bestowing its favors on the lower part of my legs. When I went on deck this morning Captain showed a flying fish that had come aboard very probably in the night. I cut off his wings and have put them to dry. They are a pretty fish, not very deep, but very full and plump, white sides and blue back. They had him cooked and we both tasted and liked it very much. Indeed I think it is as nice a tasting fish as you generally meet. These three last days we have made up tolerably for the calm in the first part. Like what we have seen of Laing and Cox very well.

Samuel Ferguson's Journal:

Just such a day as yesterday with perhaps a little less sea, not much, however. Trades so far have done well for us. Last night under royals made 11 knots. This afternoon though, wind slackened a little. Two flying fish came aboard today; cut the wings off and had the fish cooked. Tasted first rate, very delicate and rich, can't think what fish it resembles. Saw today thousands of them, wish we could catch some for breakfast. Made Cox and Laing a visit this morning and was nearly washed out of their place with a big sea. After reading the lessons and psalms, this afternoon took them some snaps and some of my tobacco. Cox gave me a tremendous lot in exchange of some of his. Have not tried it yet, in fact smoke very little indeed. Today not at all a day for reading, too hot and uncomfortable in the cabin, too windy and lively to read on deck. Last night after our games, with some whiskey drank health of dear ones at home and remembered the B.B. fraternity. The last three days we have hardly altered a sail and have, I hope, made up our average for this week. Hope Brathwaite and Lackey are enjoying a good dinner at Father's today.

MONDAY, FEBRUARY 5

Lat. 8° 15' N. Long. 28° 10' W. Dist. 235

Captain Mitchell's Journal:

Moderate trades all this day from East and fine weather. Carpenter and others at work trying to stop leaks.

Henry Ferguson's Journal:

The wind and sea have gone down very much and I am afraid before very long it will leave us in the lurch and we will enjoy the pleasure of the Doldrums as the calm latitude between the N.E. and S.E. trades is called. However, there we will get plenty of rainwater to wash the clothes in. There has absolutely been nothing today of interest to chronicle. There were a good many flying fish to be seen this morning, but none were good enough to come aboard. Paid Cox and Laing a visit this afternoon and lent them some reading. Headed South most of the day but now S. by W.½W. I believe.

Samuel Ferguson's Journal:

Very little to log today except that we still have the Trade winds, in a much more moderate degree, however. The past four days we have averaged about 220 miles which will give us over a thousand miles for our third week. Today has been fine, though very damp and close, and appearances denote rain not far off. We are rather afraid we shall be in the Doldrums before we ought to be and longer than we ought to be, but we will have to take them as they come. I rather wish we would have one or two rainy days, as we have had no clothes washed as yet and our bag is getting full. Still plenty of flying fish. Since we struck the Trades the air has been very heavy and thick, so that one cannot see very far, say 8 or 10 miles. The sun at one hour before sunset disappears in a sort of murky thickness. A few light and generally small clouds float about the sky. I suppose Mr. Mitchell preached his farewell to a crowded church last night. Wonder who they have to succeed him!

TUESDAY, FEBRUARY 6

Lat. 5° 42'N. Long. 27° 50'W. Dist. 154

Captain Mitchell's Journal:

First and middle, moderate Trades and heavy murky atmosphere. Ending very light from N. by E. About the end of N.E. Trades. A bark in company.

Henry Ferguson's Journal:

We have had quite a little breeze all day but there is great probability of its all going off. The sea is pretty still with quite a swell, the old one that never goes. We have been heading S. by W.½W. all day with the wind about North. We put up studding sails for the first time today. We have had the company of a large barque all day. We overhauled her in the night and we have been within ten miles of each other ever since as she is holding a point or so more to the Eastward than we. I doubt if we shall see her tomorrow. However, we may. Last night we tried to take a farewell look at the North Star, but he was hidden so we don't expect to see him till 5° or 10° N. on the other side. He will look like an old friend then. Have not seen the Southern Cross yet.

Samuel Ferguson's Journal:

Yesterday's appearances, like many of their namesakes' allure, proved deceitful and we had a fine day only confounded hot; wind light and shifted more to the North-Northeast as Trades should go. Everything set today: staysails, studding sails, and all. This morning saw a bark, all sails set, on our starboard quarter; she steering south by west, a half south by compass, which is, allowing for variation, due south about. Our course has been a little more westerly so that she has now appeared on our port side. Being a bark, she probably takes this course to fill her fore and aft sails better. Last night went out to say good bye to the North Star, but, as it was thick at the horizon, did not see him. Shall be glad to welcome the old fellow again after passing the Horn. Now new constellations will appear with each night. Not seeing his lordship, Henry and I contented ourselves with admiring the phosphorescence which truly beautiful and remains bright so long and is so large, pieces apparently as big as a man's hat illuminating up quite a space around it and sometimes appearing a long way back in the wake. The bark today is giving us a closer pull than any ship we have met.

WEDNESDAY, FEBRUARY 7

Lat. 4° 03' N. Long. 28° 00' W. Dist. 99

Captain Mitchell's Journal:

Very moderate airs from North all day. Murky, close, hot, and oppressive. Trades done and rain clouds threatening. Oh for a breeze to take us through.

Henry Ferguson's Journal:

Dreadful hot all day. Regular August weather, if not a little more so. Barque not in sight all day. We saw quite a lot of bonitos and we went out on the end of the bowsprit to try for them, but found them shy beyond expression. They have too much food about here to come for a piece of rag. Third mate tried the grains* and succeeded in missing them two or three times. Clouded up rapidly at about sundown and we had a regular tropical downright Doldrum shower which lasted an hour or so. As there was no knowing but that wind squalls would accompany it, there was a lively time taking in studding sails and royals and bracing round the yard, as it was, we were regularly taken aback once. Cloudy and threatening and calm all night, ship only just steering.

* *Grains were a trident, harpoon-like affair, with one tooth toggled, used to spear fish at sea.*

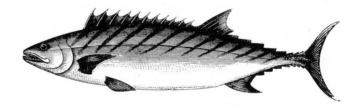

Bonito - woodcut from Fishing in American Waters, *1869.*

Samuel Ferguson's Journal:

Very hot and sultry all day, sun out most of the time. Wind still North-Northeast though very light. Bark not in sight this morning. We made today from noon yesterday, 99 miles and the Captain says he would be glad to have this amount guaranteed for the next four or five days. Saw today a good many bonitos, but they are too well fed for us yet. Third Mate tried the grains once or twice but missed them. The flying fish seem to be provided for food for the other fish in these quarters, for there seem to be multitudes of them and all other fish chase them.

   Had today a regular tropical shower which lasted about an hour and a half. Not much wind though some was expected. Bracing yards round, etc., to meet it, made a lively time for a few minutes. Opened lemons today and found that a good many had gone the way of all flesh. Had some lemonade. Shall use them up pretty fast.

THURSDAY, FEBRUARY 8

Lat. 3° 14' N. Long. 28° 10' W.

Captain Mitchell's Journal:

Begins very light airs from North. Close and hot, heavy rain clouds hanging around. Middle, light and baffling with rain. Latter, winds all round the compass and lots of rain, regular doldrums. No observation.

Henry Ferguson's Journal:

Calm all day and hot as any one could wish, no wind except just enough to make her steer. The barque came in sight again and is now a little ahead on the port bow. It is provoking to be becalmed and know that 2 degrees S. there is a good wind blowing that would take us ten knots if we could only get there. Tried for bonitos again both from the quarter and from the bowsprit, but no better luck than before. They live on the fat of the land here, that is, the poor flying-fish who seem to be the universal prey. We had a very heavy shower this morning for about two hours and collected plenty of water for washing. Out part of the time and never saw it rain so hard.

Samuel Ferguson's Journal:

This morning again very hot and sultry. About 9 A.M., we were visited by another shower and for a couple of hours the rain poured down in a regular tropical style. Wind all last night and this morning very light and from the North-Northeast, till the shower headed us off. Since then we have had the old wind, but very light indeed. Our old friend the bark is again in company. She made on us considerably during the shower which hardly slowed her, or if it did, was not adverse enough to make her alter her course. Steward caught water enough to wash our clothes today or some of them. I am mighty glad of it as the thick ones I want to put away. Nothing of particular interest going on today. Too hot at noon or about it to sit on deck as we could get no shade, so opened the skylight and sat in cabin and read *Don Quixote.*

Expect I made a mistake in getting white cord for fishing here both as to price and utility. Have seen and tried the bonitos but they won't take it, not hungry perhaps.

FRIDAY, FEBRUARY 9

Lat. 2° 20' N. Long. 27° 54' W.

Captain Mitchell's Journal:

Very light airs from North and very hot and oppressive weather all this. Ends a little more breeze from N.N.E. Bark in company.

Henry Ferguson's Journal:

Day dreadful hot, a way it has most decidedly of doing down here. The bark has been about abreast of us all day but is now fast dropping behind. We can beat her with any wind at all, but with none she goes a little easier being lighter and smaller. Went out on jibboom for bonitos but no good, they didn't see it or if they did took no notice of it. Went, for the first time, today up aloft. Only went however, so far as the mizzen-top where I read and studied Horace. A very nice cool place where you can get shade any time when the sun is not over your head. Saw much to our surprise tonight the North Star which we thought we had sunk. Charge the unexpected appearance to the refraction. Beautiful starry night.

Samuel Ferguson's Journal:

Sun out today with all his power, wind very light and shifting from North-Northeast to North-Northwest, had to change sails many times. Bark still in sight but losing ground all day. Early morning and late afternoon are splendid and always make up for the heat in the middle day. Saw tonight, much to my surprise, the North Star, about two degrees up. Captain said it was very remarkable, as in this latitude it is almost always hazy. The southern stars and constellations are gradually showing themselves and we shall soon be able to see the Southern Cross: could now, late at night or early in the morning. Notice particularly the shortness of twilight, gets dark very soon after sun down. Brought up apples and put them in cabin. They have kept pretty well and cool and are real good. The thermometer still hangs in the sun. It must come up pretty high from all our feelings.

SATURDAY, FEBRUARY 10

Lat. 0° 35' N. Long. 27° 40' W.

Captain Mitchell's Journal:

Very light variable airs from North to E.S.E. and hot clear weather. Saw the North Star distinctly last night. Never have seen it before so far South. Bark six miles astern.

Henry Ferguson's Journal:

Still another hot day without the Trades which we so fondly hoped we would have from a head sea and flying clouds. Tonight we are, I guess, past the Line. No ceremony observed at all. I never felt the sun so powerful. Both of us are pretty well burnt and my nose is quite tender. Barque well behind us all today and I guess we have seen the last of her. Went fishing again today and got my feet all tar — luckily they were bare and so washed. Went and read up aloft, very comfortable. Also discovered a good place in the channels. We saw the Southern Cross for the first time tonight. It consists of four quite bright stars in rather a lop-sided cross, thus

```
      *
   *     *
      *
```

Samuel Ferguson's Journal:

Wind still very light but as yet in the right direction. Bark dropped away astern. Should find the Southeast Trades today. Thought last night we would have them, in there was a heavy swell from the South. Took this morning for the first time a tub bath and glorious it was, it will not be long before I have another. There are lots of fish about but they don't seem to want to take hold. Saw tonight the Southern Cross and Magellan's Clouds for the first time. The former to be our "North Star" for the next sixty days.

Very hot on deck today, was in smoked glasses all day. This afternoon found a cool place in the mizzen top where I read *Tom Cringle's Log.** A first rate view from there but "nothing to see but sea". Another of the subscriber's years close tonight and Oh how old he is getting and, I am sorry to say, how confined in some ways; and to think that I shall be another whole one and perhaps half of another before I see all those at home. How long it does seem! God grant that we may all meet again in the old "Stone House".

* *This story by Scottish novelist Michael Scott was first published in book form in 1836 after appearing serially in BLACKWOODS MAGAZINE.*

SUNDAY, FEBRUARY 11

Lat. 0° 46' S. Long. 28° 30' W.

Captain Mitchell's Journal:

Very light winds from E. to South all first and middle part of this day and frequent rain squalls. Latter, breeze freshens from S.E. Crossed the Equator at 12 midnight, 26 days, 12 hours from Sandy Hook. A dull week's work.

"Pursuit of Flying Fish by Dolphins and Birds"
woodcut from The Ocean, *1856.*

Henry Ferguson's Journal:

Sam's birthday. Began the day by rising at 6½ and taking a bath in a gigantic tub on deck, a performance that I enjoyed most thoroughly, and have felt better for it all day. Sam's cough is not gone for his birthday as I had hoped, but I think that we must give anything so long settled plenty of time. Wind today light from S.E. I suppose we can call it the beginning of the Trades. Rain squall came up this morning and brought quite a stiff breeze which lasted some half hour or so and then faded. Another very hard shower this P.M. but without accompaniment. Barque nowhere to be seen any more than yesterday. We saw some fish called albacore* today after f.f. [i.e., flying fish]. They caught one poor little f.f. right near us and did it slick. Saw also a large school of porpoises, the spryest as well as the smallest I have seen.

* *The albacore is a large fish related to the tuna found in tropical waters.*

Samuel Ferguson's Journal:

Passed last night very badly, very hot and uncomfortable. Today hot and very hot in cabin; stayed all day on deck trying to get and keep in the shade. Have probably said good-bye to the bark for good. If not judging others by ourselves, should say he was very unsociable, as he might have communicated any time during two days. Flying fish never leave here, though we saw some poor sinners chased and one caught just close by the ship, by an albacore the Captain said. It was a well shaped and very handsome fish with gold spots from his dorsal fin to tail. Had two hard showers last night and one this afternoon. They last only a short time, but they are no drizzle while they do last. Drank the health of all at home today in a glass of Madeira it being the 28th anniversary of the subscriber's entrance upon this mortal scene. How good and home-like it tasted. I thank all at home today for their good wishes they have wished me. We have a Southeast wind which, I suppose, is the Trades but not yet a good wholesome breeze we look for.

MONDAY, FEBRUARY 12

Lat. 2° 46' S. Long. 30° 05' W.

Captain Mitchell's Journal:

First part light Trades at East. Middle and latter, very squally and baffling. Four weeks out today.

Henry Ferguson's Journal:

Began the day by a rain squall at about six, since which time we have had three more and are now as I write enjoying the fourth. We have had a good breeze all day except when killed by the rain. Passed a brig bound Northward today at about 2½. It has been and is now as usual hot as pepper. If I was fat I should be afraid of being sorely *tryed* by the heat. Both Sam and I began wooden chains today, but I had the bad luck to break mine while freeing the fifth link so it will have to be somewhat curtailed. There are nine left, however, and will make a tolerable chain if I get them. We have been heading S.W. by W. on average today. Expected to pass near Fernando de Noronha,* but I believe the Captain has changed his mind and will give it a berth.

* *Fernando de Noronha is a rugged, mountainous island, eight miles long, located in 3° 50' south latitude by 32° 22' west longtitude, 125 miles eastward from the South American coast of Brazil.*

Samuel Ferguson's Journal:

28 days out.
Today a good deal like yesterday, hot and showery. Wind rather more stiff, but cut up much by showers. Captain did intend making [going in sight of] Fernando de Noronha, the Brazilian convicts' place, but as it is 100 miles out of the way, he has given up the idea. The purpose of seeing the island was to verify the chronometers. This morning the Mate caught eleven small rats in a potato barrel; none had their eyes open. Wouldn't Toby have had a feast though. This afternoon saw a brig bound North, 10 miles away, however. She was going pretty fast with all sails set and was probably an English trader to some of the East Indian ports. I wish we would see a fellow bound home who would report us. 26½ days to the Equator is a very tolerable trip, hope to have a good run now to the Cape [Horn].

TUESDAY, FEBRUARY 13

Lat. 5° 39' S. Long. 32° 10' W. Dist. 220

Captain Mitchell's Journal:

First part heavy squall, winds fresh and calm alternately. Middle and latter, steady trades from S.E. by S. and fine weather. Boy Cox at work. An English steamer in company.

Henry Ferguson's Journal:

Good steady trade today and we have been going at a good rate all the time. It is well to the Southward as yet and we are now heading S.W. by S. We must have passed Fernando de Noronha sometime early this morning but even I suppose some 75 or 100 miles distant at the time. We may now say Cape St. Roque is fairly passed which is one of the bugbears, as if you cross the line too much to the West you get the S.E. wind that takes you on shore, or else N.E. by N., neither of which would be desirable. We overhauled and fairly passed today a British *steamer* bound probably for Pernambuco or Rio, who was going not only by steam, but had every sail set. We all considered it pretty well done. Have not suffered so much from heat today as there has been a good breeze, but the sun has been terrible.

Samuel Ferguson's Journal:

Splendid day, got up early and took another bath this morning. The manner is this: we get the sailors to fill a large tub made from an old cask. It is placed just by the house on the lee-ward side. Then are called and go on deck and have a real good souse which, as the thermom-eter gets high, one feels very much refreshed by it. At about 8 o'clock this evening a sail was made out to leeward, but at first too far ahead to make out what it was. We gradually made on him and by 2 P.M. she was abeam of us and proved an *English steamer*, probably bound to Pernambuco. She had all her sails set and was also under steam, so you see the *Hornet* is still good on the go. Very little now occurs to vary the routine of the day. The sunsets and clouds at that time are heavenly and really, I never saw such a variety of kinds and colors, though I don't think they are so bright as in the more Northern latitudes.

WEDNESDAY, FEBRUARY 14

Lat. 8° 53′ S. Long. 33° 45′ W.

Captain Mitchell's Journal:

Moderate Trades all this day prevailing well South. Saw an English and an American bark bound North. One box of acid burst. Threw it overboard.

Henry Ferguson's Journal:

St. Valentine's Day. We opened this morning, first thing before we were dressed even, our Valentine and it was "as good as they make 'em." We were delighted with the letters and contents, and feel most grateful to the kind givers both for the box and the manner it was given. Everything was in good order except a couple of letters that the cake had greased. Meant to have begun an answer today but the table was occupied all the A.M. and we didn't feel inclined in the P.M. Before breakfast we were called up on deck to see a couple of barks that were passing nearby, one to windward and the other to leeward. They were both American built, but the larger hoisted English colors. From the course they were holding, the English was bound for New York and the other for Europe. We spoke* them by hoisting our numbers 7306 at the gaff. One of them did the same, but they were too far off to distinguish. Hope she made out ours and will report us. Have had to head more West than is best or usual today.

* *i.e. signaled.*

Samuel Ferguson's Journal:

St. Valentine started us early this morning and kept us at work reading, talking over, and discussing our Valentine which was one of the best known. We thank most heartily the kind friends both for the articles and the kindness of thought. We found everything in good order but the two letters from Mr. Bingay to ourselves, which were a little injured with the candies and cakes getting soft. Our meditations over the above were broken in on by the Mate who informed us that there were two vessels ahead, one on each bow quite close and coming our way, so we bundled on deck and found both barks, one an American bound to England, the other an American ship under the English flag bound to New York. The latter we spoke showing our numbers (name) which brought out his, but as we both had a good breeze we soon widened the distance so that we could not make him out. The Englishman was very polite and dipped his colors. We went to breakfast and when we came up both were specks hard to find on the horizon. Page too short for today's log.

THURSDAY, FEBRUARY 15

Lat. 11° 35′ S. Long. 34° 30′ W.

Captain Mitchell's Journal:

First and middle, moderate Trades from S.E. Latter, light from South, ending nearly calm. One man, Noldt, up sick. Hard Trade this, dull work.

Henry Ferguson's Journal:

The wind has slacked up I am sorry to say today besides being more to the Southward than is becoming. Yesterday we were about off Pernambuco and only 60 miles from it. Today we are about 100 miles from land. Nothing of much interest has happened all today. We are now right under the sun and hot is no name for the weather. The butter is decidedly oleaginous and if a steak had been cut off the bullock I have no doubt but what it would be already cooked. The bright brasses are like so many stoves. Shade is very hard, too, to be got most of the day. Wrote or tried to write some nonsensical letter of thanks for our Valentine. Did not get very far. Wind pretty light and sea calm. Beautiful sunset this evening, looked like one of those chromatic lights thrown by the stereoptican.

Samuel Ferguson's Journal:

Weather fine as usual. Yesterday we were just off Pernambuco, about 60 miles from the coast. The wind very provokingly coming out about South-Southeast which has made us go all day today very close hauled. Today it has been in the same quarter but very light indeed.

Very hot, butter almost oil even in the tub. Even the claret is not a cooling drink. Today I went out as usual to take the altitude of the sun and what was my surprise to find that the maker had blunderingly made the instrument that it would not work above 88°, so that it is good for nix with the sun within 2° of Zenith either way. Blunt* should be hauled over the coals for this. Intended yesterday to have concocted a note of thanks to the Valentiners, but as the table was used in the morning could not do it.

Nothing in sight all day today. A splendid sunset again tonight, never two alike or nearly.

* *Edmund and George W. Blunt were chart and nautical instrument dealers in New York at 179 Water Street.*

FRIDAY, FEBRUARY 16

Lat. 13° 48' S. Long. 34° 40' W.

Captain Mitchell's Journal:

Begins light airs from South and calms. Middle and latter, moderate trade from E.S.E. A ship in sight bound North — wish it was this one.

Henry Ferguson's Journal:

Today the breeze has been better and I have not suffered so from the heat though all last night and this morning, I was the victim of a severe toothache. It has gone though, I am happy to say. We are now South of the sun though he is nearly directly overhead. There were two ships in sight today at different times. 1st Mate has made us a hammock which is very comfortable indeed. I laudanumed my tooth this morning and I believe that to it I can owe the departure. Saw the new moon for the first time tonight, very slim specimen indeed. Another fine sunset tonight. I am ashamed to say I have not been up at sun-rise yet, but the clouds when it is a little way up are very beautiful.

Samuel Ferguson's Journal:

Another fine day though very hot in sun. Early mornings and evenings delicious. The First Mate presented us with a hammock which he swung under the spanker boom. It is quite an installation. About noon today, discovered a large ship to windward, a good way off bound North. Mate saw another to leeward also bound North, neither were within speaking distance.

The days drag along very much alike now with hardly anything to change them. It being too hot to read with comfort, I have set to work to carve out a chain from a pretty good piece of pine wood and got 18 links cut and a place for ball and swivel with hook. The whole piece being, when whole, 18 inches long. Carpenter* has no good wood for carving or fancy whittling. Carpenter is rather at *butt* and not much of a fellow though he does his work pretty nicely, if he does take his time about it. He is a German and is rather afraid of the water working over the sides at channels, or caulking, etc.

* *B. Lawson, Sweden.*

SATURDAY, FEBRUARY 17

Lat. 15° 41' S. Long. 34° 50' W.

Captain Mitchell's Journal:

Very moderate Trades and hot weather all this day. Winds at S.E. and E.S.E. Ship sharp by the wind all the time since coming into S.E. Trades.

Henry Ferguson's Journal:

Today we had the queer (to us) sight of the sun to the North of us, thus completely changing the aspect of affairs. I believe that I will be making some mistake about E. and W., but luckily there are two compasses which can set me right. Found hammock great comfort and convenience today and think that they are a decided institution. Picked over apples today, a good many in status quo. They must be chucked to the pigs of which noble animals there are three representatives aboard, one big one, a Chileno with the most villainous long nose you ever saw, and two little fellows. Opened cask of tamarinds and drank tamarind water. Found it refreshing. Hot as blazes, not much wind and that has head us off to Westward all day. Better breeze tonight but still to the South.

Samuel Ferguson's Journal:

Again a fine day and I think that we have been particularly favored as we have not had a single rainy day since we started and never (but and excepting the Monday night after starting) have we had even to furl our topgallants. We are now blowing about not having the Trades as we should and today we have had to head Southwest by West, which is not convenient at all, the wind at the same time being very light. Today did two things, viz. picked over apples, which begin to want sorting, and got out some tamarinds, which made a good drink. Those in the keg never had molasses put over them till today. Took out about a 50 pound paint keg full to be made into tamarind water at pleasure. Today the Mate discovered an old hammock (man-of-war's) which he fetched out for our benefit, swung it in the shade and enjoyed most of the afternoon in it. Handsome sunsets continue, after which the evening comes on very quick. Southern Cross and Magellan's Clouds are now very plainly visible and early too.

SUNDAY, FEBRUARY 18

Lat. 17° 30' S. Long. 35° 54' W.

Captain Mitchell's Journal:

First and middle, light airs from S. to S.E., very baffling. Latter, steady light breeze from E.S.E., heavy swell from S.W. Very Hot. Long day, home in all my thoughts.

Henry Ferguson's Journal:

A little breeze this morning but by noon it disappeared leaving the deadest calm yet experienced with a heavy roll from S.W. Tonight at about seven, a breeze sprung up from that quarter and we are going along very nicely. Shower just passed over us. Sun dreadfully powerful in the morning and early afternoon but then overcast. Being now N. and nearly overhead, it is very hard to find shade. Saw some nautili and tried to catch one that was right up near the ship, but in so doing hit him too hard with the bucket which collapsed him whereat he sank. Sea very glassy and a sort of reddish scum upon the surface of it not beautiful to look at. Think that Trades are fickle.

Samuel Ferguson's Journal:

Very light wind all morning, towards noon became perfectly calm, not a breath except what the ship made by rolling. If the calms that we have seen before are calms I am sure this one is the deadest of the dead. In the afternoon the sun became obscured and, unless it had become so, the heat would have been almost intolerable. All day we have had a heavy head sea which denotes a Southwest wind. The Captain is rather put out that we should have no regular Southeast Trade as we should. He says we should be going here at the rate of 250 per day easy.

This evening we have been relieved a little by a smart breeze first and then a shower which, however, has turned us out of our course; the shower as usual took along our breeze. Have thought a good deal of home and Stamford today. It seems a long while since we left. Hope they have filled Mr. Mitchell's place with someone acceptable to all parties. Don't believe now that we shall be able to send home our letters. We must prepare ourselves now for showers and after them, heavy weather.

MONDAY, FEBRUARY 19

Lat. 18° 03' S. Long. 35° 47' W.

Captain Mitchell's Journal:

Light baffling airs, calms, and rain showers all the first and middle of this day. At 7 A.M. light breeze from N.E. continues through the day. Saw three ships bound North. No Trades. Ends very light.

Henry Ferguson's Journal:

Before breakfast two ships and a bark were in sight, two of them continuing in sight till afterward. They were all bound to the Northward and were a good distance off. In the course of the forenoon, saw another ship also bound North. After dinner saw a bark close by within a mile. Showed our colors, she replied with a Danish ensign, a white cross on a red ground. We then hoisted our numbers but elicited no response. Concluded she had none. Then put the ensign at the peak again and dipped it thrice. She acknowledged the compliment by doing the same thing. Hot as pepper. Breeze light from North most of the day, now there is nearly a dead calm, just enough wind to give her steerage way and no more. Squalls all around us. Saw a rainbow on one of them, very pretty one indeed.

Samuel Ferguson's Journal:

Last night showery but very hot. 5 A.M. two ships and a bark in sight, all bound North, all too far away to say anything to them by flag. Very light winds all day. All hands disappointed as we made an average run to the Line and surely expected the Trades this side; well Trades we have had, but very very light. This weather is burning us both up very much and in one place my forehead has begun to peel. We have seen the worst of it though, I guess. This afternoon met a bark and saw a ship a long way to leeward. The bark being within signalling distance, we set the Stars and Stripes, which after a while brought out the Danish flag. We then set our numbers (name) but received no reply, she probably not having a marine code. We then dipped and let hang and she replied and went. My cough still holds on and troubles me a good deal at night. I hope now that cool weather will take it off, as I am heartily tired of it.

TUESDAY, FEBRUARY 20

Lat. 19° 36' S. Long. 35° 42' W.

Captain Mitchell's Journal:

This day very light Trades from N.E. throughout. Weather hot and oppressive. Hope we shall get out from under the sun soon. Kills all the wind. Hard chance.

Henry Ferguson's Journal:

Another day with only a little breeze. I do so wish that we could get some wind to take us out of this dreadful hot weather. If we don't move on somewhat faster we will be having the *Lookout** and the *Ivanhoe*** catch us up — "Dei meliora"! Fortunately it was cloudy this afternoon and so deadened the effect of the sun a little. Hot is a very mild term for the sun's rays now-a-days. Very pretty sunset and most peculiar clouds I ever saw. Instead of laying down or being piled up in masses, you will see them standing up on end and assuming the most fantastic shapes. We saw a ship in the distance to windward today bound the same way as ourselves. Wind, what there is, is N.E., but we haven't gone more than 4 knots all day. Some swell from S.

* *The LOOKOUT was an extreme clipper built by Chase and Davis of Warren, Rhode Island, in 1853. She measured 1291 tons by 198 feet long by 38.4 beam by 21.9 deep. She was advertised in the NEW YORK SHIPPING LIST, Jan. 10, 1866, to sail on the same day as the HORNET.*

** *The New York clipper IVANHOE was built in 1847 by William Webb. She measured more than 1300 tons. There was an 1865-built merchant ship of Boston with the same name.*

Samuel Ferguson's Journal:

Again a fine day, hot as blazes though. At one time thermometer in cabin stood at 89°. North wind today which should, we would say, be cool, but down here is a hot wind. Everything is backwards, viz: sun at noon is North instead of South. Wind very light as may be seen by looking at our progress made since yesterday. Saw one ship to windward sailing the same way with us. Hope it isn't the *Lookout*, which was to start sometime after us. This unusual weather makes the Captain blow, but the worst of it is his wind don't help us. Now tonight we have a head sea and just wind enough to keep us moving through it. Fish, since we have had this calm weather, seem to have deserted us entirely. Am getting to know the ropes pretty well, have not tried a hand at steering yet, though I mean to some of these days when the sun is not so hot. Find washing aboard is no go, or at least so near it that it's no fun. Don't mean to have anything more than is absolutely necessary till we get to San Francisco.

WEDNESDAY, FEBRUARY 21

Lat. 21° 03' S. Long. 35° 52' W.

Captain Mitchell's Journal:

Very light airs all this day — tedious enough. Boys all on duty. Winds from N.N.E., ship dead before it. A ship in company bound S.

Henry Ferguson's Journal:

Another day all this tedious calm weather. It is a trial to the patience to lie like a log on the water when from all usual cases we ought to have a good breeze. However, I hope that it will not last much longer. Sun as usual dreadfully hot and shade a very desirable and somewhat scarce commodity. Somewhat to our disgust, the ship we saw yesterday has passed us and is now far ahead. Give us a breeze and I guess we can catch her. Began Thucydides today. Don't like his looks at all. We had a little shower at about half past eleven this morning, but it did not amount to anything. I wish we could have been near enough to find out that ship's name, but perhaps we may yet. Sam saw some little bits of fish this afternoon called rudder fish.

Samuel Ferguson's Journal:

As usual another fine day. Ship mentioned yesterday to windward, this morning appeared some ten miles ahead on the bow and has all day been gaining on us very fast. Our wind has been just aft all day and very light which is the *Hornet's* worst sailing point. Are in hopes before she gets too far to get a good side breeze and I guess we can fix her. Today has been again very hot and hard to keep in the shade, but next to impossible to stay in the cabin. This afternoon, had a little shower which made everything hotter than ever. Tomorrow is Washington's Birthday, hope they will think to put up the flag at home. Aboard ship, I fear, they take no notice of days, on deck at least. Find the tamarind water comes in first rate this weather, although the molasses we have is not of the choicest kind. Saw today a lot of small fish under the stern. Captain called them "Rudder Fish" and says they are a good eating fish when larger.

THURSDAY, FEBRUARY 22

Lat. 22° 28' S. Long. 36° 15' W.

Captain Mitchell's Journal:

Very light baffling airs all this day from North to East. Frequent showers and very hot. Set up mizzen rigging and back stays fore and aft. Ship ran away from us.

Henry Ferguson's Journal:

The birthday of the Father of his country, may it ever be remembered in every true American heart. Nothing particular has happened today to grace it except a slight improvement in the wind. However, to becalmed people all favors, however small, thankfully received. We are at this present moment about in the latitude of Rio and it is hot enough for any place. I fear that the wind will not last as it is less than it was. Spent the afternoon in the mizzentop. Shadiest place there is that I could find. There was a beautiful sunset tonight, not as grand as they sometimes are, but as bright colored as I ever saw one. There were some of the most brilliant green and gold clouds and all the fleecy streaks in the sky were tinged with the gold which made it look very pretty indeed.

Samuel Ferguson's Journal:

Again hot though a little better breeze. Very unfortunate we consider ourselves to have such miserable wind since we crossed the Line. I am much afraid that sixty days won't see us round the Horn and that the *Lookout* presses us closely. This month, which corresponds with our August, is the worst month to be in these parts. We honored the day by a bottle of claret at lunch and a glass of wine at dinner today, the toast being the "day and all who honor it". As I supposed, no notice was taken of it aboard otherwise.

Our adversary of yesterday was not to be seen this morning. Three-handed whist seems to wear very well and we almost every night play from 8 to 10, or 10:30. Henry and I have picked out all we could of Hoyle concerning cribbage and I guess we understand the principals though I am not quite sure we have everything right yet.

FRIDAY, FEBRUARY 23

Lat. 24° 09' S. Long. 37° 10' W.

Captain Mitchell's Journal:

Moderate breeze from N.N.E. all this day and fine weather.

Henry Ferguson's Journal:

Today is just a repetition of all that have preceded it for the last week, hot and calm though there is a better breeze than we have had. There have been three sails in sight today but they were at too great a distance to distinguish their particular rig, all except one and her we saw at night. Today for the first time I was *captured* aloft and made to pay my footing.* As I had been aloft so much and nothing said, I almost thought it had gone out of fashion. I gave the fellow half a dollar to drink my health. One of the men picked up a squid which somehow or other had got into the main-chains. It was a most curious looking thing. I would like Pynch to have seen him. The old fellow would have been delighted. How he got into the chains remains to be discovered.

* An old sailors' custom — Passengers were not supposed to climb the rigging and, if caught aloft, were required to pay a penalty to buy their way down to the deck.

Samuel Ferguson's Journal:

Still the same North-Northeast breeze as yesterday for which we are thankful, but should like a little more of it. One ship seen today from aloft far away on our weather beam, also some sort of vessel steering North, a long way off, however. Today one of the sailors found in one of the channels a squid, the funniest looking thing I ever saw. I wish I could have preserved it, but did not feel at liberty to go a bottle of whiskey on it. Fished today with accustomed luck for bonito.

We have certainly now got beyond the Trades and have for the last day or two lost the Trade clouds which are certainly very curious looking all around the horizon, raised up from it and heavy cumulus, but arranged like pillars or blocks piled up. Sometimes they break up into endless varieties of dogs, faces, toys, etc. Sunset splendid.

SATURDAY, FEBRUARY 24

Lat. 25° 50'S. Long. 37° 50'W.

Captain Mitchell's Journal:

First and middle, moderate breeze from N.E. and N. Latter, hauls gradually to the West and S.W. and S.S.W. with rain and lightning. Wind increases to a gale. Squalls and constant rain. Reduced sail. No observation.

Henry Ferguson's Journal:

Today is the first stormy day we have had since we started. It began at about 6 and has blown hard all day raising considerable sea, but has gone down a good deal and every prospect of a fine day tomorrow. We have been under three sails all day, reefed mizzen topsails, maintopsails, and reefed maintopmast staysail. Reefed fore topsail and fore course also fore topmast staysail. We have been heading S.E. by E. all day, but are now on the other tack and heading W. by S. Wind about S.S.W. End of a *Pampero** though it is uncommon to have them so far North. One of the men had a block drop from a yard above him and strike him on the back. Now though sore, he is as well as ever. Lucky it was not his head, he would have been killed.

* A storm which makes up in the pampas of the Argentine and comes off the land with great suddenness and violence.

Samuel Ferguson's Journal:

Last night was showery until about 4:30 to 5 this morning, when a regular Sou'wester set in with a good deal of rain. Blow has lasted all day with angry spurts of rain, the first rainy day since we embarked. Went on deck after breakfast and found sail reduced to reefed upper top-sails, topsails, and reefed courses with main topgallant staysail, fore-staysail and jib. Stayed under these all day until about 6 P.M., when the wind went down and we wore around and shook out all reefs. These Sou'westers have no business up here; should not fall in with one till 35° or 40° S. We certainly have been very unfortunate since crossing the Line in regard to winds. Tonight we had the most *unusual* sunset I ever saw: the whole heavens seemed lit up so that one could hardly tell where the sun did set. The change in appearance of ship and sea was astonishing, when I went on deck this morning. It was almost like travelling all night in the cars and awaking in some new place in the morning. No observations today, latitude worked out.

SUNDAY, FEBRUARY 25

Lat. 26° 26' S. Long. 38° 35' W.

Captain Mitchell's Journal:

A poor week's work. Begins fresh from S.W. by S. and S. and so continues through the day gradually dying out latter part. At 6 P.M. wore ship, head to the West. Carried away outer jib stay (rotted off at the masthead.) Great care this ship has had.

Henry Ferguson's Journal:

Nice breeze this morning but baffling and still more so towards night. We have been heading W. or a little North of West about all day, so that we will not have accomplished very much. This will be our poorest week's work yet. Beautiful day and most gorgeous fiery sunset which was not situated only in the West, but which extended over the whole sky. About sundown sighted a brig on the port tack that is going just the other way from us on the wind. She came up so that we saw her hull and distinguished her rig. I never saw such variety of sunsets as we have, no two alike and all wonderfully grand and beautiful with richer colors than I ever saw North. Twilight has returned to quite a decent length.

Cape Pigeon - woodcut from The World of the Sea, *1882.*

Samuel Ferguson's Journal:

Today a great contrast from yesterday, the wind coming from about the same quarter, say Southwest by South, only lighter. Have been on the West tack all day. The temperature was splendid. Just at sundown I discovered a sail in sight right ahead. She proved to be a brig probably bound to the Rio Grande somewhere. She was on the other tack from us. Shall probably be out of sight of her long before morning, although we are only just going along to keep up appearances. Yesterday we were visited by a couple of Cape Hens* which soar about and skim the water beautifully. They are about the size of a night hawk, but of a different shape and build, having very long wings which they use to skim with, seeming hardly ever to flap them. One stopped this afternoon to pick up a piece of meat the Mate threw over and soon after caught us up again with two others. Last night parted our jib stay so this morning the men had to go to work to rig another. I hope the rest of the rigging is not in the same condition that was.

* A variety of petrel found in high latitudes.

MONDAY, FEBRUARY 26

Lat. 26° 20' S. Long. 39° 30' W.

Captain Mitchell's Journal:

Light baffling airs and rain squalls all this day. Regular doldrums all day. Nothing done but box the yards round, first one way then other. Damn.

Henry Ferguson's Journal:

Our reckoning will tell today's story as well or better than I can. We have made only six miles difference in latitude and that to the Northward, and have been going round in a circle in a nearly dead calm all day. Water as glassy as anything and one time I even think we had sternway. Our friend the brig is ahead of us on the same course and has rather gained on us today. However, give us a breeze and I have no doubt but what we can overhaul him without difficulty. Another glorious sunset but unlike last night as possible. It has ceased, I am happy to say, to be so excessively hot as for the past three weeks it has been and we poor creatures are right glad of it. Squally all day. Most beautiful rainbow just before tea. A perfect arch showing all seven colors and part of a second outside of it.

Samuel Ferguson's Journal:

Today has been very showery and baffling. Nice breeze for ten minutes, then a shower and calm; headed in all directions. At about 11 P.M., a nice breeze sprang up from the Southeast so that we could about head our course, which continued the rest of the night. Last night our friend the brig tacked and kept by us although she did not run ahead of us all day on account of light winds. After our breeze sprang up, the Second Mate says we soon picked her up and passed her.

The temperature is certainly getting more pleasant and although the sun is hot in the middle of the day, it is not so abominably oppressive as it was; besides we again begin to notice the difference of the length of twilight.

It seems very funny to have the sun shine from the North instead of South. Our Cape Hens have kept themselves off today, because we talked about trying my pistol on one, I suppose. Today's the worst day's work yet. Six miles to North of where we were yesterday, though we are one degree to the Westward which is of no account.

TUESDAY, FEBRUARY 27

Lat. 27° 20' S. Long. 40° 19' W.

Captain Mitchell's Journal:

Calms, rain squalls, and doldrums all the first 12 hours of this day. Latter part, light steady breeze from S.E. All sail set by the wind.

Henry Ferguson's Journal:

Today there has been quite a nice little breeze from the right quarter and we have been sailing on our course S.S.W. most all day. The wind is not very heavy, but to us becalmed mariners it is very acceptable. There has been plenty of bonito about the bows today all the time and one of the sailors caught two and another three. Sam tried but without luck. I did not try. They are a most peculiar looking fish, have no scales, are very round and taper down almost to nothing, and they have a large flat tail. They have a queer custom of shaking when you take them by the tail that is as good as an electric shock. These would weigh 8 or 10 pounds. They sent some aft. I liked it, but it was very much like "Albany beef"* — but when you have been living on salt food they come acceptably.

* *Lincoln Colcord suggests that Henry probably means shad. However, bonito, a dry fish, is quite unlike shad, the "Sage of Searsport" observed.*

Samuel Ferguson's Journal:

Last night's breeze has remained steady all day today and we have all been enspirited a good deal by it, though it does come from such a quarter as to make us go quite close hauled and, therefore, not very fast. However, I reckon we have averaged five or six knots all day which is better than we have done in a long while.

This morning one of the sailors caught a bonito which certainly are the queerest fish I ever saw. Just back of the shoulder they are perfectly round and then taper off nearly so to within two inches of the tail which, in a 10 pound fish, is not one inch in diameter. Their mode of propulsion seems to come more from the lateral fins than the flukes of the tail. We had some steaks apiece for tea offered, which was very good though very dry and dark in color. Shut your eyes and you might swear it was "Albany Beef". It tasted to us more like veal cutlet than fish. I fished for nearly a couple of hours, but am afraid a squid is not the thing, the sailors say too large. Joe, the Portuguese, caught these today.

WEDNESDAY, FEBRUARY 28

Lat. 29° 32' S. Long. 41° 20' W.

Captain Mitchell's Journal:

Moderate breeze from S.E. and fine weather all this day. Latter part inclines to East. All possible sail set.

Henry Ferguson's Journal:

Nothing at all worthy of note has happened today but we have had a nice fresh breeze (though it might blow considerably harder and not hurt itself at all). We have been sailing on our course all day and hope that we have got out of the calms for the present. No bonitos to be seen today except you may say some steaks on the table this morning. Sunset as usual handsome though not remarkable. For the last two or three days we have had birds around us. They are Cape Hens which have probably been blown up here. They scale through the air in a very pretty manner. They are about the size and give you somewhat the idea of whippoorwills.

Samuel Ferguson's Journal:

Another fine day with a good breeze from about Northeast. We are going better today than for a long while. Today is the last day of winter though that seems very funny to say here when a week ago we had the thermometer at ninety degrees. I am very glad of this cooler weather as one feels much better in it. My cough has not yet left me, but I hope by the time we get to this latitude on the other side it will be gone. Very little to jot down today. I opened our thermal of ginger snaps and found them first rate, crisp and nice. During the hot and damp weather never feel like eating them. Lemons are pretty much gone, the apples want eating rapidly, which want we can accommodate them. No more bonitos today.

Chain that I cut from the 18 inch stick now measures 22-1/8 inches, which is more gain than I thought, for "what will he do with it?" I wish I could get a good flat piece of hard wood.

THURSDAY, MARCH 1

Lat. 31° 52'S. Long. 42° 45'W.

Captain Mitchell's Journal:

Moderate breezes from E.N.E. to N.E. all this day. Latter part cloudy and threatening. Bent upper and lower main topsails, best.

Henry Ferguson's Journal:

Another day with a good Northeasterly wind and we have been going on very nicely all the time. I suppose we have averaged eight knots all day. Nothing of interest to chronicle. Studied in morning and studied navigation, how to take the time, in the afternoon. Now (8 P.M.) the breeze has freshened still more and we are moving through the water nicely. It is raining a little and there is a good deal of lightning with some thunder, all pretty distant though. These signs predict a change and a S.W. blow would not surprise us. Our winds now are what they call cyclones — blow in a circle, begin one side and gradually work all the way round and, like as not, end off with a blow at S.W.

Samuel Ferguson's Journal:

45 days out at noon.
Wind today about the same as yesterday, though perhaps stiffer. Upper main topsail getting

pretty delapidated, so took it in and sent up new one made of hemp. Today is the first threatening looking day that we have had. The glasses* show a change and I suppose we may as well make up our minds for something nasty before long. Between 35° and 45° are to be expected sort of cyclones in which the wind blows for a while from every point, ending up generally with a South-wester. We have a good many birds about which the Captain says denotes that there has been heavy weather to the South of us, as these birds (which seem to delight in soaring about and going as near as possible to the water without touching) come from the Falkland Islands. Have seen no sail for some days.

Am reading Irving's *Columbus*** which is pleasantly written and very interesting. Men buying Sou'wester garments to be prepared for the Cape.

* *Barometers.*

** *Washington Irving's monumental HISTORY OF THE LIFE AND VOYAGES OF CHRISTOPHER COLUMBUS was first published in London in 1828.*

FRIDAY, MARCH 2

Lat. 33° 08' S. Long. 44° 10' W.

Captain Mitchell's Journal:

First part fresh breeze from N.E. Middle, sharp lightning in S.W., heavy thunder, and much rain throughout. At 2 A.M. wind hauls to N. and N.W. At 4 A.M. hauls to W.S.W., hard gale. Ends hard gale and heavy sea from S.W. Ship lower and two reefed upper topsails and foresail.

Henry Ferguson's Journal:

At about four this morning it came on to blow like all wrath and by breakfast time had kicked up considerable sea. It was directly ahead which seems to be the prevalent wind every where we go. We stood as well as we could on the starboard tack all day under reefed topsails and foresail, fore- and main-topmast staysails. We passed a barque on the other tack who had nothing but a reefed main topsail and foretopmast staysail. Sea runs pretty high and rolls us around and pitches us up and down considerably. Our great allowance of calm weather has spoilt me, for the pitching discomposed me again today. However, I was at every meal. In the A.M. the sea was on her quarter, but afterwards it got more ahead.

Samuel Ferguson's Journal:

Yesterday's threatening came true and very punctually. After writing last night we had a number of thunder storms and then a fresh Northeast breeze till about 4 A.M., when it died and in about 20 minutes the wind came out piping from the South-Southeast. The weather was, however, perfectly clear and these Sou'westers amount to our Nor'westers; all day today it has been blowing very hard and has raised a tremendous old sea somewhat to Henry's discomfort. Stood all day close hauled under very short sail for us, viz. fore top-gallant staysail, reefed upper fore top-, and full lower topsails, and fore course part of the day; then main topgallant staysail with reefed upper topsail, and lower topsail, mizzen lower topsail.

The sea was so boistrous that the ship rolled and pitched fearfully, looking at times as if she would bury herself entirely. Saw today an albatross, very far North for them the Captain says. Must have been blowing hard down here a good while. Met a bark early this morning with only one topsail and staysail.

Albatross - woodcut from The World of the Sea, *1882.*

SATURDAY, MARCH 3

Lat. 34° 14' S. Long. 44° 46' W.

Captain Mitchell's Journal:

Strong gale from S.W. Latter part, S.S.W. At 12 Midnight wore ship to the West. Ends fresh from S.W. by S. Top-gallants set. Second Pampero before getting to the river, encouraging.

Henry Ferguson's Journal:

Began the day by wearing round at midnight and sailing West on the port tack. Wind and sea from the same quarter but less sea, enough though to roll us about considerably and make the dishes slide round in the most playful manner. Not troubled at all with yesterday's complaint, but have been sleepy all day. Passed a homeward bound bark this morning who, though she had a fair wind, had not as much sail on her as we have. We are now under to' gallant sails and the wind is a good deal down though still ahead. I forgot to say yesterday that we saw albatrosses for the first time. Great big things that scale along in the easiest way and yet very fast. Got a head like a calf only big bill. Saw them again today.

Samuel Ferguson's Journal:

Today fine wind, the same though not so heavy; sea down somewhat, still a good deal of roll, however. Last night we wore round and now stand on the port tack heading West by North. Saw today some more albatross which do everlastingly soar, hardly ever moving their wings. This afternoon butchered pig, the cook officiating in the most butcherless manner. Her royal highness now hangs in the mizzen rigging all sewed up in canvas. All hands agreeing that the moon poisoned the meat, in what manner no one seems to know. Met early this morning another bark under short sail, bound Northeast, rolling tremendously. Two Southwesters in a week is rather opposed to our getting on very rapidly. I am afraid the *Lookout* will give us a hard push if she does not beat us out and out. However, we have made the most of what wind we have had.

SUNDAY, MARCH 4

Lat. 34° 32' S. Long. 46° 50' W.

Captain Mitchell's Journal:

Begins fresh from S.S.W., gradually moderating down. Middle part calm. At 5 A.M., light breeze from W.N.W. lasting through the day and increasing to a good strong breeze.

Henry Ferguson's Journal:

Today we have had a nice breeze from the West or West-Nor'west and have been on our course all day. It is pretty moderate now but at sunset the clouds looked as if we might be going to have another gale. The wind is very damp so that all the decks and everything exposed are quite wet, which is strange for a West wind as they are generally clear and dry. It is getting a good deal cooler and feels like autumn. There were a good many Cape Hens round the stern today, one of which kept continually going to the top of the topgallant mast and inspecting the fly which evidently troubled his mind in some way. An albatross or two came sailing by occasionally, great big things they are, but with the easiest flight imaginable. Wind has been fresh all day and this afternoon we carried away our jib topsail which was an old sail and mildewed. Split it right up.

Samuel Ferguson's Journal:

Another fine day, wind changed during the night to about West-Northwest, so we headed Southwest, about our desire. Sorry to say, however, this was too good to last and by noon our jib topsail split right across and had to be unbent to be mended. Today we have been enjoying the luxury of fresh meat again. Old pig that suffered yesterday having furnished it, and very good the liver and roast pork was. Must say I am getting pretty tired of ham and salt meat, although both are very nice indeed. Finished yesterday our first box of claret. I have no doubt this will last us well. I have been a little sparing because I thought it best to have plenty in the Tropics on the other side, when our water might not be so good as it is now. Have thought a good deal of home today from which we have been away seven weeks tomorrow. We have a pretty scaley set of men for crew, some ailing in various ways all the time; some good men though.

MONDAY, MARCH 5

Lat. 36° 16' S. Long. 47° 12' W.

Captain Mitchell's Journal:

Begins W.N.W. At 1 P.M., hauls to W.S.W. Very damp weather. At 12 Midnight, hauls South and dies away. Tacked ship. Latter part calm. Very heavy dew last night. Ends calm and hot — a sure indication of another Pampero.

Henry Ferguson's Journal:

Wind exceedingly small and from 8 A.M. to 2 P.M. there was a dead calm. A wind then rose from W.N.W. but not very much of it. Looks ugly round the horizon. We are now off the Plate River where the big blows live and I expect we will have one before very long. It's a mighty windy region down here, and the wind has had a good deal of practice in blowing. Worked out the longitude today with the aid of the Captain's chronometer. We got it within two miles of what the Captain did, which was as near as could be expected taking the observations at different times. Wind very damp which is queer for a West wind.

Samuel Ferguson's Journal:

Very light wind this morning which dies to a perfect calm by 8 o'clock, remaining so till about 2 P.M., when a slight breeze sprang up from the West-Northwest. Worked out longitude this morning by chronometer, Henry having taken observation at about 8 A.M. Are now just about off the River de La Platta, where we may expect tremendous blows. Today has been a weather breeder so I expect a blow before long. We fare much better aboard than I had expected. Soup every day, oyster, clam, oxtail, bean, pea, and vermicelli alternating. I am sorry to say our cow is running dry. Though I should have thought they would have taken plenty of cows if they took any. It is now struck off tea which don't disturb me any, we are still to have it for coffee. Temperature this morning splendid. Just cool and bracing without being chilly. This afternoon the wind is very damp, so much so that the decks, railings, etc. are all wet with it. North wind is our hot wind now which seems funny. Hope this kind of weather and wind is played out.

TUESDAY, MARCH 6

Lat. 37° 20' S. Long. 49° 00' W.

Captain Mitchell's Journal:

At 2 P.M. breeze from W.N.W. light and so continues with threatening appearance through the night. At 6 A.M. very heavy squall from South taking us all aback. Wore short round. Latter part, strong gale from S. by E. and rough sea.

Henry Ferguson's Journal:

It began the day by a very sudden shift of wind and a tolerable hard blow so sudden that for a little while we were taken square aback. Wind from N.W. all night, but now from the South. Rather ugly work if we should lose our rudder* and have to go into Rio or Montevideo. However, I hope it won't do so again. We have had a stormy wind and some sea all day and it is getting colder fast. Farther we go, worse it will be, that's plain. Great many birds about of four or five kinds. One great black fellow with wings each 18 inches or 2 feet long keeps coming up almost aboard all the time. Tried to get a shot at him, but when I went to get the pistol he departed to parts unknown.

* *By being taken heavily aback again suggests Lincoln Colcord.*

Samuel Ferguson's Journal:

This morning was awoke from a turn-over nap by pretty loud and lively orders on deck and soon after we had a regular squall, wind piped and rain pelted down tremendously. Captain had just gone on deck and had seen what was up and just got the cro'jack yard braced when it struck us and took us aback on main and foremasts. However, we soon got wind and got off. All day it has been stormy and rained in morning, but sun came out at noon. This evening the sea is pretty high and we are heading just so it takes us on our port bow, so we roll and pitch considerably. The weather has got decidedly cooler, our evenings after tea make one desire to keep in motion. A great increase of birds today, one large black fellow fully three feet from tip to tip. He hardly ever flies, but continually soars about, occasionally lighting to pick up something. Have not seen a ship for an age and now that we are off the river, shall not probably until off the Cape, as coming this way the course is generally more easterly. A game of whist is a regular constitution now of an evening. We keep a regular score.

WEDNESDAY, MARCH 7

Lat. 37° 14' S. Long. 51° 30' W.

Captain Mitchell's Journal:

Heavy gale from South all this day and heavy sea. Ship under close reefed upper and lower topsails, main topmast staysail, fore topmast staysail, and main spencer. On port tack, heading W.S.W. Hard weather.

Henry Ferguson's Journal:

Blew detestably all night and that accompanied by the heavy sea made it an uncomfortable night for unfortunates who sleep in berths 18 inches wide. We rolled and tossed about so much and the wind made such a noise that we neither of us got to sleep till 3 or 4 o'clock in the morning. I got so disgusted with my berth at somewhere round 2 or 3 I came out and lay on the cabin lounge. Had a little toothache and I had an unpleasant night of it. Head wind all day, hard in morning and ship rolling furiously. Moderated toward evening but still rolling immensely. Great many birds of all kinds from Albatrosses to Mother Carey's round the stern. We fed them and practiced pistol shooting at them, but did not succeed in killing any. They are the sauciest and most importunate birds I ever saw, came almost aboard.

Samuel Ferguson's Journal:

Last night was a roarer, the worst that we have had as regards rolling. Did not get to sleep until after 4 A.M. At about 1 or 2, shipped a big sea that came over just abaft amidships and broke over the poop with a rush, dousing the First Mate and nearly taking him off his legs. All day long stood about Southwest by compass, which is really only one point South of West. Towards evening sea went down somewhat which was decidedly an improvement.

Without meaning to boast I think I am pretty well proof in regard to sea sickness, though very likely the heavy weather off the Horn may fetch me. So far have only been sick the second day. A great increase of birds of all kinds. We wasted some powder and ball on them to no effect though there were some hair-breath escapes. The albatross are not as yet very tame or very numerous. Were under reefed topsails most all day and standing very close.

THURSDAY, MARCH 8

Lat. 37° 38' S. Long. 53° 10' W.

Captain Mitchell's Journal:

S. by E. all first and middle, fresh gale and high sea. Latter good stiff breeze from S. by W. Water discolored. If this not hard work to get South, I give it up.

Henry Ferguson's Journal:

Had a jolly night's rest which made me feel somebody. Wind and sea are both down somewhat, in fact a good deal, but wind dead ahead as usual. We have been on the starboard tack all yesterday and today and both days have been on soundings as may be seen from the color of the water which is green instead of the bright blue it usually is. There was a big turtle alongside of us this morning and just after dinner we passed a great beast of a sunfish, a most curious looking animal. Ship in sight today to the Southard and on the same tack as we, but he could not sail neither as fast nor as close as we did and he fell a little behind. At four he tacked and we also and we are now gaining on him. We can't be more than 50 miles from the South American coast now. Wind still dead ahead. Our course on this tack is Southeast by East.

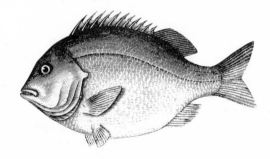

Sunfish - woodcut from
Fishing In American Waters, *1869.*

The Green Turtle - woodcut from The Monsters of the Deep, *1875.*

Samuel Ferguson's Journal:

Today fine, wind gone down as well as the sea somewhat and it again does you good to see the top-gallant sails set, which for the last day or two have been furled. This river is a hard nut to crack as may be observed by the progress we make South. Yesterday and today we have had green water instead of grey or blue of the deeper sea. All day today we were about at 70 fathoms water and towards evening, 4 P.M., tacked and now stand Southeast by East. Just after dinner saw a large ship about 10 miles to windward on our beam with all sails set. By the time we tacked we had run a good piece ahead though not enough to go to windward of her. We both tacked at same time and are now gaining on her fast, she still somewhat to windward, however. Captain saw today a large turtle. We also saw a large sunfish and a lot of birds called "Sailors Ghosts" and whale birds, a tremendous flock of them. Tom Valette's birthday about this time. I wish I had thought to tell Sarah to get him something for me though I have no doubt she will. My regular log gets along rather slowly as I find it hard to fill it with anything but the same story.

FRIDAY, MARCH 9

Lat. 37° 40'S. Long. 53° 40'W.

Captain Mitchell's Journal:

Begins fresh breeze from S.S.W., short ugly sea. At 4 P.M. tacked to the East after which wind hauls again to South. Middle part, moderates and hauls to S.E. From 4 A.M. to close, calm. A ship in company. No observation.

Henry Ferguson's Journal:

There was a dead calm all day till four P.M. when there got up a light air. However, even now it is not much. Ship we saw yesterday still in sight but some distance off to the Northwest of us, but by half past nine we were up to her and passed her as if she had not moved. We passed within an eighth of a mile of her and would, if it had been daylight, have gone close enough to hail her. Great many whale birds round. They are whitish about half the size of a duck and are very pretty looking floating on the water. We are now in whaling ground and I should not be surprised to see some. Hope that we may. No observation, but we are about where we were yesterday noon.

Samuel Ferguson's Journal:

Fine day but dead calm till 4 P.M., when a slight breeze sprang up. Cloudy at noon, so did not get the latitude ourselves. Last night while in our game, the Second Mate came in and said that we had overhauled our fellow traveler and that we were close enough to run along side to speak him. As we were to leeward, Captain concluded not to go too close. We went on deck to see the fellow and we passed him almost as if he was at anchor. When off our quarter he bore down on us. but we could not wait for him and today he was a long way to the leeward, though still in sight and has picked up somewhat with the very light winds.

The wind has now got around to the North-Northwest which will probably end again in a light old Southwester. We seem fated not to get South of this River. I hope, however, we will make up hereafter for time lost now. Steward made a capital head cheese from our old butter and today served us some pork and curry, first curry I have tasted. It was a good dish though I could live without it. Captain says I will get plenty of it in China.

SATURDAY, MARCH 10

Lat. 40° 06'S. Long. 55° 20'W.

Captain Mitchell's Journal:

Calm till 4 P.M., after which a light breeze from N.E. Middle and latter, light breeze from N.W., smooth sea and pleasant, misty. Two ships in company. Water discolored, many birds.

Henry Ferguson's Journal:

Water calm today, but I am glad to say we got a little more breeze and are going along quite nicely. Two vessels in sight, one on our starboard quarter, and one on our port bow. The one to starboard is a ship but not the same one that we were with yesterday. Though a long distance off we hoisted our ensign. He replied but we did not with certainty make out his nation. As it was red as much as we could make out, he is most likely an Englishman. The other is a bark a long way ahead. Spent most of the forenoon pistol shooting at the whale birds which were round in great numbers. Came very near to several and I am pretty sure wounded one. The sailors say they are dead sailors' ghosts. We have now dropped the ship nearly out of sight astern and the bark has done the same for us.

Samuel Ferguson's Journal:

Light breeze during night, which by morning put us out of sight of our companion of last two days, but showed us another ship steering the same way as we, but about 10 miles ahead on our starboard bow. By noon we had passed her and stood towards her showing our colors, which brought out hers, which we made out to be English, but could not be certain as the wind held out her flag directly towards us. Tonight she is hull-down astern. We have also been in company with a bark, which has showed us his heels and is some distance ahead. If fortune gives us a good breeze tomorrow or tonight, we will overhaul her. 21 feet, 7 inches is too much draft to go quickly through the water without a good breeze. All day we have been in pretty shallow water, say 40 or 50 fathoms, and about 60 miles from the coast. The greatest quantities of whale birds all morning. Henry blazed away with my pistol and thinks he wounded one. Also saw tremendous schools of fish, while every now and then a porpoise would roll up among them. Also saw marks of a whale. Today is the first day in a long time that we have been able to stand on our course with a free wind. Wind has been steady though light. Made perhaps 6 or 7 knots per hour. Saw at about 10 A.M. quite distinctly tide rips, which seems funny. "Wives and sweethearts" tonight after our game. Color of water today a rich green. Have seen the Sound just the same.

SUNDAY, MARCH 11

Lat. 42° 30'S. Long. 57° 50'W.

Captain Mitchell's Journal:

Begins moderate breeze from North and fine weather. Middle and latter, fresh and dense fog, almost rain. At 12, clears [?] and gives us an observation. See no vessels.

Henry Ferguson's Journal:

A breeze accompanied by a dense fog which moistened the sails and made them hold the wind arose last night and lasted till this noon, that is the breeze, for the fog went away in the forenoon. In the afternoon there was not very much wind but it headed us directly off so that whereas before we were steering S.W. by S., we are now only making S.E. by E. on the same tack. There were also heavy thunderings to the S.W. and as the barometers have fallen somewhat we would not be surprised if we were blessed with another Sou'westerly gale. We are now off the coast of Patagonia and on soundings which makes the water a beautiful green and tends to make the air cold and raw. There have been a great many porpoises playing about the ship evidently seeing how close they could get to the bow without getting hit. They tried to harpoon some of them, but did not succeed though there were some hair's breadth escapes.

Samuel Ferguson's Journal:

Last evening wind freshened to a 10-knot breeze. Fog arose and made everything very wet. Fog remained this morning till about 10; best day's run in a long time. Nothing seen of either of our companions; lots of porpoises, sailors tried to harpoon one but did not succeed.

Wish we were off-soundings for the air is damp and disagreeable particularly evenings, making thick clothes desirable. We are now in a corresponding latitude to Boston and only about an hour's difference in time from New York, The wind has again shifted and we now head Southeast instead of Southwest by South, our course. I hope we shall have something to compensate for our bad luck before long. Days are getting pretty monotonous, particularly when wind is very light or a calm. One can't read comfortably or rather you get tired of it and the ship does not furnish any very comfortable chairs. Suppose the journalistic letter to us at home is assuming formitable proportions. However, it won't be slighted by the two travelers. A long passage shortens Henry's stay.

MONDAY, MARCH 12

Lat. 43° 13'S. Long. 57° 00'W.

Captain Mitchell's Journal:

At 12 breeze fails. 2 P.M. hauls to S.W. and South where it continues moderate through the the day. Hard chance to get to the S.W. Fair wind one day and head winds ten. Awful progress.

Henry Ferguson's Journal:

A most uninteresting day. There has been hardly any wind at all and what there has been has been dead ahead so that we have been heading West all day. It has been overcast all day and cloudy a good part of the time and decidedly raw and somewhat chilly. There have been great lots of Mother Carey's Chickens round the stern today and we passed an albatross swimming majestically, but afterwards he took to his wings and passed us. Learnt how to make Sennit and French Sennit and also the long splice. Hope to learn a good lot of these and such things for they can't fail to come useful sometime sailing in the Sound especially. First penguin seen today, though I myself did not have the felicity.

Samuel Ferguson's Journal:

Our old luck, wind what there is, right ahead. Weather cold and raw, much more March and September as it should be down here. Nothing of special interest today. Paid Cox a visit and had a cigar offered me, the first I have had in my mouth since leaving New York. Find smoking doesn't pay. Neither Captain nor Mate smoke and it's like going on a spree alone. My pipe shows an inclination to color and I expect a little more steady smoking would put a good hue on it. Most of the birds have deserted us, a few Cape Hens and a quantity of Mother

Carey's Chickens still follow in our wake. There is some chance of Captain Mitchell going to China with the ship; if it turns out so I hope I can make it out to go with him. I don't mean to cut California or the Sandwich Islands for it, however. I have some notion of going in a Frenchman if I can find a good ship, which Captain says he thinks there is no doubt of. It would give me a good chance to pick up and speak the language.

TUESDAY, MARCH 13

Lat. 44° 04' S. Long. 57° 45' W.

Captain Mitchell's Journal:

Begins light from South. Middle very light and baffling from S. to W. Calm 4 hours. At 4 A.M. light breeze from W.N.W., thick fog. Ends moderate from W.N.W. All sail set.

Henry Ferguson's Journal:

Wind was from some chance today favorable and though not blowing hard, it has carried us along nice at an average rate of from 7 to 10 knots. If this would only keep on it would do very nicely but you can't tell where the wind won't be from next and the strong probability is that it will be from dead ahead. We are perceiving the Autumn weather more and more and I fear the sun will be at the Line before we get to the Cape. However, our days and nights will be the same length if we don't stay too long. There is somewhat of a head sea on a long swell so that it looks as if there might be more where it comes from. Coming events cast their shadows before.

Samuel Ferguson's Journal:

This morning was agreeably surprised to find the ship heading on our proper course, viz, Southwest by South. Wind pretty steady all morning though light, say 6 or 7 knots. This afternoon increased and we are now making 10 knots. Weather getting considerably cooler, making a full winter suit, *sine* overcoat, not too warm. Such weather being much more conducive to exercise than the tropical. Talk about the stove, but the pipe is still stored away. Have not seen any vessels now for a few days, expect soon to be among a number, as they all go inside the Falkland Islands.

    Captain saw today large quantities of kelp, a sort of sea-weed, very large and quite a pretty color, a redish brown. It grows like a branch with long leaves from it, thus: It is much too large to attempt to press. It is the kind used I think that iodine or some base comes from.

WEDNESDAY, MARCH 14

Lat. 45° 23' S. Long. 59° 40' W.

Captain Mitchell's Journal:

Begins good breeze from N.W. Middle, moderate hauling to South and dying away, remaining calm until 10 A.M. Ends moderate breeze from S.S.E. Damp, hazy weather, very unsettled.

Henry Ferguson's Journal:

This morning it was a pretty dead sort of calm, but a little breeze sprung up which has kept increasing so that we are now going on quite nicely. It is from the S.E. so that we sail on our course on the starboard tack instead of the port as we have been doing. They sent down the mizzen-royal yard this morning and I was surprised to see how small both it and the sail were. I had made altogether too big allowances for the height of the mast. We saw also a whale or rather to speak more correctly, saw and heard a whale blow this afternoon. He was about an eighth of a mile off. Water a very dark green, beautiful color, but not to be compared to the deep sea blue of mid-ocean.

Samuel Ferguson's Journal:

Wind lasted till about 1 A.M., then calm till about 10, then a fresh breeze sprang up from Southeast and we have been making about 5 or 6 knots on our course. Captain expects a blow, but tradition says Equinoxial gales blow off shore in this region. However, this may be, I guess we have enough water to stand a good gale. Color of water still queer, various hues, but clear. Shall not see the beautiful blue till after we round the Cape. Quantities of kelp, some almost covered with barnacles. This afternoon saw a whale spout, though he did not show his black majesty. Mate says they were blowing in numbers around the ship early this morning. Barnacles of a queer shape and enormous size are beginning to attach themselves to the ship, particularly about the stern post and rudder. Still no vessels in sight today, not even from the main top-gallant mast. Took down this morning mizzen royal, which will stay down till we have got into the 45°'s or 50°'s on the other side.

Whales - woodcut from The Riverside Natural History, *1884.*

THURSDAY, MARCH 15

Lat. 46° 42'S. Long. 61° 00'W.

Captain Mitchell's Journal:

Commences moderate breeze from S.S.E., inclining Easterly. Middle, S.E., pleasant. Latter, N.E., sea smooth, wind light and weather fine. Water green. Remarkable long time for light winds in this region.

Henry Ferguson's Journal:

Not very much of interest to chronicle today. No wind of any consequence in the morning, but it has been gradually increasing and now, though not doing wonders, still we are making on our course, which is an important circumstance in the region where head winds are so persistently prevalent. Ship came in sight today about on our beam, but a long distance off, and which caught up to which, we couldn't quite make out. We came closer all afternoon, but are about the same in relation to the course. Sometimes we would seem to gain and others she would. She is now some eight or ten miles off to the S.E. of us. Our course is S.S.W. with the wind a point or so off being directly aft, just so that the stay-sails and jibs draw.

Samuel Ferguson's Journal:

Not much to log today. Breeze very light this morning but fair. Towards noon, freshened to about a 5 knot breeze. After dinner ship noticed just abeam on our port side; remained about in relative position all afternoon, she drawing a little nearer to us. Presume she is in ballast bound to the Chinchas for a cargo of guano. Today a regular sort of a threatener all day. If ashore, I should predict a regular old fashioned Easterly three-day storm. Captain rather expects something of the sort as so mild weather is very unusual.

We must take it as it comes and be content with what we get. This cool weather agrees with the subscriber, giving him much more appetite than he has had since embarking. My cough is also better, although not yet departed. Spent part of morning in making sennet with boys, and of this afternoon, in stopping old sails. Am only waiting a good day to take my hand at the wheel.

FRIDAY, MARCH 16

Lat. 48° 30'S. Long. 63° 20'W. (Dead reckoning)

Captain Mitchell's Journal:

Moderate breeze from N.N.E. all this day. Middle part, steady rain. Latter, thick fog. A ship in company. Barometers low. Ends thick, no observation.

Henry Ferguson's Journal:

Northeast wind today with fog for most of the forenoon and afternoon till about three when it shifted to North or a little West of it, and the fog rolled off. Now (8 P.M.) it seems to be coming up again though as yet it is a beautiful clear night. We were unable to get an observation at noon today so the positions are from dead reckoning. Lit the first fire today. It was very damp on account of the fog though not particularly cold. The first attempt succeeded in filling the cabin with smoke, second was a little better, and the third made a good fire. Ship that was yesterday abeam of us is now dropped some way astern and is hidden in the fog from which we have emerged. We are evidently beating her.

Samuel Ferguson's Journal:

This morning real disagreeable with a swirling rain till about noon, then foggy and clear again till about sundown when the fog rolls in from the East. Pretty good breeze all day, but just aft; we have put our companion of yesterday pretty well astern.

Though we may make a long passage, we certainly do as well if not better than almost all we see. A good breeze, say even a 6-knot one, if not directly aft generally sends the *Hornet* through the water quicker and easier than any of our opponents, yet unless perhaps some light bark. 21 feet, 6 inches requires some wind to start.

Today being damp and cold, the Captain had the stove pipe brought in and this afternoon we have had a little fire for the first time for seven weeks nearly. Nothing new to log today in the way of sightseeing. The water here is quite dark and not clear and transparent as the deep sea blue is. Quantities of kelp pass every day.

SATURDAY, MARCH 17

Lat. 49° 35 'S. Long. 64° 10'W.

Captain Mitchell's Journal:

Light breezes from N.N.E., dark weather, thick fog, smooth sea, begins this day. Middle part, hauls to W.S.W., S., and S.E. At 5 A.M. tacked to S.W., dense fog, wind light. Latter part hauls round to East. Fog occasionally lifts. Ship in company. Ends light from E.N.E.

Henry Ferguson's Journal:

Good Easterly breeze all day which has at last taken us down to 50° S. and now rounding the Cape is the matter of greatest interest. Our friend was on our lee beam alone most of the day, but all of a sudden another fellow made his appearance and came up close to him and spoke him and had quite a conversation. Then another ship appeared well off to leeward which, when she lifted, proved to have a white hull from which we judge she is a Frenchman. Soon the two who had had the talk seemed to think that they wanted some more, so one of them waited for the other and they had another friendly confab. We could not make out their flags. After tea we saw in the dim distance another sail which we think is a bark though we could not make her out plainly. Fog in morning, but cleared off.

Samuel Ferguson's Journal:

Foggy and disagreeable all morning. Sun out at intervals, but horizon very bad for an observation for longitude, though the above [position] is the mean of four sights taken. Got up from below my box of ale thinking the pleasant weather was more suitable to ale drinking.

When judge my sorrow and constination at finding only five bottles out of the two dozen whole! Some had burst, though most had blown out the corks. I am very sorry but after being out five days it got too warm for ale. This afternoon we had more company than we have had yet: three ships and a bark. Two of the ships during the afternoon had two confabs, the foremost one bracing up and waiting for the other. They then sailed close along side one another for some time. Later in the afternoon the foremost one appeared to have forgotten something and layed to again. The third ship was painted white and appeared to be a Frenchman. The penguins seem to be very numerous down here by their crying. I have not yet seen one, however, although the Mate said he saw some quite close to the ship.

SUNDAY, MARCH 18

Lat. 52° 10'S. Long. 65° 30'W. (Dead reckoning)

Captain Mitchell's Journal:

Fresh wind from N.E. first part and thick fog. Sunset fog lifts, three ships and a bark in sight. Middle part, good breeze from E.N.E. Latter, wind hauls to E.S.E., dense fog. Ship sharp by the wind. Hard chance, dark, thick, gloomy weather. No observation.

Henry Ferguson's Journal:

Last night the wind edged round to S.E., which, seeing we are as far West as we want to be and that we are in a sort of a corner here, was a little too much of a good thing. Nevertheless, we have been sailing S. and S. by W. all day and just now (at 8 P.M.) have tacked and are standing off to the N.E. I suppose that we will not stay very long on this tack as the Falkland Islands are only 100 miles to the E.N.E. of us, and we only want offing enough to make Cape St. John or Le Maire Straits, whichever the Captain thinks the best. Cape St. John is the Easterly end of Staten Land and is the furthest East of any of the land here. Heavy fog all morning which lifted after dinner, but we were unable at any part of the day to get any satisfactory observations. Penguins screaming considerably.

Penguins - woodcut from The Ocean, *1856.*

Samuel Ferguson's Journal:

The most thoroughly disagreeable day we have had yet. All morning foggy with cold wind from East-Southeast. Lifted about noon enough to give us an uncertain sight for observation.

As by reference to map one will see, we are about half way between the Falkland Islands and the mainland. Having sailed pretty fast this afternoon, Captain thought best to tack at 8 P.M., so we now stand on the starboard tack, heading about Northeast. I saw this afternoon a couple of penguins; they are much smaller than I imagined, and seem to stay under water much more than above, only coming up like porpoises to breathe; the two I saw were not longer than a good sized duck, white underneath and a very dark grey or black on the back. I hope to have a better view of them. Have seen nothing today of any of our friends of yesterday though I expect tomorrow will bring them around us. Steward seems to have had quite a life of experiences, twice wrecked and once went down. Has sailed with Captain Samuels in the *Dreadnaught*.* One of his wrecks was on Lake Erie near Buffalo, the other on the North coast of Iceland.

* *The clipper DREADNAUGHT was built in 1853 by Currier and Townsend of Newburyport, Massachusetts, and measured 1413 tons by 200 feet long by 39 wide and 26.6 deep. This big vessel made history under the hard-driving skipper Capt. Samuel Samuels. She was lost off Cape Horn on July 4, 1869, flying the flag of the Red Cross Line. David Ogden and others of New York were her owners.*

MONDAY, MARCH 19

Lat. 52° 46' S. Long. 65° 00' W. (Dead reckoning)

Captain Mitchell's Journal:

Fresh S.E. by S. winds all this day. At 8 P.M. tacked off shore to the E.N.E. Middle part moderate. At 7 A.M. tacked in shore again. Hard luck this to be hemmed in this bite [bight]. Glorious wind if one was only round St. John. Ends fresh from S.E., cool weather, land in sight. This is hard to bear. No observation.

Henry Ferguson's Journal:

Saw the first penguins I had seen today and they surely are most serious looking birds. They come up to the top of the water and stay there a little while and scream like a baby, bob in and out a little while, and then dive like a fish and you don't see them any more for they have most wonderful powers of submersion. We had a visit from a little land bird today, a pretty little fellow that seemed glad to get somewhere to rest. Getting colder and colder. No sail to be seen today, so I am afraid they may have got ahead of us. Great expectation of seeing land which is near by, but though there were some false alarms, we have seen nothing of it yet, but will certainly by daylight tomorrow.

Samuel Ferguson's Journal:

Thermometer has been at about 45° all day, weather feeling much colder. Cloudy almost all day. Took various observations, as in this latitude there is no telling when the sun will shine. Captain is, therefore, very anxious to verify all observations taken. Spent most of the day in the cabin. Nothing of our companions today, am afraid they got the best of us, though we head the set. A little bird came on board today, evidently a land bird resembling a chippy.

He rested himself and finally departed. Saw some more penguins today. We are not far from Staten Land, will probably see it before 8 o'clock tomorrow and the wind at time will determine as to whether we take the Strait or go round the island. The tide runs very swiftly here, 7 knots at half way in the Strait, so unless we have a strong, favorable breeze, I suppose we will go round. We still continue to play whist every night, generally from 8 to 10, or as long as it takes to play seven games, except Saturday when we make up the full tally.

TUESDAY, MARCH 20

Lat. 54° 12' S. Long. 64° 27' W.

Captain Mitchell's Journal:

Begins moderate breeze from S.E. and cloudy weather. Middle part very moderate at E.N.E. Calms from 6 to 9 A.M. Ends very moderate breeze from N.E. All possible sail set, sea smooth as a mirror. Staten Land bearing S.E. by compass (body of island). Oh for a breeze.

Henry Ferguson's Journal:

Today we have seen the first land since leaving New York, and we liked to see it though a more bleak barren rugged place no one could imagine. We could see both the mainland and the island and have been sailing along the island for Cape St. John at a distance of about 20 miles from it. We now have the cape about South of us and though we are still heading East, will soon fall off a little. It is the most desolate looking place I ever saw. Mountains which rise right up from the water to the sharpest of peaks, with bare shiny sides all the way up — it is as jagged as a hacked knife and I wished all today I could draw so as to give an outline. Three sail in sight, ship, bark, and brigantine. Ship and bark ahead.

Samuel Ferguson's Journal:

Was awoke this morning with the information that land was in sight, both the main and Staten Land. Both coasts are very bold and rugged. Sailed by Staten Land today and a more serrated coast can hardly be imagined, the sharpest kind of peaks. Saw one ship, one bark,

Penguin - woodcut from The World of the Sea, *1882.*

and a brigantine; passed the latter at about 6:30 P.M. nearly off the end of Cape St. John. Wind has been favorable but light all day. Passed great quantities of weed of various kinds. Caught some kelp which is quite pretty. Dried some to keep, but it all shriveled up so we chucked it overboard. Quantities of albatross, all at rest, so could catch none. On deck walking now becomes necessary in order to keep warm. Am disappointed that my cough holds on so, as I hoped after the hot weather the cooler would nail it; patience though I suppose! For the next two weeks now we may expect to have a gay old time of it, unless we are to be especially favored. So far all agree we have had a most remarkable calm and quiet passage. I wonder where the *Lookout* is now.

WEDNESDAY, MARCH 21

Lat. 55° 50' S. Long. 64° 13' W.

Captain Mitchell's Journal:

Begins moderate breeze from N.E. hauling East. A brig and bark in company. At 7 P.M. Cape St. John, S.S.E. 12 miles. Middle, fresh breeze from N.W. which continues nearly through the day, ending W.N.W. 8 A.M. Staten Island N. by E. 35 miles. 12 Noon, fine weather.

Henry Ferguson's Journal:

The sun is North of the equator today, but equinox or not I have seldom seen a finer day than it was this morning. The sea is calm and all morning we had an eight or nine knot breeze, and made use of it well. In the early part of the P.M. it was calm, but gradually the breeze sprung up from the North and we are now going on nicely. We passed Cape St. John last night as expected and took I hope our last look at Staten Land this morning. We have been heading S.W. by W. and W.S.W. all day sailing free. Cape Horn bears about W. by S. now and we hope to pass it before morning. Captain and everybody says that this is most unusual weather. Certainly we could wish no better than it. Cool but not unpleasant. Fancy that land is in sight, but probably clouds which shape themselves like the land they shadow very much. Brig in sight way to the windward.

Samuel Ferguson's Journal:

When we started I believe the Captain thought he had on board a couple of "Jonahs", but today he told Henry that if we would bring him this mild weather always he would give us our passages. After rounding Cape St. John everyone expected to find an old Southwest sea, but no, and today has been as fine as anyone could wish, almost like one of our clear cold October days. Noticed this morning our friend the brigantine some distance nearer land than we; though we have caught up with her, she has decidedly the inside track. The wind has been about Northwest by compass and our course about Southwest, though the variation down here is over 22°. This afternoon saw a quantity of whales quite close, of the Grampus description. They were between 30 and 40 feet long, Captain said.

This evening we had a beautiful sunset which the Captain says he has never seen before here, though he has been round 17 times. By tomorrow I suppose we will feel the swell from the old Pacific. Very few birds about which indicates that the weather here has been very mild for sometime past. Certainly all the accounts of weather in this latitude do not agree with our experience thus far, but we have not yet got out of the woods yet.

PART III—FROM CAPE HORN TO THE LINE

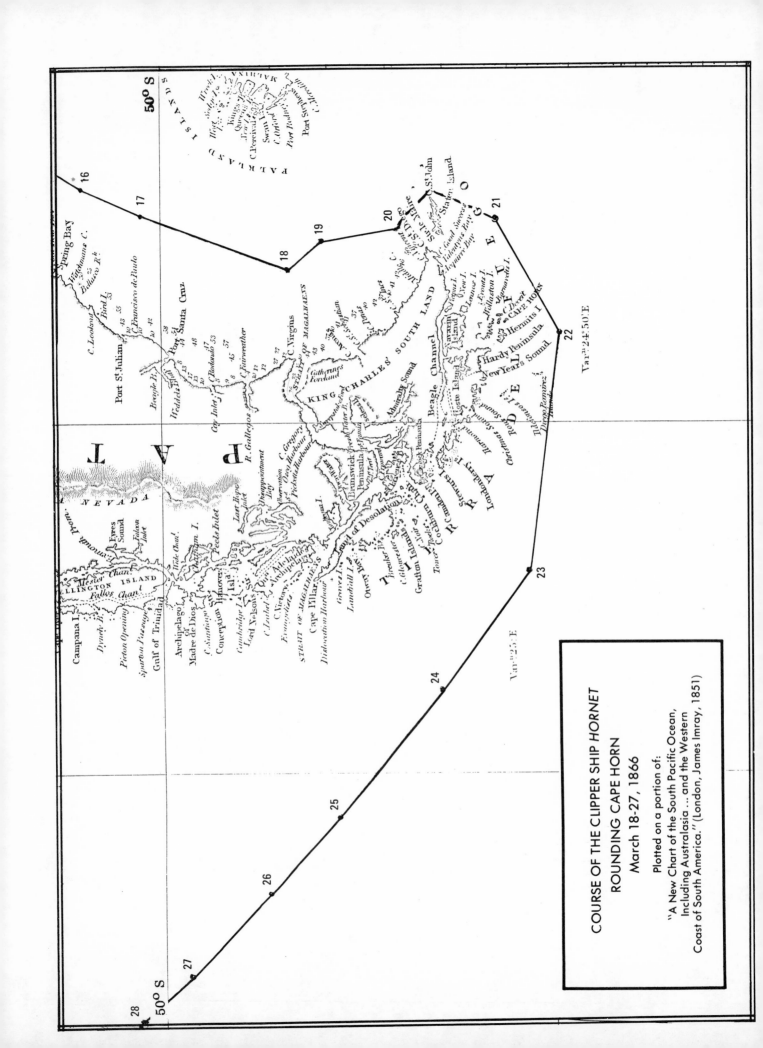

COURSE OF THE CLIPPER SHIP *HORNET*
ROUNDING CAPE HORN
March 18-27, 1866

Plotted on a portion of:
"A New Chart of the South Pacific Ocean,
Including Australasia ... and the Western
Coast of South America." (London, James Imray, 1851)

THURSDAY, MARCH 22

Lat. 56° 49' S. Long. 67° 40' W.

Captain Mitchell's Journal:

Begins wind N.W., fine weather and smooth sea. Middle part, wind same, very light. At 6 A.M. wind N.E., foggy, very light. Ends light breeze from N.E., smooth sea and fog clouds. No such weather ever seen in this latitude. No birds, warm and pleasant. Strong tide rips.

Henry Ferguson's Journal:

Early in the morning Cape Horn was in sight well aft of our quarter and before I got a chance to look it was out of sight altogether. We have been heading West and W. by N. today with a Northeasterly breeze and are now going and have been all afternoon full 9 or 10 knots. At about three saw land from aloft bearing about North of us which must have been the Diego Ramirez rocks,* the furthermost South of America. We have made a good run today and are making good use of our wonderful weather. Water green this A.M. and M., but this P.M. we emerged into the blue waters of the Pacific. Brig in sight astern with studding sails set. We are now past the Cape without any weather that could not have been borne by a good sail boat. In fact ever since we left the River Plate it has been so. Some southwesterly Pacific swell and our Northeast wind is raising the water a little.

* *Diego Ramirez islets lie about 60 miles southwest of Cape Horn in 56° 25' south latitude, by 68° 44' west longitude.*

Cape Horn - woodcut view from Gleason's Pictorial, *July 30, 1853.*

Samuel Ferguson's Journal:

Passed the "Stormy Cape" early this morning and have been sailing first rate all day with a Northeast breeze, this afternoon amounting to 9 knots per log. Passed Diego Ramirez Rocks this afternoon and are now headed West by South which, adding two points for variation, heads us about West by North, so that we have now probably gone as far South as we shall unless we get a Southwester. All day this has been a beautiful day with enough sea to give motion, but not very much though. Tonight when we are really on the Pacific we feel somewhat of a swell. We certainly have had so far a remarkable passage round the Horn. This afternoon saw the brigantine a long way astern of us with her studding sails set which, however, she took in towards 4 P.M. So far we have seen no homeward bound vessels which the Captain thinks a little curious as we are now just in their track. Hope to show our numbers to some tomorrow so that they will report us round in case we have poor luck in getting to San Francisco. Tried peaches and found them excellent. Thanks to aunt for her kindness, our stores hold out very well except ale, even Valentine cake.

FRIDAY, MARCH 23

Lat. 56° 18′ S. Long. 74° 20′ W. (Dead reckoning)

Captain Mitchell's Journal:

Begins fresh breeze from N.E. At 4 P.M. passed Diego Ramirez. Saw the hermaphrodite brig in the fog astern dragging all studding sails, breeze increasing fast and weather thick. Middle and latter part, strong gale from E. by N., thick dark weather and high sea. Ship carrying main royal, two reefed topsails, fore and mizzen, and whole foresail. No observation.

Henry Ferguson's Journal:

Today we have had a tolerable Easterly gale which has kicked up quite a considerable sea especially as this afternoon there came up a swell from the Northwest. We have been going along finely, never I suppose less than eight knots. Very pretty bird flying around the ship today. He is perfectly white about the size and shape of a dove and flies like one, only as is the way with all of them down here, he is web-footed. Ship said to have been seen ahead of us, but I rather suspect it was a myth. This Easterly wind is helping us along splendidly and if it will last a day or two longer, it will be all right. The sea helps us along, nevertheless we could dispense with some of it as it makes her roll a good deal. Lots of albatrosses around the stern today almost coming aboard. Are now under reefed topsails and foresail. In the morning had main to'gallant and royal set.

Samuel Ferguson's Journal:

Although round the Horn, still we have not got off certainly. The wind is Northeast, pretty stiff, and we are now meeting a Northwest swell which causes considerable motion, more than we have had for a long time. From the River La Platta after our last "Pampero" to today, the *Johnson* would have done first rate and made better than perhaps we have done, although we have beaten the average all hollow. Today is thick, morning foggy so that we have had no chance at an observation. Worked out though, the Captain makes our position as above. This is a great place to make longitude, there only being about 33 miles to a degree. Think it strange we have seen no vessels, but the foggy day will perhaps account somewhat for it.

Kept cabin most of the day being too disagreeable and rough to walk with any degree of pleasure. Henry is growing as fat as a pig though he complains this weather of not sleeping well.

SATURDAY, MARCH 24

Lat. 55° 00′ S. Long. 78° 30′ W.

Captain Mitchell's Journal:

Strong gale from East. At 4 P.M. heavy head sea making. Took in royal and reefed the foresail, furled upper mizzen topsail. Middle, strong gale, high sea, rain and fog. Frequent long lulls in the breeze. Latter moderate and hauling to the North. No observation.

Henry Ferguson's Journal:

Gale moderated a good deal in the night but nevertheless we made by noon some 200 miles, which is not to be despised especially in these regions. We were able to get sights today which we were not yesterday. If we had wished it we could have been at 53° today and 50° tomorrow, but the Captain thinks best to make Westing down here where the degrees are short. After dinner it scared us by beginning to blow pretty strong from ahead, but after a few hours it shifted round to the East again. We put on more sail and are going now nine or ten knots on our course which is N.W. by N. true bearing, not magnetic for the compass varies some 25 degrees here. We have certainly had the most remarkable good fortune in getting round the Cape. It makes up for the calms and head winds South of the Line [Equator] on our way down.

Samuel Ferguson's Journal:

Weather not very pleasant though the wind still favorable. Considerable sea which makes us roll and pitch about rather uncomfortable. Nothing particular to write today. Every hour this wind holds makes it better for us and we now stand a good chance of making a pretty good passage. Saw no ships bound either way today, but at night always now set our big light which used to belong to the steamer *Ericsson*,* so is a strong one for a ship.

Am going to try a little Balsom of Capevid for my cough which troubles me at night a good deal. We head now about Northwest which means North-Northwest, and are going about 8 knots (8 P.M.). A good many albatross about today, but we went too fast to catch them as they have to light on the water and then pick up any bait that is thrown them. Penguins seem to have deserted us entirely. I expect they don't come so far as we are out. They are very different from what I ever supposed and seem more fish than fowl in their habits.

---

*   This vessel, named for the Swedish-born inventor John Ericsson, was originally equipped with his newly invented "caloric" engine installed in a 2200-ton ship, 248 feet long by 40.4 beam by 27.6 deep. She capsized on her trial trip in 1852 and was subsequently raised and given a conventional side-wheel steam engine. In the late 1860's she was converted to a sailing ship.

SUNDAY, MARCH 25

Lat. 53° 15'S. Long. 81° 30'W.

Captain Mitchell's Journal:

Begins fresh breeze baffling from N.N.W. to N.N.E., heavy sea coming from West. Middle part, hard squalls, plenty rain, wind still veering in squalls from N.N.W. to N.N.E. Reduced sail to two reefed topsails and mainsail. Latter more moderate, wind steadier from North, ending pleasant. Heavy head sea. Main topgallant sail set. Plenty of birds indicating a change.

Henry Ferguson's Journal:

There were some pretty heavy squalls last night from the N.W. which drove us a little off our course, but all today we have been heading N.W. pretty close hauled. There has come up a pretty big head sea which rather looks as if the wind might be coming from that quarter, but I hope not. It pitches us up and down considerably. I fancy it is not very pleasant on deck and is likely to be a stormy night. We are under reefed topsails, and some staysails. Great many albatrosses round — big and small, old and young, a fact which looks as if we were going to have a Southerly wind. I hope we may if it don't blow too dreadful hard as S.W. winds have a way of doing down here.

Samuel Ferguson's Journal:

Last night squally with heavy rains, wind remaining, however, this day about the same, allowing us to keep our course Northwest. Fine day, sun very pleasant and comfortable. Remains of a good old sea which increases considerably towards evening. A good many albatross and Molinux* around today. Next Sunday is Easter; how little it seems as if it could be! I should like much to be able just to drop down on Saturday night and spend Sunday with all at home. Here we have no service but what we read ourselves. The Captain is a sort of Swedenborgian, but is pretty well mixed up and not very well-read even in his professed sect. We have made up I expect for our lost time on the other side, which will I hope give us our original chance for a 120 day passage. Tonight it looks very stormy and Captain is a little apprehensive of a hard Nor'wester. We must take it as it comes, however, and be mighty thankful to have been let around the Cape so easy.

* *It is suggested by George E. Watson of the National Museum of Natural History that Molinux is a bastardization of Mollymauk, a sailor's name for the smaller albatrosses such as the Black-browed and Grey-headed that are abundant in the Cape Horn region. They are about three feet long with a seven-foot wingspread.*

MONDAY, MARCH 26

Lat. 51° 52'S. Long. 84° 00'W.

Captain Mitchell's Journal:

Begins fresh breeze from N.N.E., very heavy head sea. Ship pitching heavily and taking in a good deal of water over the bows. Middle part very squally, baffling, rain, and calm alternately. Strong contrast between Westerly and N.E. wind. First the S.W. prevails, then the N.E. has it, very squally and calm between squalls. Latter part steadier from North. Topgallant sails set.

Henry Ferguson's Journal:

Squally like it was yesterday and headed us off somewhat, nevertheless we ought not to complain after the easy and quick run we have had. Maury* gives the average time from 50⁰ to 50⁰ as 18 days, and we, if we had chosen, might be there now, certainly will be tomorrow. Our course is now about N.W. when we can do it and we want to cross the Line in about 115⁰ West, San Francisco being in 123⁰. Weather is getting a little warmer, but the thermometer still averages only about 50⁰. Soon I hope we will be in warmer latitudes and be able to dispense with the stove which is dreadful gassy. We opened and partook of some of our home gingersnaps, and they are as crisp and nice as the day that they were baked.

* *Lieut. Matthew Fontaine Maury, USN, the famous oceanographer, nicknamed "Pathfinder of the Seas." See note for April 10.*

Samuel Ferguson's Journal:

Cloudy all morning, got an observation through at noon. Afternoon cleared and was sunshiny and pleasant. Very little to chronicle, in fact here one day is so much like the previous one that log writing is no easy job. A contest today between the Northeast and Northwest winds, resulting during the morning in one or two squalls. Northeast finally came out and won, so that we now stand on our course Northwest. Have seen no vessels since the day we passed the Cape. I suppose the brigantine is to the Eastward, a mistake on her part if she is, as she must make Westing and when she gets the Trades she will have them dead aft. Besides, Westing is easily made down here where the degrees are short. In 57⁰ latitude a degree of longitude is only a scant 33 miles. The water has again got to its perfect blue and clearness. Barnacles are forming a good deal on the rudder and rudder post, a very funny shaped set too, almost like the claw of an animal, quite long and pointed, not like ours on the *Fannie*.**

**Their family boat on Long Island Sound.*

TUESDAY, MARCH 27

Lat. 50⁰ 27'S. Long. 85⁰ 50'W.

Captain Mitchell's Journal:

Fresh North winds all day with heavy head sea and frequent squalls. At daylight a bark on weather bow. 12 noon, bark a point abaft the beam, carrying hard. Ship and bark both sharp by the wind.

Henry Ferguson's Journal:

Wind better today and backing round so that we are heading our course and going about seven knots although pretty close-hauled. Barque in sight on the weather bow this morning whom we overhauled and neared and expect tomorrow to be to the windward of him. He is way astern anyhow. He is a light fellow apparently in ballast for Chinchas's, Iquique, or some of those guano and saltpeter places. Quite a heavy, long swell from the Southeast like the ground swell at home which looks as if we ought to have the wind from that quarter. I hope we may, for a Sou'east would carry us along famously and perhaps help us up to the Trades. Squally in afternoon and there was a very beautiful rainbow. Looks squally also now, 8 P.M.

Samuel Ferguson's Journal:

Northeast wind still holds. Frequent squalls, however, head us off a little from our course. Sighted, came up with, and passed the bark that was ahead of us in rounding the Cape. She is very light and probably bound to the Chinchas for guano. Was too far off to telegraph to. Most of the day very fine on deck. Quite a sensible difference in the six degrees of latitude, though the Northerly wind has something to do with that.

Steward is a regular darkey and it's fun to get him on some of his experiences, he gesticulating and going wholly in as do all his race in what they are interested in. Very few birds today, our chance at catching an albatross is getting smaller and smaller.

A good deal of sea today and increased tonight by a Southeast swell, which makes us pitch considerably. Our sailorship is I think now pretty tried out as far as sea sickness goes. The remaining bottles of my ale prove first rate, making me very sorry for the loss of the others.

WEDNESDAY, MARCH 28

Lat. 49° 30'S. Long. 87° 12'W.

Captain Mitchell's Journal:

Baffling winds from N.N.W. to N.E. and frequent rain showers, calms, &c., all this 24 hours. One man (Peter) laid up sick. Ends very light at N.E. No observation.

Henry Ferguson's Journal:

Bark just in sight this morning to the S.E. of us and went out of it before noon. She probably was a Valparaiso trader or something of that sort. Wind very light, but abaft the beam all day and what we made we made directly on our course which is well. Rain squall came up at noon, nevertheless we got a very tolerable sight which placed her in the latitude above. All the latitudes and longitudes I have down are for noon. The former being taken then and the latter being taken in the morning or afternoon and reduced to it. Ship in sight this evening on the wind with nothing set above topgallant sails. We bent on our fore royal today which had come down stairs for repairs.

Samuel Ferguson's Journal:

Wind about the same today, sea gone down a good deal from yesterday morning and till afternoon cloudy, with sun out at intervals. Afternoon cleared off and gives us splendid evening. This afternoon saw a ship ahead on the wind and, therefore, about across our bows. She had apparently no top-gallant sails on her, but as to where she was bound we could not make out and, from the way she headed, Captain thought she might be a whaler cruising about. The bark was still in sight in the morning, but stood in towards shore so we soon lost sight of her.

No birds today and very little of interest to chronicle. Were employed today in scraping starboard side of the ship, beginning at the stern, so we shall go in looking gay. Will probably have to paint a good deal before we make our port. The hot weather of the tropics blisters if the paint is not put on well. Wrote a good full sheet of notes home, being connected in account with the one written in January.

THURSDAY, MARCH 29

Lat. 48° 09 'S. Long. 87° 56 'W.

Captain Mitchell's Journal:

Very light winds all this day from N.E., E., and S.E., and ending S.W. Frequent light showers through the night. Sea smooth and weather fine. Such a long spell of moderate weather, I don't believe was ever known here before.

Henry Ferguson's Journal:

Today we have had it pretty calm, just a little breeze blowing and now much to our disgust, after having gone all the way round against the wind, it has set in the Northwest with every prospect of a storm. Well, we are in a good position for it if it does come, though it is rather provoking to have W. and N.E. the best courses we can steer. None of our friends in sight today. A few birds round whom I tried in vain to catch. They would light at the bait readily enough, but would only try for it once or twice and then sit and look at it float away from them. We were going a little too fast to catch them with. I am afraid we won't be able to bring home any albatrosses as I had wished.

Samuel Ferguson's Journal:

Last night a most splendid night. Marched the deck after tea till the stars came out bright. Saw the Southern Cross not having seen it in a good while, it almost always being too cloudy by 10:30 P.M. However, we have had a number of showers which soon passed off though.

Today fine in morning but got cloudy and chilly this afternoon, wind changing to Northwest after going gradually round by the South. We now have to head by compass North-Northeast with two points against us. Henry saw today a whale blow. We also saw a lot of porpoises playing and posting off the windward. We also had some birds following us which Henry fished for but with no success, both albatross and Molinuxes with one black ugly looking fellow with a grey back. Nothing today in the way of companions. Water beautifully blue and clear.

FRIDAY, MARCH 30

Lat. 45° 56 'S. Long. 89° 00 'W.

Captain Mitchell's Journal:

This day begins with light winds from West hauling to Northwest and increasing. 8 P.M. wind N.N.W., tacked to the West. Middle part hard gale. Wind hauling to N.E. and East and going all the way round to S.W., blowing a hard gale with a very heavy head sea running from N.W. Ends strong gale from S.W. All possible sail set.

Henry Ferguson's Journal:

Moderate gale last night and all today, blowing round from East to West and most of the day about S.S.W. Very heavy head sea all day which has made us toss round a good deal and has prevented us carrying as much sail as otherwise we would. I think the old sea we have had on today is by far the heaviest we have seen as yet. Immense bodies of water they are that don't take any more regard of the ship than if she was a chip. Today the pin in the tub of the mizzen topsail yard broke and fell overboard and the yard came down on the halliards which, luckily, were plenty strong enough and they slacked it down. Fine clear night.

Samuel Ferguson's Journal:

Upon looking at compass this morning was glad to find ourselves heading on our course, the wind having again hauled to the South. We have, however, a heavy head sea. As the day grew, the wind freshened and this afternoon we are under topsails going about 7 knots. Head sea increasing and bringing her up short every now and then. Day clear and fine but wind cold. Sea pretty high and in long swells with neat white fresh looking combings. Walking on deck a pretty difficult matter, i.e., walking anything like straight. Today is Good Friday and how little like our usual Good Fridays it seems! Have thought a good deal of all at home today and may God in His goodness bless them all.

Tonight in civilized regions the moon should be totally eclipsed, but way down here in the South Pacific I'm not so sure we will have it so. Just now the East is cloudy, so that it may be a total after all. Rats getting very plenty and bold on board, mean to make a trap and catch some if possible; have not yet got into the cabin.

SATURDAY, MARCH 31

Lat. 43° 52'S. Long. 88° 50'W.

Captain Mitchell's Journal:

Begins W.S.W. hauling to N.W. with a very large sea from N.W. Middle part, fresh from N.W. A total eclipse of moon this night. Raining, squally. At 9 A.M. hauls to S.W. in a hard squall. Ends S.W., strong gale. Ship under reefed courses and double reefed topsails. Very large sea from W.N.W.

Henry Ferguson's Journal:

Gale increasing all today and sea with it and we are rolling a good deal. We were unable to get a sight of the eclipse last night when total, but saw it both before and after it had been on fully. Only a few birds round the ship, not the numbers we had further South. This is setting in plainly for a stiff Sou'wester and I am very glad we are here instead of off the Cape where it must be blowing everlastingly hard. In spite of rolling we had our game all regular tonight and we have not missed playing some three games at least every night round the Cape.

Samuel Ferguson's Journal:

Sure enough, last night the moon was totally eclipsed. We saw it first at 9:30 our time. It was then two thirds eclipsed. The clouds, however, hid it except now and then. Today we find the inhabitants of these parts, viz. Southwest winds and a heavy sea, at home. We have been under very short sail but still going some 7 or 8 knots. Wind blowing like blue blazes. Ship rolling worst than any day yet and occasionally shipping something of a sea. The swell is different from the Atlantic, being much longer. Ship rides over these well enough, but the waves caused by the stiff breeze she pitches into and makes spray fly sometimes as high as the main yard. Walking still more difficult today. The weather, however, is fine except squally which means frequent hard blows and rain which is rain if it is not hail; why it seems to rain more in five minutes than I have ever seen it before do in an hour!

EASTER SUNDAY, APRIL 1

Lat. 41° 28' S. Long. 89° 00' W.

Captain Mitchell's Journal:

Begins brisk gale from W.S.W., hauls to West. Middle strong from W. At 3 A.M. hard squall from S.W. with hail and rain. Squalls numerous and hard until 10 A.M. when it settles down to a very hard gale from S.W. with large sea running. Carrying all possible canvass.

Henry Ferguson's Journal:

Gale increased still more today with very heavy hail squalls and rain in the morning during which it blew like concentrated Blue Blazes. All day it has been a stinger, but nevertheless we are under double reefed topsails and foresail. We have not yet had in the upper topsails. In the afternoon we had no squalls, but blowing hard and tremendous sea rolling. We are about in the trough of it and she is wonderfully dry, but rolls things round in a way that is a caution. Some pretty good seas have come aboard, but no bad ones. Hardest blow and biggest sea we have had. Tremendous big rollers they are.

Samuel Ferguson's Journal:

At noon today we are 76 days from New York. Easter Sunday, I hope they have at home a less windy and squally day than we have. Was woke up this morning at 4 by a tremendous clatter against my window and the noise also of the wind howling through the shrouds and though we have had a fine day in general, we have had a succession of squalls. Wind still Southwest, only stiffer than yesterday, amounting to a regular gale. Sea just astern and very high and though we have double reefed upper topsails on fore and main and lower on the mizzen, we are making our 8 to 9 knots. The ship rolls tremendously with the sea where it is, but wins praises from everybody for her good sea qualities. From the Second Mate particularly, who is generally rather down on everything.

I hope they have had a good fine day at home and all things agreeable to the joy of the day. Hope Brathwaite will give himself a little rest now that Lent is over. I wonder if Redding has settled down in Stamford. I hope he has got a house for We, Us, and Co.

MONDAY, APRIL 2

Lat. 38° 20′ N. Long. 89° 00′ W. (Dead reckoning)

Captain Mitchell's Journal:

Strong gale and high sea from S.W.   At 4 P.M. kept the ship off N.N.W., sea large on the beam. Middle part, gale continues with high sea. Ship under lower and two reefed upper topsails and reefed courses. Latter part more moderate. Made sail as wind dies. At 11:30 under topgallant sails. No observation.

Henry Ferguson's Journal:

We have made pretty good use of the gale and are getting well to the Northward. It has moderated a great deal and we have gradually put on sail all day, till now we have topgallant sail and royals set and are going along very nicely indeed. Sea has gone down but there are still big rollers in plenty, one of which dosed me as I was standing by the weather rail pretty considerably. Good many birds about which they say are a kind of stormy petrel. Wind has hauled more aft and is I think dying away gradually. It has served us a good turn though and we ought to be thankful for it. It must have been a tremendous blow off the Cape.

Samuel Ferguson's Journal:

Yesterday and last night expended the force of our Southwest gale, though there was some of it left this morning, also a pretty heavy sea. Henry got a good ducking today by a sea breaking over the rail just by the corner of the house. Towards noon became cloudy and wind dropped so as to allow putting up our topgallant sails and this afternoon, royals and courses. This afternoon is again like old times and is comparatively quiet in the cabin although the barometers and so forth do swing about to some extent.

    This morning we had a quantity of "Stormy Petrels" about us, about the size of whale birds but they soon left us. This afternoon also we had a lot of porpoises, one of which one of the men struck with the harpoon but did not get him. We have been very unfortunate in all our fish and fowl catching. Began on our third box of claret (quarts) today. Fancy it will hold out well.

TUESDAY, APRIL 3

Lat. 36° 04′ S. Long. 89° 30′ W.

Captain Mitchell's Journal:

At commencement wind from S.W., moderating fast. Middle part very light with high rolling sea. Latter very light from S.E., ending calm. Unbent all best jibs, topgallant sails, and lower topsails and bent others. Prospect of an Easterly wind. Oh if it would only come and run us into the Trades.

Henry Ferguson's Journal:

Weather evidently delights in contrasts for today we have had the very deadest kind of all dead calms. Of course we have the old swell left by the gale. We have got well to the Northward and yesterday's work is very much better than we anticipated. It is provoking getting becalmed, but we have to take what comes. It is getting very much warmer and the stove is out, not to be lit again I hope and pray this voyage, for it made the cabin, except in the very cold weather, hot and stuffy to say nothing of half the time nearly suffocating us with coal gas. Yesterday there were a lot of porpoises round the ship. Men tried to harpoon them. Hit one, but bent the iron and so missed him.

Samuel Ferguson's Journal:

Today has been a regular calm all day, don't suppose we have made 5 miles from 8 A.M. to 8 P.M. A tremendous contrast in regard to the sea even from yesterday. There yet remains, however, some of the old Southwest swell. The men today have been very busy in bending and unbending sails and we have now on our summer suit as the Captain calls them, namely, the old and patched lighter ones, for it is in heavy weather that a ship dresses in her best. About 11 A.M., Captain called out to us to have a look at a bottle floating by us and sure enough there was one corked and sealed with something white like a paper inside. The boats being all up and inboard, it was not thought worth the while to lower one for it. I am sorry such was the case and think the Captain regretted it afterwards, for we were not going very fast. We are, I suppose, some 500 miles from land so that must have come from some ship, though perhaps it might have been some passenger's foolishness. I wish we had lowered and got it.

WEDNESDAY, APRIL 4

Lat. 35° 46′ S. Long. 91° 02′ W.

Captain Mitchell's Journal:

Light baffling airs and calms all this day. Little progress.

Henry Ferguson's Journal:

Another calm day though not quite as bad as yesterday, for we have steered all today and at one time had quite a little breeze. Had a line in the water for the benefit of an albatross this morning and when I went to haul it in this afternoon, I found a big fish on much to my delight. I got him in and he proved to be what they call albacore on this coast, though different from those of the same name in Atlantic. He must have weighed 15 lbs. Very stout indeed and shaped a good deal like a bonito, but had fins eight or ten inches long which I have cut off and preserved. He, like a bonito, had great faculty of shaking and shivering, almost as good as a shock. Had some fried steaks tonight. Very good indeed, infinitely better than bonito, very rich and fat. Great many little jelly fish round today, countless in fact. Sam, Mr. Thomas, and I made a rat trap this P.M. for we are horribly infested with rats.

Samuel Ferguson's Journal:

One of the most beautiful days that can be imagined. One can hardly realize the rapid change from almost winter to early summer that we have today. Five or six degrees makes a great difference in this particular [region] and by having for three days a good strong Southwest or Southerly breeze, the change to a calm or light Northerly wind is very manifest. Tomorrow I shall make some change of garments. Today has been marked by Henry's catching a very curious fish, a fine fellow that would weigh perhaps 12 or 15 pounds. No one on board had seen the like of it. In some respects it was much like a bonito but was light meated and very fat, which they are not, and again it had two very long fins coming from just behind the shoulder. The most curious part was that all the fins, dorsal and all, had receptacles for them as if the fish was in the habit of taking a start and sliding a long way. Wind Northeast to North by East.

THURSDAY, APRIL 5

Lat. 34° 59'S. Long. 93° 00'W.

Captain Mitchell's Journal:

First and middle part of this day, very light breeze from North. Latter, steady breeze, moderate from N.N.W. Fine pleasant weather and sea smooth as a floor throughout.

Henry Ferguson's Journal:

Delightful day, but the wind heads us off more than yesterday. None of our vast preparations against the rats have succeeded, they *sabe* too much altogether. Our beautiful box trap we made yesterday has not been troubled at all. Captain put some mixture on some fish which we hoped would kill them, but no success though they eat it all up. The mixture I believe was calomel, jalap, oil cloves, and essence of cinnamon. The clouds are more broken up than they have been lately and I hope that before very long we shall have the Trades. It certainly is the finest weather I ever saw. No fish today though both lines out at stern.

Samuel Ferguson's Journal:

Another splendid day, wind heading us off more than yesterday, but very genial and pleasant. This morning we were disappointed in not finding any of our machinations against the rats successful. Third Mate, Henry, and I made an old fashioned box trap, but it did not succeed. Captain tried a lot of poisoned fish which was a good deal eaten but no signs yet of any mortality. No more fish yet, though we have had both lines out all day.

Clouds again begin to assume the Trade shapes and soon I suppose we shall have more of those splendid sunsets. The old Southwest swell still holds; it is very long and is even more a slow respiratory motion than the Atlantic. Have set more traps for rats today. Mostly they are very cunning and very plentiful. Captain laments daily this not having a cat and rather blames Captain Harding*. There is no doubt about it that the change of captains was a great thing for us as well as the ship.

* *The HORNET's previous master.*

FRIDAY, APRIL 6

Lat. 34° 50 'S. Long. 94° 20'W.

Captain Mitchell's Journal:

Moderate breezes and baffling from N.W. to N.N.W. all this day. Tacked once. Hard getting along this, bound to make a long passage. Some sick today, violent pains across the back.

Henry Ferguson's Journal:

We were headed off so much by the wind, what there was of it, this morning, we tacked and are now standing N.E. which is a hard course. Another of the most delightful days I ever saw. In forenoon there were some signs of a change of wind but no results as yet. Captain and Third Mate fixed up a barrel with a head on a pivot so as to move with a rat's weight and set it between decks, and was rewarded before night with two poor little devils. This evening Cook came and said that the box trap had caught some so we held it over the side and launched three little fellows into the Pacific. How long this wind will last we can't say, but we most fervently hope not very long.

Samuel Ferguson's Journal:

Wind headed us so much that this morning Captain tacked and we now stand about North-Northeast, or about Northeast true. Wind light, but the air is very pleasant and day very fine. Today Captain rigged a barrel with a moveable top for rats and was successful this afternoon in taking two small ones. My trap was also successful and about dark the cook brought it in to the door of the cabin and said there were two in it, so we held it over the ship's side and found three small ones, however.

Today they have been mending some old duplicate sails and one that they have got bent is something like a bed quilt, it is so patched and with so many different kinds of cloth.

Three-handed whist is still the go and we have kept it up nightly for a long while, there having been only one night that it would have been too much motion to play comfortably and that was Sunday last.

SATURDAY, APRIL 7

Lat. 33° 33' S. Long. 92° 27'W.

Captain Mitchell's Journal:

Steady light N. W. by N. wind all this day. Damn bad wind and no sign of change.

Henry Ferguson's Journal:

Our course today is just the same as it was yesterday and I can't see any signs of improvement. However, the moon quarters Sunday morning and it will most probably bring a change of weather with it. No rats today and they certainly are the cutest creatures out and remind us all of "J.B. sly, devilish sly" which they certainly are. Wind light and it is another day just like the foregoing, as pleasant as possible with a head wind. I wonder why it is that wherever you go, you find more head wind than anything else. It certainly is the case whatever Maury may say about it.

Samuel Ferguson's Journal:

Course today the same as yesterday though with a little fresher breeze. Captain is much provoked at being thus headed off and I am afraid made to loose all our gains in getting round the Cape so well. Still we are ahead of Captain Harding's last passage and hope we will catch a good sound Southeast Trade before long, that will take us across the Line. The air again was very balmy and pleasant, wind a little cool, but not chilly. Fine day for a long walk if ashore. No more game today, either finny or leggy. Rats certainly are "J.B. Sly", etc. Have seen no ships since the 28th. ult. and are rather looking for them, as we ought to be in the track of homeward bound ones. Birds also are very few, as are also porpoises or whales, although we shall soon come into the region of flying fish. The fish Henry caught the other day had one in him, so I suppose they are not far off.

SUNDAY, APRIL 8

Lat. 32° 18'S. Long. 91° 06' W.

Captain Mitchell's Journal:

A miserable week's work. Very moderate all this day with airs from N.W. to W.N.W. Lovely day if we were only making some progress. Weather fine and sea smooth. Saw a ship a long way off bound South.

Henry Ferguson's Journal:

It will seem I am afraid rather like Falstaff's "d--nable iteration" to say that this has been a most lovely day, but nevertheless it has been. Hardly a cloud to be seen and just warm enough, and not too hot. One rat fell a victim to the barrel's allurements last night, but he was the only one. All my figure of 4's have had bad luck, something has been the matter, and the rats have carried away 3 bait, spindle, and all. Saw two sail today, one a bark bound Southward and another whose rig we could not distinguish, but apparently bound the same way as we. We could only see her from the topgallant yard.

Samuel Ferguson's Journal:

Today one of the most beautiful days that can be imagined, wind, however, about the same. In the afternoon, however, hauled more Westerly so as to allow us to head about North-Northwest. I suppose we have averaged 3 knots all day. This week's work will be a very bad one and it is very disappointing for after having made the good passage round the Cape we were set up again for time lost on the other side. Saw today a bark a long way to leeward, heading South; also from topgallant yard, a vessel supposed to be a ship on the same course with ourselves. We could not see her from the deck, however.

Sunday aboard (such a day as this) is one of the most marked even more so than ashore. No noise, the men all forward and no work done and regularly a day of rest. The sea has been calm as could be, just rippled by the light breeze with the same heaving that old ocean always has. The *Fannie* would have made many more miles here than we today. Some prospects of a change of wind.

MONDAY, APRIL 9

Lat. 31° 06′ S. Long. 91° 16′ W.

Captain Mitchell's Journal:

Light airs from W.N.W. and calms make up this day. No prospect of a change. This is tedious and provoking. Hope on, hope ever.

Henry Ferguson's Journal:

Still another delightful but disappointing day to us weary mariners, but it now (evening) looks more hopeful of a breeze and we have been able to inch up to our course, which is a great gratification. After dinner we saw a bark in the dim distance heading S.E. dead ahead of the wind. Went up to the topgallant yard and so raised her hull and had a good look at her. She probably is bound home round the Cape. I never saw such a clear atmosphere as it is here. You can see a wonderful distance on the water and at night the stars are brighter than any I ever saw North. Several times we have seen stars rise right out of the water so that they looked like a ship's light.

Samuel Ferguson's Journal:

Again another very fine day with a very light breeze from the old quarter, viz, about West. This afternoon saw a bark a long way off standing South. She had everything set that would draw and was going along pretty lively. Nothing particularly interesting to jot down today. Men all employed in scraping the outside of the ship preparatory to painting, so that we shall go into port looking quite gay.

Last night the First and Third Mates' watches, a hugh rat got into the house and got up and stole from the table a whole biscuit (hard tack). He dumped it off the table then carried it in his mouth up quarter-deck steps and cut under one of the boats to eat it. Pretty good for a rat. Our traps have only caught small ones and not many of them. This evening from looks and appearance of clouds a change is predicted, which we are all heartily glad of, for this last week since Monday we have only made about seven degrees of latitude and one of longitude.

TUESDAY, APRIL 10

Lat. 29° 00′ S. Long. 92° 00′ W.

Captain Mitchell's Journal:

First part light breeze from W.N.W. Middle, good steady breeze from W.S.W. Latter part baffling, squally, and rain. Some hope of a change now. Ends thick and rainy. No observation.

Henry Ferguson's Journal:

Today I am glad to say I have something different to put down. We went very well last night, but this morning it was calm with rain squalls, many and hard, lasting till afternoon so that we were unable to get observation. I fell asleep after dinner and on waking received the grateful intelligence that we had caught the Trades and were travelling on nicely. And so it was and I hope we will keep them now till well North of the equator. Rain squalls all gone ahead now and it is another beautiful clear night. One unfortunate rat caught. The other night one was seen to get on the table in the house and take a whole hard-bread and carry it off in his mouth up the steps on the quarter deck and under the boat and there he enjoyed it. Mates say they are as big as good sized rabbits.

Samuel Ferguson's Journal:

Last evening's appearances have proved true. This morning we had frequent showers and calms until about 12:30, when we hope a regular Trade set in. The wind is just about Southeast and is taking us on at the rate of about six knots. Our course is Northwest, so that brings the wind dead aft which is not so good as it might be, but still much better than all our last week's work. This now, we hope, will stay by us and take us to 8° or 10° on the other side. Have been reading Maury on winds, etc.,* and very interesting and curious it is and how true and simple the theory seems to be. He has undoubtedly done a great deal both to shorten and make safe the ocean navigation. Yesterday I had an application from one of the sailors (a very decent sort of fellow) for an old pack of cards, so I gave him our second pack which by candle light we thought a pretty fare pack, but when I took them to him, I felt like apologizing to him they were so dirty. There are some nasty little islands** just sticking up somewhere about here according to some charts, they put them down but mark them doubtful. I expect they are not here as no two maps or charts agree to where they are. Our captain has never seen them.

* *Lieut. Matthew Fontaine Maury, USN, A NEW THEORETICAL AND PRACTICAL TREATISE ON NAVIGATION (Various updated editions from 1836 to 1845) — also his U.S. Hydrographic Office Wind and Current Charts which were undoubtedly carried on board the HORNET despite the fact that Maury, being a former Confederate naval officer, was discredited after the war by Yankees.*

** *There are no "nasty little islands" in this position — most probably they represented misplaced sightings of Juan Fernandez, 360 miles west of Valparaiso, or its neighboring island, Mas-Afuera. They are located respectively in 33° 37′ South latitude by 78° 50′ West longitude and 33° 44′ South latitude by 80° 45′ West longitude. Both are high, volcanic islands, the one 12 miles long by 4 wide and the other 8 miles long by 5 wide. Juan Fernandez was the island on which Alexander Selkirk was marooned in 1705, providing the inspiration for ROBINSON CRUSOE. The only other possible islands in this general area West of the coast of Chile were the more Northerly pair of San Ambrosio in 26° 20′ South latitude by 80° 54′ West longitude and San Felix eleven miles due West. Like Juan Fernandez, they are also bleak volcanic "desert" islands. (SOUTH AMERICAN PILOT, III. H.O. No. 174. Washington, 1928)*

WEDNESDAY, APRIL 11

Lat. 27° 15′ S. Long. 93° 40′ W.

Captain Mitchell's Journal:

At 1 P.M. wind comes out light from S.E., rain ceases, clouds disperse, and weather becomes fine. Middle and latter fine steady Trade and beautiful weather. All possible sail stretched on the ship.

Henry Ferguson's Journal:

Moderate tradewind all day now. In the evening there have come up squalls which blow from all quarters and kill the wind. However, I hope that they will not last long. We saw today a peculiar looking white bird which is only seen near the tropics and is called the "Tropic" bird and by the sailors the Marlinspike bird.* Some islands laid down in the charts as hereabouts, but we have not seen anything of them as yet. Our Trade is not quite as fierce as we should like, but it is a vast improvement of the calm of last week. Feel now that we have got them that we are almost at our journey's end though we have seven or eight weeks yet.

* *So called because its tail feathers come to a single point like a marlinspike. This sea bird is a member of the PHAETON family. It is also known as the Boatswain Bird.*

Samuel Ferguson's Journal:

Trade still holds, but has hauled more Easterly which is considerably to our advantage, giving us I should say two knots more speed in that it allows all sails to draw. We have today all sail set, even to main topmast studding sail and fore topgallant sail. Last night went on deck just before turning in, the phosphorescence very beautiful. Every wave breaking would roll out in fiery splendor. The wake you could follow a long way back. This afternoon I went out on the bowsprit to the spritsail yard and looked at the ship cut the water. The color today and always out here is a very clear blue, which as it shows out through the white foam that flows off from her cutwater, made a very pretty sight. I could distinctly see the bottom of the cutwater and some distance back along the keel. At the end of the jib-boom the ship looks as if it were another object and one is impressed to find himself nearly as high as the fore top. Saw a strange bird about today; Captain had no name for him but called him a "Tropic Bird." It was white with dark feathers under and along the wings and was web-footed. Although he flew high all the time, I saw him. Did not stay about long.

Tropic bird— woodcut from The World of the Sea, *1882.*

Lat. 25° 23 ' S. Long. 95° 40 'W.

Captain Mitchell's Journal:

First part fine fresh Trade. Middle, wind very baffling and frequent rain squalls. Latter pleasant, light Trade at N.E. Saw a Prussian bark steering S.W. Where can he be going?

Henry Ferguson's Journal:

Squally last night, but we have gone on tolerably today, though now it is again squally. These squalls kill all the wind for some time and very often head you off your course which ain't pleasant. This last one has not, though, I am glad to say. Saw a bark this A.M. heading S.W. She passed astern of us before noon and hoisted her colors which on examination proved to be Prussian, white with a chicken hawk in the center. We showed her ours and then she saluted us by dipping, which compliment we acknowledged by doing the same thing. Before dinner she was out of sight. She was probably bound for Australia. I believe the Captain's trap took a rat last night. Often heard of the kind, but this is the first I ever saw in operation.

Samuel Ferguson's Journal:

Last night showery which took our wind; still on the whole we made a pretty good day's run. Today it breezed up a little better again, but frequent showers break the steadiness. This morning sighted a bark that was heading West-Southwest. She passed astern of us near enough to show us her colors, which we made out to be Pressian. We then showed him the Stars and Stripes, when she was polite enough to dip hers which we returned. After dinner she was out of sight. She is on a queer course, Captain did not know where she could be going, unless Australia and then she is not on her right course. Saw today a few flying fish, the first that we have seen in the Pacific. They were very large ones and took very long flights. Have the same queer stand-up clouds that we saw on the other side, of all kinds of shapes. I wish I could sketch them as they look. This afternoon my gold pen rolled off the table and broke off one of the diamonds on the nib for which I am very sorry for I have had it ever since I went into the office in Pine Street, May 1858.

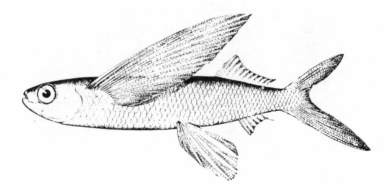

Flying Fish - woodcut from The Shore Fisheries of Hawaii, *1903.*

FRIDAY, APRIL 13

Lat. 23° 55' W. Long. 98° 00' W.

Captain Mitchell's Journal:

Begins good breeze from Northeast. Middle and latter, wind very baffling from North to Northwest and squally. Ends strong squally Norther. Great wind for N.E. Trades. Surely everything contrives to retard our progress.

Henry Ferguson's Journal:

Today was ushered in by a pretty sharp squall which played the old scratch with our fore-topmast studding sail boom, snapping it in two in fine style. They got the sail in all safe though. Also it snapped the main topgallant stay and let the staysail flap round in a most ferocious manner, making noise enough for two dozen. Wind has been adverse all day, most provokingly being North and Northwest, right in the heart of the South-East Trades though we be. Head winds seem to be our lot. We have headed West half the time and never up to our course. Some tropic birds round, but very few if any flying fish. Wind is a pretty good breeze and we are going on nicely which only is the more tantalizing.

Samuel Ferguson's Journal:

Woke up this morning with a tremendous noise and row on deck, wind howling through the rigging in great style. Pretty soon the noise was increased by a sort of crack and then a great flapping and slapping of a sail, I looked out and saw that the main topgallant staysail was loose and only held by the halyards and sheet. Soon, however, the squall went over and I found out that the fore topmast studding sail boom had been carried away, having broken off right at the boom and while the men were saving the sail, this main topmast stay parted and for a short time it was pretty lively. Both sails were saved.

A real fine day but wind had been fooled with by squalls so that all day it has been about North, heading us off to West-Northwest and sometimes West. This is funny for a Southeast Trade, but we put it down to disturbing influences. Scraping the deck has been the order of some days past and this morning holystoning commenced. The inside of the ship is also getting the priming for painting.

SATURDAY, APRIL 14

Lat. 23° 26' S. Long. 100° 19' W.

Captain Mitchell's Journal:

Wind steady and light from N.W. all this day. Whoever heard of the like in the heart of the S.E. Trades to have a regular N.W. wind! Patience. Patience. Scraping ship outside.

Henry Ferguson's Journal:

Today is even worse than yesterday, whereas we headed West, today we have been S.W. and at one time even got to S. by W. Wouldn't do, so we tacked and now, of course, we are headed off to the East of North. It is hard lines if we can't steer either North of West on one tack or West of North on the other. Bad toothache last night. Applied oil of cloves which did it good and relieved me exceedingly. More of those birds about today. Getting hot. Got a hammock and spent the afternoon in it. These are most peculiar Southeast Trades certainly. What business it had to blow from the Northwest is hard to say. *Chi sara, sara*, is poor consolation, but we must take the wind as it comes.

Samuel Ferguson's Journal:

Wind more contrary than ever, heading us off to Southwest at times. About 5 P.M. tacked and now head just about North. This tacking is the best fun of anything done aboard ship to lookers on. Both watches are called and every man has his place at some of the braces. When everything is ready, the order is given to put the helm hard-a-lee and while the ship is coming up in the wind there is regular silence all over the ship except perhaps the flapping of some sail. As soon as her head is fully up in the wind, Captain sings out, "main topsail haul". Then if ever there was a bedlum let loose it seems to be now, for the men start with the braces and run forward hauling the yards round with a sort of yell there as they get in the slack and come to the hard pulling. Each set at each brace set up their ho-hoing making a regular racket. The foresails are the last to do and the quickness and competence of the men make the difference between a quick clean tack or a slovenly one. All the ropes being off the pins just after a tack, everything is at loose ends which adds somewhat to the effect. Soon, however, everything gets to its place again and we are under good headway.

SUNDAY, APRIL 15

Lat. 22° 52' S. Long. 100° 06' W.

Captain Mitchell's Journal:

First part winds N.W. Middle part, W.N.W. Tacked to North. Winds light and baffling two to three points. At 9 A.M. tacked again to the West. Ends light, wind from N.W. as usual. Did every anybody ever see the like! No S.E Trade on the other side, none on this.

Henry Ferguson's Journal:

Another provoking day just the same as yesterday if not worse. Tacked in the morning and again at midnight. It is real interesting and amusing to see them tack ship. The helm is put hard down and the order is given for the men to be at their stations. Then "hard a-lee" is sung out at which the fore-topmast staysail and jibs are let fly. Then as she gets round into the wind, Captain sings out "mainsail haul" and in place of the hush that there was while she was coming up, comes the singing out of the men and the swinging of the main and cro' jack yards with all above them. The sails on the foremast are left aback to draw her round and when the mainsails, etc., begin to fill, the order "fore bowlines" is given, and when they are let fly, the order "let go and haul" comes and the yards swing round and she fills and comes up. We have always as yet in tacking hauled up the main course and cro' jack, but they do it without and the fixing the tacks and sheet make it lively work.

Samuel Ferguson's Journal:

The same baffling winds all day today heading us off in the afternoon to Southwest. About 3:30 we went about and now stand heading nearly North. The air and weather has been very pleasant, sea calm yet with motion enough to give it life. Captain feels much disappointed that our chance for a good run is cut off by these "out of place winds". We should have a good strong Southeast Trade here, but Maury says that this month here the winds are much broken and disturbed. Have thought much of the houseparty today; how I would enjoy a few days with them all. No ships in sight today nor any birds or fish. This ocean does not seem to abound in life as the Atlantic, but I suppose here we are far away from any land which may account for it. Occasionally we see some tropic birds, but they do not follow us like the gulls and albatross. A little further North I suppose we shall find plenty of fish of various kinds. No flying fish for a few days past.

MONDAY, APRIL 16

Lat. 22° 20´ S. Long. 100° 14´ W.

Captain Mitchell's Journal:

Same as yesterday, light baffling winds from W.N.W. to N.N.W. Tacked often, but soon after tacking, off she would go no matter which tack she was on. It is enough to provoke a saint, utterly impossible to gain anything.

Henry Ferguson's Journal:

Today resembles in the closest possible manner its predecessors and it does not improve at all. We had hoped that it would change with the moon, but the new moon has come and still no change. We saw it tonight and a slimmer one I never saw, nor did I ever see the dark part of her so clearly. The stars must give a tremendous quantity of light down here. Tacked once today and are now on the starboard tack heading W.S.W., eight points nearly off our course. Tacking don't improve it for as soon as we tack we get headed off however we go. Some sea come up from the South. We most fervently hope it may be the fore-runner of a wind from that quarter. Such is life!

Samuel Ferguson's Journal:

Last night squally, wind in every direction and one time allowing us to go upon our course and deluding us into hopes of its continuance, but after a half hour's duration, it came out from the Northwest, just our desired course, and has continued so all day, seeming to shift a point or so according as we tacked.

Very little to chronicle today. All are down in the mouth and disappointed about our prospects that were so good and now seem all upset again.

Saw the new moon tonight with the old one plainer in its arms than I ever saw before. Also noticed the very narrowness of the said moon. Saturday night saw the old and welcome lights of the Dipper, all but the upper pointer. It seemed quite natural to see his old handle again. It was 11:30 P.M., however, so we have some way to go yet before we raise the North Star, which Dana* says is the first land made going north and is always welcomed by sailors from around the Cape.

* *Richard Henry Dana, Jr.*

Lat. 22° 22′S. Long. 101° 30′W.

Captain Mitchell's Journal:

The same cussed damnable winds baffling from N.N.W. to W.N.W. light and rain squalls. Heavy appearance in the South and a strong strife of winds for six hours, but the Northerly wind at length prevailed, destroying the last hope. No observation.

Henry Ferguson's Journal:

Today there has been an evident battle between the Northerly and Southerly winds which is gratifying as it shows the Trades yet live and we may get them sometime again. The Northwest wind seemed to get the best in the morning and to keep back the other and we could see where they met by the clouds and showers. The afternoon was a calm roused I have no doubt by the meeting of the winds. We are now heading North a half West, but are not going scarcely at all. Have the best hope for tomorrow that my birthday may be graced by a return of a good fair wind. I hoped that we would be farther North when it came. The Captain has come down and joy! he says that the wind is aft what there is of it. So we may hope for the best.

Samuel Ferguson's Journal:

Monday night and this morning very like its predecessor, squally wind in every direction. When we went on deck we headed Southwest, but the old wind stood out again and blew till about noon when it died entirely and left us in as still a calm as can be imagined. Mr. Hardy [First Mate] and I improved it by seeing how deep we could see in the water. At first I threw over a china button about the size of a three cent piece, which we saw for a long while. I then went and got my white blue fish squid and fastening the line to it threw it overboard and let it slowly sink till we could indistinctly see it. We then measured the line and it was 72 feet; a larger object we could have seen at a much greater distance.

This morning we were in a tantalus position, behind us we could actually see where the Northerly and Southerly winds met and stopped. What little wind there was rippling the water till it met the other where it was perfectly flat and calm and very black from the clouds overhead. By 10:30 the Southeast wind so far conquered as to give us a motion which with the swell moved us at about three knots which was increased somewhat as the night went on.

WEDNESDAY, APRIL 18

Lat. 21° 10′S. Long. 102° 00′W.

Captain Mitchell's Journal:

First part calm. At 6 P.M. light breeze from S.S.E. continuing through the day. Latter part moderate breeze from S.E., which I hope is the commencement of a permanent trade. Finished scraping outside.

Henry Ferguson's Journal:

The first day of my nineteenth year finds us, I am happy to say, with a fair wind which I hope will last till well North of the Line. It is not very strong yet, but we must allow it time to rest itself after its exertion yesterday. In all other respects my birthday finds me about the same as yesterday. I will put down here that Sam's cough has been less and he himself has improved much since we left the Cape. Yesterday he coughed more than usual now, but does not today. He got out a bottle of sherry to drink my health in and it tasted very nice and homelike. It is the first sherry we have had opened. Gingersnaps are now as good as when made, but if they stand exposed to the air for any time, grow soft. It is wonderful how they have kept.

Samuel Ferguson's Journal:

Steward reported wind dead aft this morning, but enough to give us 5 knots. As the day grew, the wind got round more East and gave us more chance. Captain set *everything*, studding sails, staysails, and all.

Am sorry to say there is considerable sickness aboard; one man has had a bad fever for nearly a month. There are three now down in the First Mate's watch (Port), so that one has been transferred from the other. Henry's birthday today which we celebrated by opening and drinking his health at dinner in a bottle of sherry. We also remembered absent friends. The home-made gingersnaps still hold out and are very good if eaten when first taken out of the can. Although such things are very good and nice I never should take so many again to sea, for there is really no time you feel like eating them. Breakfast at 7:45, dinner at 12:15 and tea at 5:30 hardly gives you much time to get very hungry between times. They are very nice, however, whenever taken and are fully appreciated by the Captain.

THURSDAY, APRIL 19

Lat. 19° 45′ S. Long. 103° 20′ W.

Captain Mitchell's Journal:

Very light baffling Trades all this day. Winds from North to E.S.E.

Henry Ferguson's Journal:

Today we have been moving along nicely over our course and doing well though a little stronger wind would not hurt us. It is the North of East which is better than being dead aft as everything draws nicely. It headed us a point or so but soon came back to its original place where I guess it will stay. We saw this evening one of the prettiest sights I ever saw. There was a fine sunset with a few clouds a little above the horizon, but it itself was clear and we saw the evening star set in the sea looking quarter as big as the moon. It is wonderfully clear and the moon and stars give a great deal more light I ever noticed them to give on land.

Samuel Ferguson's Journal:

This morning wind freshened to a fine breeze about abeam and strong enough to give us full 6 knots. Water and sea both splendid today. The former, one cannot imagine or appreciate without seeing. The air also is exceedingly clear, allowing us to see stars right down to the horizon and go out like the sun. Sailors busy today setting up the back stays which soon work slack. Some also have been employed in painting, so that we will go into San Francisco looking gay. Have not seen a sail for nearly a week or anything else in fact except ourselves.

What a lot we shall have to read up and study when we get ashore, which it looks now as if a 130-day passage would not be far out of the way. No fish of any kind to be seen lately except porpoises. I suppose it is rather far South yet for flying fish.

FRIDAY, APRIL 20

Lat. 17° 18'S. Long. 104° 40'W.

Captain Mitchell's Journal:

Moderate Trade all this day and fine weather. Finished painting bulwarks and waist. Tarring down fore rigging.

Henry Ferguson's Journal:

The breeze continues steady as it ought to do and has freshened up quite a good deal so that we have been going I suppose at eight knots all afternoon and are now if anything going a little more. In calm weather like this with the water still a breeze does more service than one thinks. We have got nearly everything set we have, everything in fact but a storm spencer and a lower fore studdingsail. She does not carry a complete set of studdingsails, but has only four in all, two topgallant, one topmast, and one lower. I guess we must be satisfied to get in by the 20th. of May even if we could do that, although it would be hard papers (?) if our bad luck compassed us all round.

Samuel Ferguson's Journal:

Wind the same, a good stiff breeze nearly Northeast instead of Southeast as they should be. Captain has been reading up Maury and looking out various logs of vessels up here in this month and nearly all agree in reporting the Trades South of the Line much broken and disturbed. We hope now, however, that we are going to keep those we have until well across the Line.

Very little now going on today, still painting and tautening backstays. The sun is getting intensely hot during the morning particularly as we get very little shade then. The air, however, is very pleasant and agreeable.

When I started this log I was in hopes of making it readable, but one day is so much like another that it really comes very hard to vary one day's jottings from another. Henry has got along very well with his studies and is, I guess, now much ahead of his class in everything but perhaps French, which they seem to have such a crazy way of pronouncing, according to his dictionary, that I have not been able to be of much service to him. Nor have I studied myself preferring to be on deck all the time I can.

SATURDAY, APRIL 21

Lat. 14° 48' S. Long. 106° 00' W.

Captain Mitchell's Journal:

Very moderate Trades all this day. Doomed to a long passage. Took all the sick men out the forecastle and put them in the poop.

Henry Ferguson's Journal:

Today we still have propitious breezes, but moderate, and I am sorry to see they are working aft. However, they are not to be sneezed at. It is getting dreadfully hot again, what it will be when we get under the sun I'm sure I don't know. Nothing particular to put down. Several tropic birds around (these are also called "boatswains") and they can utter the most inharmonious note of any bird I ever heard. Filing a saw is nothing to it. Quite a good many flying fish round. I have not seen very many myself, but Sam says he has seen more this afternoon than all put together that he saw in the Atlantic. Boatswains fish for them, diving into the water like good fellows after them, though they generally try to catch them in the air.

Samuel Ferguson's Journal:

Trades still hold and from about the same quarter. Seem today to have run into the region of flying fish especially this afternoon. Hardly five minutes would elapse between the flights and in some flocks I should think there were thousands. We had a lot of tropic birds about and what with the fish starting them out and the birds pitching on them when out or alighting, the poor fellows have rather a precarious sort of existence.

I am sorry to say my cough still holds on and in this warm and close latitude troubles me. I am much better, however, and have filled out my cheeks somewhat. Not having had our hair cut since we started, both Henry's and mine are in a very lengthy condition. I mean to have mine clipped though pretty soon and then it will be ready for another cut soon after we arrive. John, one of the sick men, has inflamation of the lungs the Captain thinks. These three sick ones are all moved down to the booby hatch. Whether they like the change from the forecastle or not I can't say. Big ring around the moon tonight. So far we have had no real storms such as we would call it on land, though we have had gales.

SUNDAY, APRIL 22

Lat. 12° 44' S. Long. 107° 20' W.

Captain Mitchell's Journal:

Very moderate Trades all this day and fine weather. A poor week's work considering we are in the best of the Trades. Four men sick.

Henry Ferguson's Journal:

Today has been another lovely Sunday and indeed I don't think we have had but one un-pleasant Sunday since we came out. The wind is here, but light and getting more and more aft, which makes quite a difference in our speed. Thousands of flying fish about. The ship frightens them I suppose and they rise from near her continually in flocks, some of which must be of over a thousand. I never saw such a quantity of fish. "Boatswains" are actively employed all the time, between fishing and squawking their delight when they have had a very palatable one. Hot. Breeze is cool and pleasant which is a blessing. Saw the other day a blue billed bird which Captain calls a "Booby", also a black bird, name unknown, that looks like some kind of a hawk.

Samuel Ferguson's Journal:

Again a beautiful day, getting, though, after 10 A.M. too warm on deck for comfort till about noon when you can get into the shade from some of the sails. I am afraid we have two pretty sick men aboard; one I doubt whether he will see San Francisco, his disease is venereal, the other has a sort of low intermittent fever.

Flights of flying fish today even exceed those of yesterday, thousands and thousands in each flock, making the water just where they hit perfectly white. The birds making a dash at a flying fish must catch them with their beaks not feet as most birds do. Found today a bar-ber in Mr. Hardy, the First Mate, who promised to clip us both tomorrow and a great relief it will be, for this hot weather makes long hair very unpleasant. Hope all at Stamford had as pleasant and fine a Sunday as this has been here. It is always a very marked day aboard.

MONDAY, APRIL 23

Lat. 10° 17' S. Long. 108° 35' W.

Captain Mitchell's Journal:

Moderate Trade as usual all this day. Sick men about the same, I see no improvement.

Henry Ferguson's Journal:

Another delightful day with a brisk Trade and we are speeding along towards our haven at a very nice rate. It is one of the most charming nights imaginable, bright as day and a pleasant breeze blowing. It would be a lovely night for music on the water if we had a party of feminines. Stars somewhat thrown into the shade by the moon, but still very bright. We saw the "Dipper" for the first time about a week ago and it looked like an old friend. Saw it to-night and it looks as if the North Star could not be far off, though I suppose we shall not see that till we are well North of the Line. If the wind we have got now keeps up, we will I hope cross certainly by Friday. Both Sam and I were barberized today. Mr. Hardy acted as execu-tioner and shingled my hair very nicely indeed. Father's birthday, many happy returns of it to him.

Samuel Ferguson's Journal:

Captain's three patients rather better this morning. Antonio, the sickest one, is pretty weak and suffers a good deal of pain. John the third one, is somewhat better but worse than a darkey to be sick. This being Peter's well day, he was feeling much better.

Wind has got a little more aft, but comes over the quarter enough to make bracing the yards a little necessary. We head Northwest by North, a half North, the wind being about Southeast and part of the time giving us 8 to 9 knots. Again lots of flying fish, but no signs of any others, the ship starting up the flocks we see. This afternoon Mr. Hardy barberized both Henry and I and vastly more comfortable does it feel. N.B., if advice is asked, advise plenty of silk but not many white pocket handkerchiefs to be taken by any young man making a long voyage. The white look out of place at sea anyway and get very quickly soiled and are not washed to perfection by any means.

Many happy returns of the day to Father, even if the 23rd is not the day, but I think it is.

TUESDAY, APRIL 24

Lat. 7° 47 'S. Long. 109° 50 'W.

Captain Mitchell's Journal:

First and middle fresh Trade. Latter moderate, ending nearly calm. Caught several bonitos for a change. Sick about the same.

Henry Ferguson's Journal:

Today pleasant but very hot indeed all day though worse in the forenoon than in the afternoon. Wind not quite so brisk but more on our quarter. We are heading N.N.W. Great many bonitos about the bow and indeed all around catching their fill of flying fish. One of the men caught three this morning and in the afternoon I tried but with no success. One was speared this afternoon, but no more took the bait. The ones he caught were very large indeed and must have weighed from twenty to twenty-five pounds, ditto the one that Tom, the boy, speared. There are a great many flying fish and some we saw today could not have been more than an inch long. These were snapped up by the bonitos as very dainty tidbits and at times there would be quite lively scenes.

Samuel Ferguson's Journal:

Breeze held splendidly last night and this morning to about 6, when it caved in and was very light all this morning and as a matter of course the sun pelted down awfully, making it hot everywhere. Today has been distinguished by the catching of four bonitos, three by hook and one with the grains.* They were most abundant but were after flying fish and showed that they preferred them to our piece of white rag. I wish I could have caught some flying fish I saw today, regular infants and not more than an inch and a half long. These poor little fellows would come out of the water like a large fly, but would almost invariably be caught by a bonito before he had gone four feet. Joe, the Portuguese fellow, was the successful fisherman and certainly a very patient one he is.

Tomorrow noon we are a hundred days out, how the time does go! Still, it seems an age since we left New York, and we are now in our second summer since that time.

* *Multi-barbed fish spear as cited previously.*

WEDNESDAY, APRIL 25

Lat. 5° 10'S. Long. 110° 50'W.

Captain Mitchell's Journal:

Very moderate Trades and fine weather all this day. Another man sick. Former sick ones about the same, I don't see any improvement.

Henry Ferguson's Journal:

There is very little, in fact nothing to put down today. There have been no bonitos and only few flying fish to be seen and the breeze has been lighter than we could wish. One day in these parts is exceedingly like another. They are tarring down all the standing rigging and have been setting up the topgallant and royal backstays. Everything that has been tarred looks very nice, but is exceedingly sticky and detrimental to any clothes that chance to run against any of it. They have done the stays forward and all the fore shrouds and backstays and are at work on the main and mizzen shrouds today. We have, I am sorry to say, several sick men, one of whom is very sick indeed with intermittent fever.

Samuel Ferguson's Journal:

Trades still hold as they should do, but slackened considerably today and have got rather more aft, to meet which, the Captain has changed our course to North by West. He thinks, too, that we have a Westerly current here. Both bonito and flying fish scarce today. The sun is getting very hot and pours down on deck pretty heavy. I only hope we don't have to knock long about in the doldrums. It seems a long time since we have seen anything at all but ourselves. If the Chiliean ports were open we ought to see vessels bound there, but nary one have we seen since the Prussian bark. All the standing rigging is newly tarred down and looks first rate all shiney and black. Tomorrow I believe they begin painting the outside of the ship. Pretty hot weather to paint in, but I believe they make three coats go for one by putting it on very thin. The chains and windless, etc., is all painted red.

THURSDAY, APRIL 26

Lat. 3° 48'S. Long. 111° 10'W.

Captain Mitchell's Journal:

Very moderate Trades. Middle part light from S. by E. Latter very light ending calm and awful hot. Sick about the same as yesterday.

Henry Ferguson's Journal:

Furiously hot today and indeed it has been for some time. They finished up the tarring the rigging today, sending men on chairs to tar the stays. Rather ticklish looking it is swinging in mid-air high above the deck and greasing and tarring as hard as they can. Hot is no name for

- 110 -

the weather; it is beginning to be perfectly awful. What it will be when we get beneath the sun I don't know. The Captain quotes,

> "O for a lodge in some vast wilderness
> Some boundless continuity of shade,"

and that will be the wish of all when he shines down straight perpendicular. Sick men pretty bad. One has pleurisy and there is now a fourth laid up with swelling on his back which looks, so the "Old Man" says, like the effects of an old fall.

Samuel Ferguson's Journal:

Today looks very much like a break up of what Trades we have had. I hope, however, they are not going to leave us in the lurch now, to drift to 8 or 10 degrees on the other side. Another man was added yesterday to the sick list. Peter still very sick and had today a violent chill. Antonio suffers a good deal of pain in his legs and can walk with difficulty. John is only so-so and still in a good deal of pain which seems to be in the lungs, though it does not put him in a fever.

Weather very hot and in the morning very sultry; better breeze after noon which died to about a 2-knot one by night.

We have the good and familiar sight of the Dipper every night now and very soon must see the North Star, although the Southern Cross is still pretty high. Three-handed whist still runs and we have increased the number of games to ten.

FRIDAY, APRIL 27

Lat. 2° 50'S. Long. 111° 20'W.

Captain Mitchell's Journal:

Light baffling airs from S.W. to S.S.E. and calms all this day. Great Father, when are we to get any wind to go along! Peter had another awful chill, is getting very weak. Cloudy, no observation.

Henry Ferguson's Journal:

Today is much the same as yesterday. Hardly any wind all day and the little breeze that has sprung up now is heading us off which is an abomination. At least it would be a little comfort to be right on our course though we don't go but two or three knots. The sick men are pretty sick and Peter, the one with the chills, was this morning and yesterday very low indeed, but is rather better this evening. The others are about the same. Squally today which has made it dreadful hot and close, and tonight there is quite a hard rain which drops through the skylight and comes on the table. Cabin as hot as Sahara. Don't like to think what the berths will be.

Samuel Ferguson's Journal:

About a 2-knot breeze all night and very hot and close this morning. About 11, however, we had a good shower which I think really did cool us off a little. Peter, the sickest of the invalids, is very low this morning. Captain told me this morning he hardly expected him to live 24 hours.

The Captain has taken very good and kind care of all those sick men and seems to feel a good deal about them. My brandy has come into service and I hope it will help to do them good. Peter, I have taken quite an interest in; he always seems in such good spirits, although poor fellow, he is as weak as a kitten and this morning can hardly raise his head.

If we see San Francisco by the first of June, I believe we will be lucky, for since I began to write this the wind has come more North so as to head us off about Northwest. The worst part is that if the Southeast Trade leaves us here we may be a month or more before we catch the Northeast.

SATURDAY, APRIL 28

Lat. 1° 32'S. Long. 112° 12'W.

Captain Mitchell's Journal:

Light baffling airs, calms, and plenty of rain showers all through the day Peter decidedly better, Antonio worse, no improvement in John, Neil the same.

Henry Ferguson's Journal:

Today is only a repetition of its predecessors and has not done very much for our onward course. There has only been about enough wind for two moderate breaths all day. However, it is one consoling thing that we have been on our course all day. Men have been scrubbing the topgallant, forecastle, and paint work round the forward part, and the removal of three months' and over's dust and dirt makes quite a perceptible difference. Most beautiful night. Moon very brilliant and gives a splendid light. Although we don't go much we raise the "Dipper" and drop the Cross tolerably fast. If the moon was not so bright I really believe we might see the North Star tonight if the moon was not so bright and the horizon were clear.

Many happy returns of the day to dear Sarah. I wish we could see her and wish her them today.

Samuel Ferguson's Journal:

This morning began the day in a cleanly manner at any rate, viz. by have a good tub bath, which has decidedly comfortable and to the right spot. Wind today very light and just sending us through the water and the Mate reports it the same all last night with heavy showers of rain. The men are rather better on the whole today, although it must have been a trying night as it was very close. Remembered Sarah today and wish her long life and happiness.

I am glad to find that we are so far four days ahead of the *Hornet's* last passage, which was about the same time of year, he being 108 days to the Line and 128 to San Francisco. I hope we may have the good fortune to get a good Trade soon the other side and take us right along. I want to beat that passage anyway. One voyage this ship made home in 84 days to the Line on the other side, running through both Trades in nine days. About the Bermudas she was caught by very light winds and calms.

SUNDAY, APRIL 29

Lat. 0° 47'S. Long. 112° 24'W.

Captain Mitchell's Journal:

Very light airs from N.N.E. to N.E. and calms all this day. Very hot. Sick men appear little better. O Patience, don't desert men.

Henry Ferguson's Journal:

Dreadful poor work today for it has been frightfully calm and is so now. It does beat all, the way that these calms stick to us. If we had had only moderate good fortune in winds we doubtless would now be pretty near San Francisco, whereas we are not even across the Line yet, a thing that we ought certainly to have done last Sunday. Can't see the North Star yet nor won't for a month if this weather keeps on. Tried to get the latitude by the moon last night, but did not succeed very well as I could not get a decent horizon when I took my altitude. However, know how to do it now and intend to do it again and see if shall not have better luck.

Samuel Ferguson's Journal:

Another fine day, as usual the wind pretty nearly nix all day, just moved that is just kept steerage way. Sun poured down in true tropic style making the deck as hot as blazes. Noticed today a great number of worm-like objects in the water, some would be quite straight while others would be sort of kinked up, all, though, had the power of twisting and moving about. Saw also a lot of jellyfish.

  The invalids are all better this morning, John seeming now to be the most out of sorts. Peter has escaped his chill for three days, and if he goes over the fourth, the Captain hopes he will get all right again. He was mighty low one day. Last night while reading I heard a rat in the pantry, so shutting all the cabin doors, I opened the pantry one and pretty soon the Captain and I had about the liveliest rat hunt one can imagine. Of course we finished him and a rouster he was and very saucy.

MONDAY, APRIL 30

Lat. 0° 40'S. Long. 112° 50'W.

Captain Mitchell's Journal:

Dead calm all this 24 hours. It's awful trying. Sick men about the same. This hot weather without a breeze will soon kill them. Some current.

Henry Ferguson's Journal:

Speaking of this forenoon and part of the afternoon, (like the man when the boys let down the back board of his wagon when he was going up hill and so lost his potatoes for him) I can't do justice to the subject. We have actually made six miles of latitude from noon yesterday to noon today. A little breeze sprang up this afternoon which promised better things, but we must not build our hopes too high. Portugee Joe caught some more bonito today. He is certainly the greatest hand at catching fish I ever saw. Saw tonight before coming down stairs a very beautiful shooting star that was visible for quite a time and drew a trail of fire behind it like a meteor.

Samuel Ferguson's Journal:

As will be seen by the above we have not made much progress since yesterday noon. Six miles Northing a big day's work. Today has beaten yesterday till about 2 P.M. when a nice little breeze sprang up from the South-Southeast. All morning it was powerfully hot, almost intolerable in the sun on deck. Captain got an old sail stretched over the poop raised up on the spanker boom and took off the skylight entirely so that made us pretty comfortable down here in the cabin. I find my stateroom intolerably hot and the other night was troubled also with bedfellows, so I spent the night on the cabin lounge, which I think I shall continue to occupy at night until the weather gets cooler at any rate. Today Joe caught three more bonitos. We have not tried for them as the rigging forward as well as aft is all newly tarred.

TUESDAY, MAY 1

Lat. 0° 12' N. Long. 112° 10' W.

Captain Mitchell's Journal:

Very light airs all this day from S.S.E. and hot. Sick men about the same. Painting outside.

Henry Ferguson's Journal:

Deceptive breeze all died away before this morning but we have managed to scrape across the Line, which I had almost begun to despair of ever doing. I did a thing this morning I have not done before all the time we have been out, namely I got up at 5 A.M. to see the dawn and sunrise and very pretty indeed it was, although it was not a clear sunrise. It is a great deal finer than a sunset, but it is hard to describe exactly where the superiority lies. Took a morning cup of coffee with Mr. Hardy and it sat remarkably well. Shooting stars again tonight though none as fine as last night's. Peter has not had his chill now for four days, and we hope now he will get all right soon.

Samuel Ferguson's Journal:

At last we have managed to get across the Line, but all today have been just creeping along. By some unaccountable way we seem to have drifted over two degrees Eastward, for the last week we have been steering to the West of North. The Captain tried two observations in morning and afternoon which coincided, so whether we have been mistaken before or have drifted I don't know. The drifting seem too great a notion.

The invalids generally improved. John is still the sickest now and the Captain seems to think it is his liver; he suffers considerable pain and has a mean little cough and complains that it hurts him to lie on either side. Peter I hope has shaken off his chills, though I don't believe he ever will be a sound man again. The phosphorescence tonight is very bright and comes often in large sort of lumps which light up all around. North Star not yet to be seen, though it must at times be above the horizon (early in the evening).

WEDNESDAY, MAY 2

Lat. 1° 28′ N. Long. 111° 56′ W.

Captain Mitchell's Journal:

Very gentle breeze all this day, say from 1½ to 3 knots. Sick folks improving.

Henry Ferguson's Journal:

Calm day with a little breeze and a great many fish about. They caught nine bonito and an albacore. An albacore that must have weighed sixty or eighty pounds got hold of a hook, but broke the hook off and left. Albacore and shark beneath the stern, but would not bite. Shark staid some feet beneath the surface of the water.

Mark Twain's Comments: *

When the following paragraph was written the ship was about one hundred and twenty days out from port, and all hands were putting in the lazy time about as usual, as no one was forecasting disaster.

* *Taken from his 1899 article, "My Début as a Literary Person" - see pages 224-228.*

Samuel Ferguson's Journal:

Again another hot and sluggish day. At one time, however, the clouds promised wind and there came a slight little breeze, just enough to keep us agoing. The only thing to chronicle today is the quantities of fish about. Nine bonitos were caught this morning and some large albacore were seen and after dinner First Mate with my line and white squid hooked a fellow which he could not hold, so let the line go to the Captain who was in the bows. He, holding on, brought the fish to with a jerk and snap went the line, hook and all. We also saw astern, swimming lazily after us, an enormous shark, he must have been 9 or 10 feet long. We tried him with all sorts of lines and a piece of pork, but he declined to take hold; I suppose he had appeased his appetite on the head, etc., of the bonitos thrown overboard. It was a true bell about the current; we now head Northwest a half West.

The Hornet on fire, May 3, 1866. From a painting by Burnell Poole, 1927. Courtesy Mr. Henry L. Ferguson

PART IV—FIRE! THEY TAKE TO THE BOATS

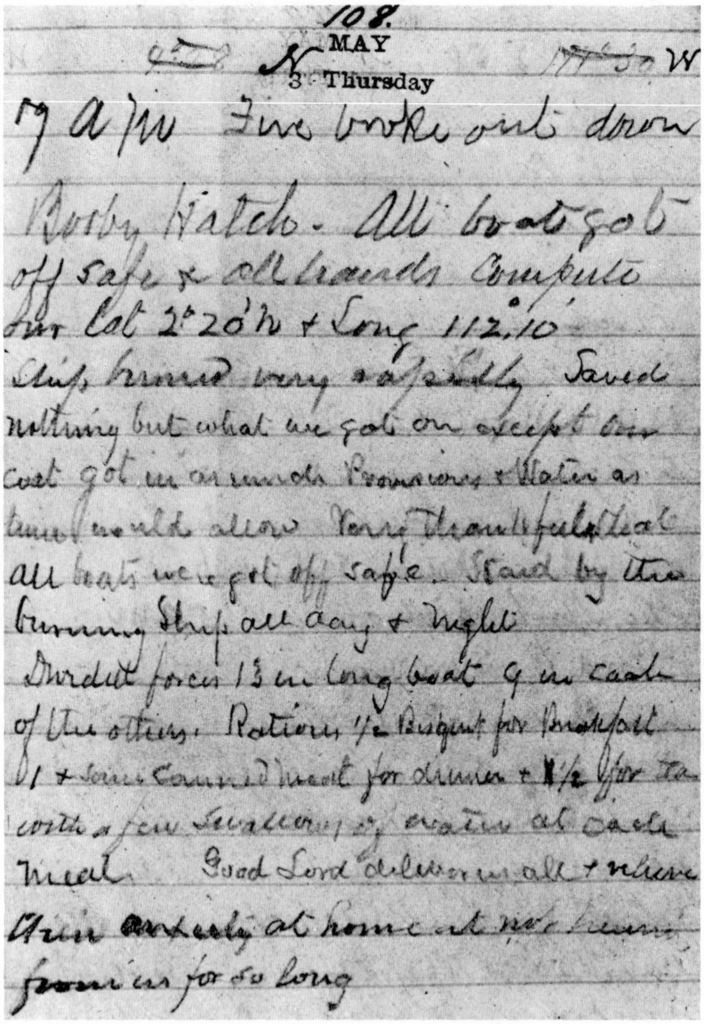

108.

N MAY W

3 Thursday

7 A M Fire broke out down
Booby Hatch. All boats got
off safe & all hands Compute
our Lat 2° 20' N & Long 112° 10'
Ship burned very rapidly Saved
nothing but what we got on except our
coat got in as much Provisions & Water as
time would allow Very thankful that
all boats were got off safe. Stand by the
burning Ship all day & Night
Divided forces 13 in long boat 9 in each
of the others. Rations 1/2 Biscuit for Breakfast
1/ & some Canned Meat for dinner & 1/2 for tea
with a few swallows of water at each
Meal. Good Lord deliver us all & relieve
their anxiety at home at not hearing
from us for so long

Samuel Ferguson's journal entry for May 3.

Actual Size

<h1 style="text-align:center">THURSDAY, MAY 3</h1>

Lat. 2^O 04 'N. Long. 112° 00'W.

Captain Mitchell's Journal:

7 A.M. Lat. 2^O 20 , Long. 112° 10 .
At eight left *Hornet* in three boats. Ship on fire and enveloped all over. Just enough time to launch boats and get a little provisions. At 9 masts went overboard. Stay round the ship in the boats hoping some ship would be attracted by smoke and take us off.

Henry Ferguson's Journal:

Most horrible to tell. The ship took fire this morning between decks in some varnish and oil, which soon got such headway that it was impossible to save her and so we had to take to the boats. We were most fortunate in getting all these safely into the water and getting some provisions in and all hands. Hardly any clothing saved. We got off all right with all hands and soon saw the flame seize the whole ship and run up the sails. Soon the mainmast went over, carrying with it the mizzen topmast. The fore- and mizzenmast lasted longer but were soon gone. Sam and I with the captain and third mate got into one of the quarter boats, and at night into the longboat. Ship blazing very bright.

Samuel Ferguson's Journal:

7 A.M. Fire broke out down booby hatch, all boats got off safe and all hands. Compute our latitude 2^O 20 N. and longitude 112° 10 . Ship burning very rapidly. Saved nothing but what we got on except our coats. Got in as much provisions and water as time would allow. Very thankful that all boats were got off safe. Stayed by the burning ship all day and night.

   Divided forces, 13 in longboat, 9 in each of the others. Rations half biscuit for breakfast, one and some canned meat for dinner, and one and a half for tea, with a few swallows of water at each meal. Good Lord deliver us all, and relieve their anxiety at home at not hearing from us for so long.

Mark Twain's Comments:

This day's entries record the disaster. The three boats got away, retired to a short distance, and stopped. The two injured ones were leaking badly; some of the men were kept busy bailing, others patched the holes as well as they could. The captain, the two passengers, and eleven men were in the longboat, with a share of the provisions and water, and with no room to spare, for the boat was only twenty-one feet long, six wide, and three deep. The chief mate and eight men were in one of the small boats, the second mate and seven men in the other. The passengers had saved no clothing but what they had on, excepting their overcoats. The ship, clothed in flame and sending up a vast column of black smoke into the sky, made a grand picture in the solitudes of the sea, and hour after hour the outcasts sat and watched it. Meanwhile, the captain ciphered on the immensity of the distance that stretched between him and the nearest available land, and then scaled the rations down to meet the emergency; half a biscuit for breakfast; one biscuit and some canned meat for dinner; half a biscuit for tea; a few swallows of water for each meal. And so hunger began to gnaw while the ship was still burning.

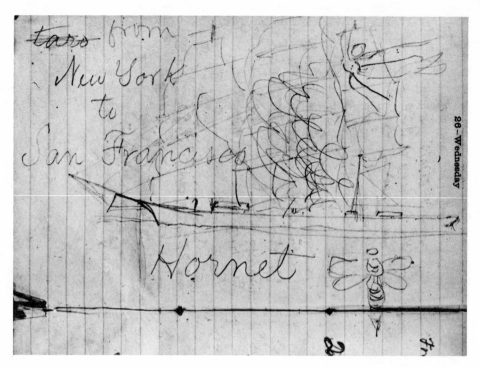

The Hornet *on fire as drawn by Henry Ferguson on a back page of his journal, May 3, 1866.*

FRIDAY, MAY 4

Lat. 2° 50' N. Long. 112° 45'

Captain Mitchell's Journal:

Begins ship still burning. No relief. At 6 P.M. divided the men in the boats, 9 men in each yawl and 13 in longboat with water and provisions. At 5 A.M. ship went down still burning. At 6 A.M. kept off N. by E. for Clarion Island,* hoping to reach it as nearest land.

*   *Clarion Island is reported in the pilot book for THE WEST COAST OF MEXICO (U.S. Hydrographic Office Publication No. 56, Washington, 1880, pages 197-198) as a volcanic island five miles long and from a mile to two miles wide. Its highest elevation is given at 1,282 feet. Doves, fish and sea turtles were described as being numerous in the vicinity. The anchorage in the Northeast part of Sulphur Bay (named for H.M.S. SULPHUR) is given as 18° 20' 55" North latitude, by 114° 44' 17" West longitude. THE NORTH PACIFIC PILOT, PART II by W.H. Rosser (London, 1870, page 292) states that "neither wood nor other necessaries can be obtained. Still a vessel in great distress might have her wants to some extent relieved." Clarion might well have served the HORNET'S crew for a short period at least. The 1866 revised edition of Lippincott's COMPLETE PRONOUNCING GAZETTER, OR GEOGRAPHICAL DICTIONARY OF THE WORLD (Philadelphia, 1872, page 459) lists "Clarion or Cloud's Island" in the North Pacific, so suggesting an alternate name.*

Henry Ferguson's Journal:

Ship sank at five this A.M. and we are now alone on the ocean. Longboat ahead with its 'gallant studding sail set as a lug and the quarter boats with sail set but all linked together. We stayed near the ship till she sunk and are now heading N. by E. for some islands** that are about North of us. We hope to be picked up before then. Pray God will have mercy on us and grant that we may be saved. We are 14 in the longboat and 8 and 9 respectively in each of the others. Two crackers and a pint of water is our allowance. We hope to be in the doldrums and catch some more water. Sun is terribly hot and blistering. All in pretty good spirits. Good breeze all today and yesterday.

** *These islands were undoubtedly the Revilla Gigedo Islands (Revillagigedo) located in THE WEST COAST OF MEXICO pilot book as being between 18° 20′ and 19° 20′ North latitude, and 110° 45′ and 114° 50′ West longitude. Including Carion, there are four of them, all of volcanic origin and were said to have been discovered by Spanish navigators in the sixteenth century. They were named in 1793 for the Spanish Viceroy of Mexico. Socorro is the largest, being roughly circular, ten miles in diameter and rising to an elevation of 3,707 feet. San Benedicto is a barren island three miles long and 975 feet high lying to the North of Socorro. Roca Partida is merely a barren rock, 300 feet long and 110 feet high, lying Westward of Socorro and looking "like a vessel under jury masts." Clarion Island (see above) lies 214 miles almost due West of Socorro. Socorro, in turn, lies about 500 miles West of the mainland at Cape Corrientes, Mexico. Captain Sir Edward Belcher in his NARRATIVE OF A VOYAGE ROUND THE WORLD . . IN H.M.S. SULPHUR . . IN 1836-1842 (2 vols., London, 1843, pages 346-347 of volume I) referred to "the almost unknown island of Socorro," stating "I found this island to be placed 52 miles farther to the West than laid down in the charts; but its latitude, correct."*

Samuel Ferguson's Journal:

Ship burned all night and blazed brightly. Our hopes are that some ship has seen the light and borne down to it. None seen, however, this A.M., so we have determined to go together, North and a little West to some little [islands] in 18° to 19° North latitude, 114° to 115° West longitude, hoping to be picked up by some ship. I put full confidence in the Almighty, who will do for us as He thinks best.

The ship sank at about 5 A.M.

Find the sun very hot and scorching. We all try to keep out of it if we can. Men stand it so far well, though we have three of the four sick ones. Though we have not yet, we hope in this latitude to have plenty of showers which work two ways though, as they kill our provisions and also our wind. Our course today has been North-by-East. Water rations increased while we are in the doldrums, where we have too frequent showers.

Memorandum in back of Captain Mitchell's Journal:

Stores in boats this May 4th.
About 100 lbs. bread in all.

       7 small pieces salt pork.
       4 Hams.
      14 cans oysters, clams, &c.
      ½ box raisins.
      3 bottles Brandy.
      Lot raw potatoes.

Where are we to go, in God's name with this small lot of stores? No chance but to be picked up by some vessel or gain the Windward Islands in the doldrums. At all events we must live as long as we can and trust in God for wisdom to guide and to direct us. For this I pray.

Mark Twain's Comment:

They did a quite natural thing now; waited several hours for that possible ship that might have seen the light to work her slow way to them through the nearly dead calm. Then gave it up and set about their plans. If you will look at the map you will say that their course could be easily decided. Albermarle Island* (Galapagos Group) lies straight eastward nearly a thousand miles; the islands referred to in the diary indefinitely as "some islands" (Revill-agigedo Islands) lie, as they think, in some widely uncertain region Northward about one thousand miles and Westward one hundred or one hundred fifty miles. Acapulco, on the Mexican coast, lies about Northeast something short of one thousand miles. You will say random rocks in the ocean are not what is wanted; let them strike for Acapulco and the solid continent. That does look like the rational course, but one presently guesses from the diaries that the thing would have been wholly irrational — indeed, suicidal. If the boats struck for Albemarle they would be in the doldrums all the way; and that means a watery perdition, with winds which are wholly crazy, and blow from all points of the compass at once and also perpendicularly. If the boats tried for Acapulco they would get out of the doldrums when half-way there, — in case they ever got half-way, — and then they would be in lamentable case, for there they would meet the Northeast Trades coming down in their teeth, and these boats were so rigged that they could not sail within eight points of the wind. So they wisely started Northward, with a slight slant to the West. They had but ten days' short allowance of food; the longboat was towing the others; they could not depend on making any sort of progress in the doldrums, and they had four or five hundred miles of doldrums, in front of them yet. *They* are the real equator, a tossing, roaring, rainy belt, ten or twelve hundred miles broad, which girdles the globe.

It rained hard the first night, and all got drenched, but they filled up their water-butt. The brothers were in the stern with the captain, who steered. The quarters were cramped; no one got much sleep.

* *The Spanish name for Albemarle is Isabella. It is the largest of the Galapagos Islands.*

SATURDAY, MAY 5

Lat. 4° 00'N. Long. 111° 30'W.

Captain Mitchell's Journal:

Run North by East 5 knots until 6 P.M. Night dark, calm, and rainy. Filled up everything with water. At 6 A.M. breeze from Southeast, fresh. A good deal of cobbling sea.* Run North by East. Cloudy and rainy in the doldrums. Hot. Half biscuit a man.

* *By "cobbling sea", the Captain apparently means choppy or confused. Cobble-stone-paved roads would be familiar to him as providing a bumpy ride and apparently he made a nautical adaptation of it. A search in many dictionaries failed to disclose its use in this connection. However, "cobbling" might well be a corruption of the old English term "cockling" seas which are short and quick ones.*

Henry Ferguson's Journal:

All well. Rain in plenty.

Samuel Ferguson's Journal:

Last night was very unpleasant one, rained very hard, and it was mighty hard stowage. We all, I guess, got some sleep though. The men and all of us stand by our misfortunes thus far well. Today fortunately has been overcast, so we have not suffered from the burning sun as we otherwise should. Caught a good deal of water last night; have now more than when we left the ship. Captain computed our latitude at about 4° North. Captain, Henry and I and Third Mate and 9 men lead in the Longboat which, having more sail,** tows the other two, the First Mate coming next and the Second Mate coming third, each with eight men. Made a real good day's run till about midnight, when wind lessened a good deal. So far everything goes on as well as could be expected. Men in good spirits though we all have a pretty hard time. Kept on our course till shower, squalls headed us off.

** *HORNET'S main top-gallant studding sail (Mark Twain).*

SUNDAY, MAY 6

Lat. 5° 11$'$ N. Long. 111° 05$'$ W.

Captain Mitchell's Journal:

Strong breeze from South and rough sea. Running North by East until 12 midnight, dies. Torrents of rain and awful doldrums. Bread and everything soaked. Boat very uncomfortable. At A.M. breeze from South-Southwest, fresh. Hard chance.

Henry Ferguson's Journal:

Doldrums.

Samuel Ferguson's Journal:

This morning began very stormy and squally, rained very hard and the sea at one time very wicked. Everybody soaked of course. Bread got somewhat wet, with fresh water, however. Wind from Southeast and rather light till about 1 P.M., then a rain squall. Keep on the lookout all the time for a sail. P.M. it rained, making everything very disagreeable. This boat, the longboat, is very inconvenient, what with the large water-cask and the bags of bread and other bags there is hardly any room left. Thought a good deal of all at home and was glad to remember that it was Sacrament Sunday and that prayers would go from their inmost hearts for us, although they know not our peril. Read and said our prayers as best we could for the rain. Stood about the same course with not much wind. First part of the night very rainy and uncomfortable.

Mark Twain's Comment:

Stormy and squally the next morning, with drenching rains. A heavy and dangerous "cobbling" sea. One marvels how such boats could live in it. It is called a feat of desperate daring when one man and a dog cross the Atlantic in a boat the size of a longboat, and indeed it is;

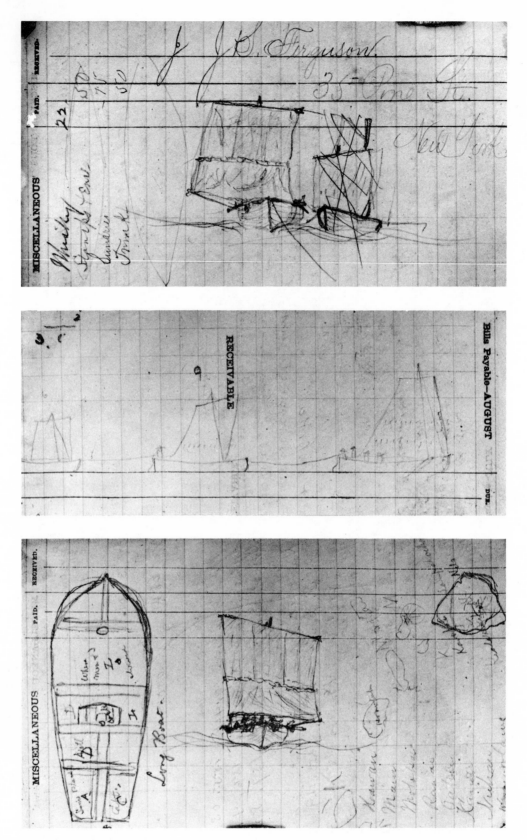

Sketches from the Ferguson brothers' journals showing the longboat and the two quarter boats.

but this longboat was overloaded with men and other plunder, and was only three feet deep.*

* *The same year in which the HORNET disaster occurred, two men and a dog successfully crossed from New York to a port on the English Channel in a 26-foot, ship-rigged, metal lifeboat named the RED WHITE AND BLUE. Probably this was the voyage that Mark Twain had in mind when the above was written. The RED WHITE AND BLUE, reported at the time as the smallest craft to cross the Atlantic, was, subsequent to her arrival in August 1866 after a 37-day passage, exhibited at the Paris world's fair. Captain J.B. Hudson, Captain Fitch and "Fanny" comprised the ship's company.*

MONDAY, MAY 7

Lat. 6° 12' N. Long. 110° 00 W.

Captain Mitchell's Journal:

Winds light and baffling with calms and cobbling sea. Latter strong breeze from Southwest, a good deal of sea from Northwest. Soaking rains at intervals. Very bad sea. Doing the best we can in a crowded boat. The three boats still attached. Made North by East when we could. Have to go easy. Steering East-Northeast.

Henry Ferguson's Journal:

Doldrums.

Samuel Ferguson's Journal:

Henry got the best sleep last night he has yet, the Captain also got a few good winks, the first he has got since we came aboard. Wind light till about 7 or 8 o'clock, when it freshened up and gave us a high and cobbling sea, the worst sea we have seen in a good while. The other boats got on well and are much better sea boats than this chunk we are in, not that I have any reason to complain of her action. Upon consultation the Captain thought best to steer more Easterly, to an island called Clipperton Rock* which is decidedly the nearest. Suppose we do not find it we are exactly on the highway of ships and again we get a good piece of Easting by which we are better able to make the islands farther North, they being in latitude 18° to 20° and longitude 111° to 131°. About 10 we head East-Northeast and hope to find Clipperton Island in 10° 28' Lat, and 109° 19' Long. Our bread provisions are decidedly our weak point. Captain places no reliance upon the chronometers, though he means to take sights now and then. They keep together pretty well.

* *Clipperton Island (or Rock) is reported in THE NORTH PACIFIC PILOT, PART II by W.H. Rosser (London, 1870, page 289) as being "most dangerous" and, being "but little known, is thought by many not to exist." It does, however, and the pilot book locates Clipperton in 10° 17' North latitude, by 109° 10' West longitude, stating that from a distance "it appears not unlike a sail, but a nearer approach it presents the appearance of an immense castle." The British explorer, Captain Sir Edward Belcher visited Clipperton in May 1839, gave a fine description of the place and first determined its position accurately (See Belcher's NARRATIVE, Vol I, pages 255-257). Clipperton could have afforded the HORNET'S people but scant and temporary relief.*

Mark Twain's Comment:

The Captain got not even a cat-nap during the first three days and nights, but he got a few winks of sleep the fourth night. "The worst sea yet." About ten at night the Captain changed his course and headed East-Northeast, hoping to make Clipperton Rock. If he failed, no matter; he would be in a better position to make those other islands. I will mention here that he did not find that rock.

TUESDAY, MAY 8

Lat. 6° 21' N. (Long. 109° 99' W.)

Captain Mitchell's Journal:

Light breeze first part. Steered Northeast towing the small boats. Night, wind light, all round the compass. Perfect torrents of rain. Latter part calm. Had both boats along side and had a good talk. Men cheerful and hope to be taken out; for myself, I see and feel no prospect. Ends hot, calm, and cloudy. No observation.

Henry Ferguson's Journal:

Doldrums.

Samuel Ferguson's Journal:

Last night a series of calms and light breezes, during which we had head winds in all directions. Rained, but not hard till A.M. when about 6 A.M. it began and kept it up pretty decidedly and wet us all again and everything. No wind all day. About noon it cleared off and came out hot. Went into Second Mate's boat during the A.M. We were put last and each boat took to the "white ash" — that is to the oars.* Saw plenty of dolphins today but could catch none. I think we are all beginning more and more to see the awful situation we are in. It often takes a ship more than a week to get through the Doldrums, how much more then such a craft as we, who cannot sail within 8 to 10 points. We are so crowded that we cannot stretch ourselves out for a good sleep, but have to take it when we can get it. I am glad I managed to get aboard all my brandy which will do us a good service. God have mercy upon us!

* A "white ash breeze" is a sailor's expression for rowing, oars being usually made of ash wood.

Mark Twain's Comment:

On the 8th of May no wind all day; sun blistering hot; they take to the oars. Plenty of dolphins, but they couldn't catch any. "We are so crowded that we cannot stretch ourselves out."

Of course this feature will grow more and more trying, but it will be human nature to cease to set it down; there will be five weeks of it yet — we must try to remember that for the diarist; it will make our beds the softer.

WEDNESDAY, MAY 9

Lat. 6° 50' N. Long. 108° 00' W.

Captain Mitchell's Journal:

All well as yet, doing best we can. Men all cheerful. Steered when we had a breeze, North-Northeast and North. All the first part calm toward until 7 P.M. I got a nap of two hours last night, the first I have had. We are now on the 7th. day since leaving the ship. The prospect of being saved is small. God be merciful to us.

Henry Ferguson's Journal:

Doldrums.

Samuel Ferguson's Journal:

Last night a pleasant one. No rain of any account, so most of the day we spent in drying our wet clothes and biscuit. Early in the evening 2d Mate's boat took the lead rowing when shortly a breeze sprang up and they made sail continuing to row. We reefed our sail and set it and so soon caught up that we took the lead, then shook it out. We have been highly favored in being able to keep together so well. Sun very hot indeed, and gave me a warning to keep out of it, in a very peculiar doubling of the sight with both eyes while with either one it seemed right. With both eyes the horizon crossed thus:✕. Lying down in the shade, however, soon took it away. I am all right now. Henry keeps well but broods over our trouble more than I wish he did. Caught today two dolphins; had some of one cooked in a pan which went well. Turned in about 7½ and slept pretty well till 12, then turned out to Henry. Had no rain and a good breeze. Course North-Northeast most of the time. Captain noticed the compass out of the way about 2½ points which, however, don't prove so by the North Star which is a welcome sight.

THURSDAY, MAY 10

Lat. 7° 03' N. Long. 110° 32' W.

Captain Mitchell's Journal:

Calm and hot. Afternoon caught two dolphin. Through the night, breeze from Northwest. Steered by the wind, boats fast together. This is the 8th. day. Men begin to look famished and dispairing, almost out of resources for encouraging them. Latter part calm and scalding sun. Got a sight with chronometer. The diet beginning to affect us all. 2nd Mate's boat very improvident and troublesome.

Henry Ferguson's Journal:

Doldrums.

Samuel Ferguson's Journal:

A series of calms and drifting all day. As the Captain says, all romance has long since vanished, and I think most of us are beginning to look at the fact of our awful situation full in the face. We are still in a good place to be picked up but seem to make little or nothing on our course, viz. the [Revillagigedo] isles. We are so cramped up that it makes it more trying than all else.

Rather a bad spirit is beginning to develop itself in the 3rd boat. They are not at all provident and having eaten up all the cooked meats, etc. brought from the ship, they now are discontented. Not so with the Mate's boat which is careful and contented, recognizing the awful position we are all in. The chronometers are going but differ somewhat so cannot be depended upon. We have been most mercifully guarded against sudden squalls and have all the water we want. Today Joe caught some more dolphins and a nice turtle, the former, Charlie cooked some of.

Mark Twain's Comment:

They have made about three hundred miles of Northing since they left the region of the lost ship. "Drifting in calms all day." And baking hot, of course; I have been down there, and I remember that detail. Bad news from the rearmost boat: the men are improvident. Not so with the chief mate's people — they are evidently under the eye of a *man*.

FRIDAY, MAY 11

Lat. 7° 00′ N. Long. 109° 03′ W.

Captain Mitchell's Journal:

Begins light airs and scalding sun and calms. Through the night, slow drizzling rain. Wind light from North. Could not succeed in catching any water. At 6 A.M. calm. My own strength failing fast. Never can get anywhere in these calms. Ends hot and calm. We are all failing fast.

Henry Ferguson's Journal:

Doldrums.

Turtle - woodcut from The World of the Sea, *1882.*

Samuel Ferguson's Journal:

More than we made yesterday we lost last night. We caught some little rain but not enough to fill up or make the allowance good. The sun in the middle of the day is very powerful and made it necessary to cover your head. Today Mate's boat caught a turtle so we have some animal food, if we have to eat it raw. The cock which was picked up while the ship was afire still lives, and crows with the morning, cheering us all a good deal.

Second Mate's boat again wants water today, showing they overdrink their allowance. Captain spoke pretty straight to them. From appearances they ought to be able to catch enough tonight.

Have no reported sights of sails yet. In these latitudes the horizon is filled with little stand-up clouds that look very much like ships. The men keep up well in our boat and Captain serves out two spoonsfull of brandy and water, half and half to our men. I offered our bottle to the Mate but he declined saying he could keep the after boat quiet and we had not enough for all. God has protected us so far, I can't but think we will all come right bye and bye.

SATURDAY, MAY 12

Lat. 7° 00´ N. Long. 109° 00´ W.

Captain Mitchell's Journal:

Another day of calms, burning sun, baffling airs, rain drizzles, etc. alternately with a good deal of cobbling sea. Nothing gained. Shall be obliged to separate the boats, all very crowded. I feel tolerable well yet for which I am truly grateful. God preserve us.

Henry Ferguson's Journal:

False alarm of a sail in the morning and nobody but those who have experienced it the feeling it gave at first and the disappointment. God send one soon is our constant prayer. All tolerably well. Captain pretty much worn out. Sam affected by the sun a little yesterday but has not been troubled today. Had a glorious rain and caught a good deal of water which is life for us. Please God we are saved we will all have an awful lesson against carelessness. If we do not live better lives than we have if we are saved we deserve worse than we have now.

Samuel Ferguson's Journal:

A good rain last night during which we caught a good deal though not enough to fill up our tanks, pails, etc. Our object is to get out of these doldrums but we can't seem to do it. Today we have had it very variable and hope we are on the Northern edge though we are not much above 7°. This A.M. we all thought we had made out a sail, but it was one of those deceiving clouds.

Had no chance for an observation today, rained a good deal, made all hands very wet and uncomfortable. Filled up nearly all our water-pots. I hope we will have a fine night for the Captain certainly wants rest and while there is any danger of squalls or anything he is always on hand. I never would have believed open boats such as ours, with their loads, could live in some of the seas we have had. Thank God we are all right so far, and as comfortable as could be expected. I feel the fatigue and the lack of exercise with the insufficiency of food, considerably. Henry seems to bear up pretty well, though looking at times pretty miserable.

Mark Twain's Comment:

They have lost three miles of the three hundred of Northing they had so laboriously made. "The Captain spoke pretty sharply to Second Mate." It is true: I have the remark in my old note-book; I got it from the third mate in the hospital at Honolulu. But there is not room for it here, and it is too combustable, anyway. Besides, the third mate admired it, and what he admired he was likely to enhance.

They were still watching hopefully for ships. The Captain was a thoughtful man, and probably did not disclose to them that that was substantially a waste of time. Mr. Ferguson saved three bottles of brandy from his private stores when he left the ship, and the liquor came good in these days.

They stood regular watches — four hours on and four off. The chief mate was an excellent officer — a self-possessed, resolute, fine, all-round man. The diarist makes the following note — there is character in it: "I offered our bottle of brandy to the Mate, but he declined, saying we had not enough for all."

Henry Ferguson's diary is of the economical sort that a person might properly be expected to keep in such circumstances — and be forgiven for the economy, too. His brother, perishing of consumption, hunger, thirst, blazing heat, drowning rains, loss of sleep, lack of exercise, was persistently faithful and circumstantial with his diary from the first day to the last, — an instance of noteworthy fidelity and resolution. In spite of the tossing and plunging boat, he wrote it close and fine, in a hand as easy to read as print.

They can't seem to get North of 7° North, they are still there the next day.

SUNDAY, MAY 13

Lat. 8° 08′ N. (Long. 109° 00′ W.)

Captain Mitchell's Journal:

Suffered much from thirst. Very dark, squally, rainy weather. Awful hot. Midnight clears up, wind South which lasts through the day. Steered North by East, boats still together. Chances dark. Ends squally appearance. Oh for more rain, this thirst I can not stand.

Henry Ferguson's Journal:

A nice breeze arose last night which has continued all through today varying from Southeast to South but generally we have been getting along nicely and find that a breeze is a great aid to the spirits. We live in continual hope and trust that God will send us succor before long. Last night there arose the cry of "light ho" but looking steadily at it the supposed ship's lights turned out a star. It was a bitter disappointment. We have had a squall or two today which luckily did not hurt our wind, while they gave us water. We ought to be very thankful for this great blessing of water which we have had.

Samuel Ferguson's Journal:

Last night one of the finest nights we have had, no rain nor squalls, though a variable set of winds. This morning found us all pretty cheerful. During the night had a cry of a ship, but it proved to be a star rising out of the water. Have thought much of all the loved ones at home today and the disappointment next Sunday of the not hearing from us.* May God grant it good news when they do hear. Today our rations are reduced to ¼ of a biscuit a meal with about a half pint of water. We hope to catch more turtles and fish to eke out our small stores. All day long we have had a Southerly wind and have headed North by East which we think very fortunate. We can place no dependence on the chronometers though they are both going, for no piece could stand the jolting and shaking about they have had and 4 minutes only make a degree.

I still feel confident that God will help us out of our calamity, read Gospel for today. The men I am sorry to say are improvident. They don't waste what they have but would take three times as much as is necessary if they could get and eat it instead of keeping it.

* *By telegraph from San Francisco. It will be many weeks yet before the telegram is received, and it will come as a thunder-clap of joy then, and with the seeming of a miracle, for it will raise from the grave men mourned as dead (Mark Twain).*

Mark Twain's Comment:

During the night, 12th-13th, there seemed to be the glimmer of a vessel's signal-lantern rising out of the curve of the sea. There was a season of breathless hope while they stood watching, with their hands shading their eyes, and their hearts in their throats; then the promise failed; the light was a rising star. It is a long time ago, — thirty-two years,* — and it doesn't matter now, yet one is sorry for their disappointment.

Rations reduced on the 13th of May, with more than a month of voyaging in front of them yet! However, as they do not know that, "we are all feeling pretty cheerful."

* *Mark Twain was preparing his CENTURY article in 1898.*

MONDAY, MAY 14

Lat. 9° 06′N. (Long. 109° 00′W.)

Captain Mitchell's Journal:

Condition not bettered. Still alive and together. Some doldrum weather, squalls and baffling winds and calms, burning sun, and nights torrents of rain, thunder, and lightning. Crowded this boat, no room to move. ½ biscuit per day, can any thing be worse? God is our only help. I pray continually.

Henry Ferguson's Journal:

Calmish all the morning but still we went on tolerably for which we are thankful. Mr. Hardy paid us a visit. Calm toward noon and beginning of afternoon when there came up the biggest rain squall I ever saw with thunder and lightning and some wind. It headed us off to all points of the compass and lasted till after dark making a most awful black night. Thank God we have got plenty of water now, everything filled. Wet night and uncomfortable. Pray God will send us relief soon. Bread going pretty fast. Allowance now ½ of a biscuit and a gill of water to a meal. We (Captain, Sam and I) soak ours in half our water, and think besides being more palatable it goes further.

Samuel Ferguson's Journal:

Today very showery, [though] last night was the most comfortable one we have had. In the P.M. had a regular thunderstorm, which toward night seemed to close in around us on every side, making it very dark and squally. 119th Hymn seemed very appropriate, with great gratitude we saw the clouds break and the stars once more appear. Our situation is becoming more desperate, for we have very little steady wind to make Northing and every day wastes our small stock of provisions. We want to get to 18° North and hit some of the Islands.* But even at their best we will have the Northeast Trades to contend against. They would be a good steady breeze, but with our sail and boat I doubt if we could sail within eight points, certainly not towing the other boats. We have two large compasses, we one and 2nd Mate one. My little one that Helen gave me I have lent to the Mate. The time must soon come when we must separate.

* *All of these islands cited in Samuel Ferguson's journal, with the exception of Clarion, Roca Pardita and Clipperton, were non-existent, representing the supposed sightings of not too reliable navigators — mostly whalemen — who reported encountering what they thought was land. Until definitely disproven, these mythical islands continued to be indicated on charts and in sailing directions. Captain Sir Edward Belcher in H.M.S. SULPHUR, with her consort H.M.S. STARLING made a concerted effort to find Freshwater, Cloud, New Blada and Best Islands. but without success, as he reported in his NARRATIVE (Vol I. pages 48-49). Among others, New Blada and Cooper were still listed in Bowditch's THE NEW AMERICAN PRACTICAL NAVIGATOR .. (29th Edition, published by L. and G.W. Blunt, New York, 1860, page 375). This edition of THE NAVIGATOR was probably the one carried on board the HORNET and taken along into the longboat by Captain Mitchell. The actual copy is said to be in possession of Henry Ferguson's decendents today.*

Note written in the back of Samuel Ferguson's Journal on a page listed "Bills Payable, May."

Clipperton Island	Lat. 10° 28'	Long. 109° 19'
New Blada	Lat. 18° 12'	Long. 114° 85'
Clarion	Lat. 18° 21'	Long. 114° 23'
Cloud	Lat. 19° 43'	Long. 114° 57'
Freshwater	Lat. 19° 22'	Long. 115° 08'
Copper	Lat. 20° 06'	Long. 131° 43'
Roca Pardita	Lat. 19° 06'	Long. 111° 52'

TUESDAY, MAY 15

(Lat. 9° 40' N. Long. 109° 40' W.)

Captain Mitchell's Journal:

Still the same dreadful weather, steering North whenever I can to get over into a breeze for this is getting awful. Drenched through and through again last night. Thunder and lightning terrific. Would that we could get a breeze. Still I am truly thankful we are preserved. What our fate is to be God only knows. No observation, ends calm.

Henry Ferguson's Journal:

Today was calm in the A.M. and very hot. After dinner a Southwest wind began to pick up and has increased and also has worked around to North so we are heading no better than

East-Northeast. It looks ugly to windward, as if we were going to have another uncomfortable night. Boobys and some other kind of Island birds around, one of whom lit on the yard or gaff whichever it was called. They most probably came from Clipperton Rock. If we could find it even if it were not habitable it would give us our Long. Chronometers cannot be much depended upon, with so much wetting as they have had. Sam still well, but is I fear growing weaker under our low diet.

Samuel Ferguson's Journal:

From 10 P.M. last night we had a more comfortable night, though everything was in a perfect sop. Wind baffling and very light. Headed most of the night from Northwest to West though made a little progress. Spirits keep up and I trust all will be well, but it is a terrible thing for us all so cramped and with no change of clothes. Sun out again hot, drying our wet things but making it very scalding. We manage to head about North but make very little progress. One blessing we have is a continued supply of water which as we must soon take the Trades is very important. Captain took a longitude sight this A.M., but noon was too cloudy for latitude. This P.M. wind headed us off to nearly East, and threatened squalls and showers late in the P.M. Joe caught another dolphin today. In his maw we found one flying fish and two skip-jacks. Had visit from a land bird today which perched on the yard for a while. This shows that we cannot be far from Clipperton Rock, but whether we shall hit it or not is very very doubtful. Good Lord deliver us!

Mark Twain's Comment:

They realize that the boats must soon separate, and each fight for its own life. Towing the quarter-boats is a hindering business.

That night and next day, light and baffling winds and but little progress. Hard to bear, that persistent standing still, and the food wasting away. Soon the sun comes out and roasts them.

There is an event, now, which rouses an enthusiasm of hope: a land-bird arrives! It rests on the yard for awhile, and they can look at it all they like, and envy it, and thank it for its message. As a subject of talk it is beyond price — a fresh, new topic for tongues tired to death of talking upon a single theme: Shall we ever see the land again; and when? Is the bird from Clipperton Rock? They hope so; and they take heart of grace to believe so. As it turned out, the bird had no message; it merely came to mock.

WEDNESDAY, MAY 16

Lat. 10° 16' N. Long. 110° 18' W.

Captain Mitchell's Journal:

Comes in very light air from North. Opened a S. & B. tin, 14 good dinners. All getting hungry. No rain today. Middle and latter very light airs from Northeast. Caught a dolphin. Got a sight this morning. Chronometer running. Very hot and scalding. About ½ bushel bread crumbs left. What are we to do then? God in Thy mercy help us. Winds very light from Northeast, hot and cloudy. I want to reach Clarion Island,* it's our only chance. God be with us.

* *See note for May 4.*

Henry Ferguson's Journal:

Contrary to my expectation last night was a pleasant one and we saw the new moon. God grant it may not be the last one. He has preserved us so long that I have confidence that He will still keep us in His Fatherly protection, and bring us safe home again. Last night brought the Trades, and we have quite a nice light breeze this morning, though it heads us off farther to the westward than we would choose. But God knows what is best for us. Great many birds about us this morning, from Clipperton Rock I suppose. I hope we may be permitted to make it for even if there is no water on it, it would show us exactly where we are. Our great hope is to be picked up and we try to remain cheerful as day after day passes and no sail in sight. Came up to rain dreadfully hard at about four and has lasted ever since. Tried in the early afternoon how the boats would go separate. Second Mate went ahead of us, but we beat the other. I think there would be more chance of some of us being picked up if we should separate for good.

Samuel Ferguson's Journal:

Last night a very quiet and comfortable night as regards rain, though our limited space makes it very hard sleeping for any length of time. We all keep well yet, thank God; but are getting weaker. Today we have the wind from the Northeasterly which we hope will settle down to a good steady trade and take us either to the Islands or across some vessel's track. The 1st Mate's boat is in good spirits but they have lived very close and are pretty weak. The cock that escaped the fire still lives and daily carols forth His praise. Neither of the turtles have we eaten yet and must, when we do so, eat them raw, for want of means to cook with. No more fish caught today. Bids fair for a rainy night which I do not mind if we can fill up our water butts full.

THURSDAY, MAY 17

Lat. 10° 40' N. Long. 109° 30'W.

Captain Mitchell's Journal:

An awful day and worse night. Wind and squalls from all quarters, a good deal of sea, much thunder and lightning, and perfect torrents of rain. Everybody and everything drenched. The most anxious night I ever passed, dark as Erebus. These three boats together. If I had but this one it would not be so hard. But I cannot cast them off. No observation, dark and rainy.

Henry Ferguson's Journal:

Passed a most awful night, rained hard nearly all the time and blew in squalls accompanied by thunder and lightning from all points of the compass. It slacked up about six, but began again and kept steadily at it till I suppose two P.M. We went in every direction last night so it is impossible to say how far we went to the West. It has partially cleared off now, but is nearly a dead calm, and the sun has been unable to fairly break out. I never saw such rain. It is an utter impossibility to keep dry. It rained five times as hard as I ever saw it anywhere else. Joe caught a dolphin this A.M. and a little while ago gaffed a bonito which had fled for refuge from a large swordfish to the shelter of our stern. I think we must have passed near the Rock, I wish we knew which side.

Samuel Ferguson's Journal:

Was stopped writing last night by the rain which continued steady all last night with a heavy and dangerous sea. Passed the most dreadful night I ever remember. All day today till 2 P.M. rained steady, and a more uncomfortable set of wretches one cannot imagine, than we are to-day. However, we are now drying a little. Were fortunate today to catch a dolphin and a bonito, the latter seemed to take shelter under our rudder from a large swordfish that was swimming around and which we dare not try to catch. Today we have been two weeks in these egg-shells and it certainly seems as if we are to be saved. I trust we are all devoutly thankful for the many and great mercies that have been vouchsafed us. God grant an end to our captivity may soon be sent. The men in all boats seem pretty well. The sick one wonderfully recovered.* A great increase of birds this A.M.

* Antonio Possene. This is the Third Mate's detested "Portyghee" that raised the family of abscesses (Mark Twain).

Mark Twain's Comment:

On the 17th one of those majestic specters of the deep, a water-spout, stalked by them, and they trembled for their lives. Young Henry set it down in his scanty journal with the judicious comment that "it might have been a fine sight from a ship."

It rained all night and all day; everybody uncomfortable. Now came a swordfish chasing a bonito; and the poor thing, seeking help and friends, took refuge under the rudder. The big swordfish kept hovering around, scaring everybody badly. The men's mouths watered for him, for he would have made a whole banquet; but no one dared to touch him, of course, for he would sink a boat promptly if molested. Providence protected the poor bonito from the cruel swordfish. That was just and right. Providence next befriended the shipwrecked sailors: they got the bonito. This was also just right. But in the distribution of mercies the swordfish himself got overlooked. He now went away; to muse over these subtleties, probably.

FRIDAY, MAY 18

Lat. 11° 12´ N. Long. 109° 10´ W.

Captain Mitchell's Journal:

God in his goodness has preserved us another day. Boats still together. First and latter part calm. A good deal of sea, weather cloudy, very sultry through the night. Nice breeze from East to South. Steer North whenever I can to get out of doldrums. All well yet.

Henry Ferguson's Journal:

Forgot to say yesterday that there was a water-spout in the morning not far from us. May be very nice to look at from a ship's deck but situated as we are it is not pleasant. It broke and disappeared however. God be thanked. Last night was tolerably clear until about three when it began to rain. Kept it up till morning, but not very hard. Stiff breeze all night but died away and is now very light indeed, 12 M. and dead aft. No signs of change in weather. Last night had raw dolphin for supper, and this A.M. raw bonito. They have managed to cook some which I hope will serve for dinner and tea. They have killed their turtle in the stern boat. Ours is still alive. Sultry and hot though the sun is not fairly out. Same all the afternoon. Expect we will separate soon as there will be more chance for some of us to reach safety.

Samuel Ferguson's Journal:

Last night no rain of any consequence, had a pretty good night, managed to keep going last night but first Northwest then Northeast till about 2 A.M. when we got a good breeze which gave us our course.

Mate came aboard today and reported all well with him but Peter, who has again got the fever, poor fellow! The 3rd boat cooked the turtle the second boat caught, and the Mate reports the meat first-rate. We talk of separating and must soon do so, we can take one boat in tow but not two. It seems too bad but it must be done for the safety of the whole.

At first I never dreamed but now hardly shut my eyes for a cat-nap without conjuring up something, to be accounted for by weakness I suppose.

We very likely could have been in by tomorrow or next day had not our disaster happened. I should like to have sent Bess* the telegram for her birthday. May God grant we may keep it all together again. At about 2 P.M. we took a nice little breeze in the Southwest which allows us to run our course North by East.

A young sister (Mark Twain).

Mark Twain's Comment:

So they have averaged but forty miles of Northing a day during the fortnight. Further talk of separation. But for the disaster, they think they would be arriving in San Francisco about this time.

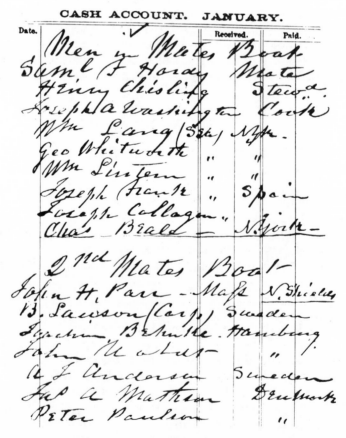

List of crew in First and 2nd Mate's boats in Capt. Mitchell's journal.

SATURDAY, MAY 19

Lat. 11° 20' N. (Long. 110° 00' W.)

Captain Mitchell's Journal:

Calms and light rain squalls and hot scalding sun burning us up and no progress. The Mate with eight men cast off this morning by himself. Divided the water and provisions. Ends calm, burning hot. We are too weak to pull and unless we get a breeze soon, must all perish. No observation.

Memorandum in back of Captain Mitchell's Journal:

May 19th. Mate cast off this day after sharing stores and left.

Henry Ferguson's Journal:

Dead calm nearly all day, the deadest and flattest that I have seen yet. The sun's heat was terrible and we were almost thankful when at about 4 P.M. there arose a little breeze and clouds obstructed it. We had a most painful parting this morning thinking that the chances of some being saved greater separate than all together. The Captain asked the second mate if he was willing to separate, he not being so Mr. Hardy took his (Second Mate's) compass and sail into his boat and separated. Laing, cook, steward and five men. We divided stores and water fairly and bade them good-bye, and they left us. They were in sight till about four when we lost them. God grant that we may all meet again in safety. These calms are using up our time and provisions fearfully, but He knows what is best for us. Bessie's birthday today. God bless her and grant that we may see her again.

Samuel Ferguson's Journal:

Calm night last night, rested pretty well, This A.M. Captain called up the two quarter-boats and said one would have to go off on its own hook. 2nd Mate would not go, so first Mate took his boat and with some six of 2nd Mate's men who volunteered to go with two of his own, in all nine, started early and by 5 P.M. were out of sight to windward. Was very sorry to have the Mate leave us but all considered it for the best. This morning we have had a most scorching and burning sun making it almost intolerable. Very calm all day to about 4 P.M. when a light breeze sprang up, which lasted not very long, however. I was in hopes that we should have sent Bess a telegram for her birthday. The Mate's boat nowhere to be seen this morning. Hope he was more successful in catching water than we were. Water now will be a scarce article, for as we get out of the doldrums we only now and then get showers in the Trades. Must admit that this life is telling pretty severely on my strength. Henry, I am happy to say, holds out first-rate.

Mark Twain's Comment:

On the 19th, the Captain called up the quarter-boats and said one would have to go off on its own hook. The longboat could no longer tow both of them. The Second Mate refused to go, but the Chief Mate was ready; in fact, he was always ready when there was a man's work

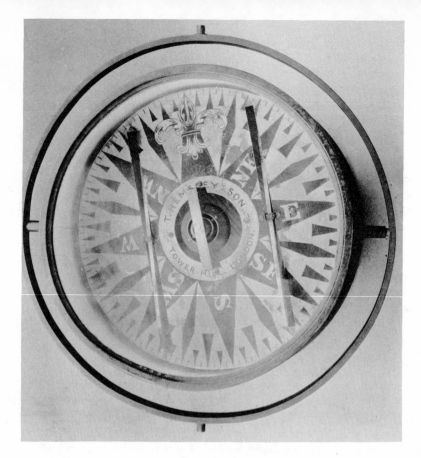

Photo of the boat compass from Hornet *longboat owned by Mrs. C.L. Tilden.*

to the fore. He took the Second Mate's boat; six of its crew elected to remain, and two of his own crew came with him (nine in the boat, now, including himself). He sailed away, and toward sunset passed out of sight. The diarist was sorry to see him go. It was natural; one could have better spared the "Portyghee." After thirty-two years I find my prejudice against this "Portyghee" reviving. His very looks have long since passed out of memory; but no matter, I am coming to hate him as religiously as ever.

Henry Ferguson did not start well, but under hardships he improved straight along.

SUNDAY, MAY 20

Lat. 12° 10' N. (Long. 110° 50' W.)

Captain Mitchell's Journal:

First part calm and hot. Through the night cool and light breezes, baffling. Steering North, two knots. At daylight Mate's boat not in sight. God grant some of us may be picked up. Sabbath. Oh how glorious if one could be anywhere else. A lovely day but oh what a place to pass it in. Very little hope, I am getting very weak. Ends hot sun and calm.

Henry Ferguson's Journal:

Nice breeze in the night but in the morning died away, and we had another dead calm which lasted till after M. [Meridian, i.e. noon] Then it gradually picked up and now we have a gentle breeze, which is a great deal better than a calm. Nothing seen of the Mate's boat. Beautiful day. Hot. Sun very oppressive in the morning but pleasant in the afternoon. Night before last there was the finest rainbow and most beautiful sunset I ever saw. This morning's dawn and sunrise surpassed anything I had seen. Killed our turtle yesterday and cooked him. Eat half yesterday, very good it tasted. Wish we might catch many more. Boiled him and the soup was excellent. A booby flew aboard the stern boat this afternoon whom they caught and intend to make a good meal of. God has been very kind to us in giving us fish and turtles, etc. and preserving us so long. May He continue His Gracious Protection and preserve us.

Samuel Ferguson's Journal:

Very little rain last night, none that we could save to put in the cask. A light breeze last night but very little. It is very strange we do not get the Trades which usually come at 8° or 10°. Breeze today light again but enabling us to head nearly North.

   We all watch anxiously for a sail but have as yet had only sights that looked like it. God grant that the time is not far distant when we shall be picked up for that is my greatest hope. The turtle that Joe caught served us for dinner yesterday and today, and very good it was. Have no fish about us today. We are daily in hopes of catching something for it helps out our stores wonderfully.

   When not a sparrow falls to the ground without our Heavenly Father's knowledge, He will certainly take care of us. 2nd Mate this P.M. succeeded in catching a "booby," a bird as large as a wild duck. As they have no other meat it will go well, so are we helped and preserved.

Mark Twain's Comment:

They ought to be well out of the doldrums now, but they are not. No breeze — the longed-for Trades still missing. They are still anxiously watching for a sail, but they have only "visions of ships." The Second Mate catches a booby this afternoon, a bird which consists mainly of feathers.

MONDAY, MAY 21

Lat. 13° 00'N. (Long. 111° 40'W.)

Captain Mitchell's Journal:

Begins light air from Northeast, increasing to steady breeze. All hands encouraged by it. Middle rough and squally, wind North-Northeast to Northeast, very uncomfortable. Latter part strong squally Trade, heavy sea. Boat pitching and rolling fearfully. Pitched away mast. Reduced mast and sail. Cloudy and fresh with heavy sea, ends. No observation. Caught several boobies.

Henry Ferguson's Journal:

Blew fresh all night and has done the same all day with squalls which headed us off to the Northwest and still more and we hope and pray it may get more to the Eastward. There is such a sea on that it throws us off from the wind. It is now breezing up very fresh. About one we broke our mast just below the step and we had to lower it and cut it off to trim it.

- 139 -

Also fixed the sail reducing it in size. Stern boat caught three boobies one of which they passed aboard. God send us a ship or a shift of wind for if we can make no better course than this we will never fetch anywhere. A breeze is better than a calm and we thank Him for sending it. Sea high still. All well in our boat but getting weak very fast.

Samuel Ferguson's Journal:

Fine breeze all last night about East, quite as much as we could well stand. It soon brought us up a sea but we made a great night's work of it. No rain today; more squally, and the wind not steady. 2nd Mate has been fortunate enough to catch three more boobies, and gave us one. For dinner today we had a half can of mince-meat served round which strengthened us all somewhat. Just after dinner during a little squall and rolling a good deal, we sprung our mast so badly that it had to be taken down and cut off and reshipped. The sail also was altered and we may now be said to be in our Trade Trim. Our rigging, like ourselves, is rather weak, however. I believe I have not before stated that in getting this longboat off the ship's deck, a hole was stove on the starboard side of our keel. It has been caulked the best we could do, but still keeps one bailing all the time. One of the quarter boats also had an oar handle staved through her. We have headed today about Northwest which is perhaps well, for we hope we have Easting enough to make some of the Islands; if not we are in a better position to be picked up.

Mark Twain's Comment:

They strike the Trades at last! The Second Mate catches three more boobies, and gives the longboat one. They have to keep a man bailing all the time; the hole knocked in the boat when she was launched from the burning ship was never efficiently mended.

They hope to have Easting enough to make some of those indefinite islands. Failing that, they think they will be in a better position to be picked up. It was an infinitely slender chance, but the Captain probably refrained from mentioning that.

TUESDAY, MAY 22

Lat. 13° 20′ N. (Long. 112° 35′ W.)

Captain Mitchell's Journal:

Begins strong Trade and rough sea, winds North-Northeast. Very rough night. Daylight saw the Mate's boat ahead. Thought it a sail and we saved. The disappointment was bitter. Came up and spoke him, all well and cheerful. At 8 A.M. divided water and stores with 2nd. Mate's boat, bid them farewell, and left them. God have us all in His keeping. A beautiful day, but what a situation to enjoy it. Took one man out of 2nd. Mate's boat.*

* *James Cox*

Memorandum in back of Captain Mitchell's Journal:

22nd. Saw the Mate's boat again this day. Thought it a sail. Great disappointment. Again divided stores with 2nd. Mate's boat and bidding him farewell, parted. We are left now with 3 cans of oysters, one can soup and bouillon, 2/3 of a ham, and about 6 quarts of bread crumbs, and ¼ box of raisins, and 20 gallons water. What's to become of us. God in his wisdom knows. In Him we will trust.

Henry Ferguson's Journal:

This morning was roused by the cry "Sail ho" and sure enough there was some vessel dead ahead of us. We cast off the Second Mate for a time and made for it as fast we could, but when we neared it to our most bitter disappointment found it to be the Mate's boat. The most dreadful disappointment and sickness of heart that it caused. We waited for the Second Mate and as we found that towing him there was no chance for either, divided stores and water again and bade him Godspeed. We soon dropped him out of sight and caught up with the Mate, passed him and are now a long way to windward of him. God save us all and grant we may meet again in safety. We have a stiff Trade, North-Northeast, which accompanied by a heavy sea is heading us off badly. God knows what is best for us, and we thank His merciful goodness in preserving us alive and well so long, and trust that yet, in His good time, He will save us. Blew fresh all day. Ate our bird and caught another.

Samuel Ferguson's Journal:

Last night wind headed us off, so that part of the time we had to steer East-Southeast and then West-Northwest, and so on. This A.M. we were all startled by a cry of "Sail-ho!" Sure enough we could see it and for a time cut adrift from the 2nd Mate's boat and steered so as to attract attention. This was about 5½ A.M. After sailing for about 10 minutes we made it out to be the 1st. Mate's boat which had left us on the 19th. Of course we were glad to see them and to hear them report all well, but it was a sad disappointment to us all. It seems to be impossible now we have the Trades to make North enough to make the islands.* We have determined to do the best we can and get in the route of vessels. Such being determined, it became necessary to cast off the other boat which after a good deal of unpleasantness was done. We again divided water and stores and taking Cox into our boat making our number 15. 2nd. Mate wanted to all get aboard this boat and cast the other adrift. It was a very painful separation. This P.M. caught a booby
 Thank God for His mercies.

* *These are all mythical islands with the exception of Clarion.*

Mark Twain's Comment:

So those isles that they have struggled for so long and so hopefully have to be given up. What with lying birds that come to mock, and isles that are but a dream, and "visions of ships that come to naught," it is a pathetic time they are having, with much heartbreak in it. It was odd that the vanished boat, three days lost to sight in that vast solitude, should appear again. But it brought Cox — we can't be certain why. But if it hadn't, the diarist would never have seen the land again.

WEDNESDAY, MAY 23

(Lat. 13° 45' N. Long. 113° 25' W.)

Captain Mitchell's Journal:

Comes in fresh Trade and rough cross sea. Boat jumping a good deal. Caught a booby. God seems to provide for us. Middle and latter part sea smoother and Trade moderate. Sky overcast, a great relief to us. Men getting weak and sleepy. Steering by the wind all the time, heading about Northwest going three knots. Read prayers in boat today. God send us relief. Ends cloudy. No observation. Sea making and wind increasing.

Henry Ferguson's Journal:

Cloudy and overcast in the morning. We head a little Northwest and hope we may get her up still further. All well, pretty weak. No observations this noon. Eat our booby raw for dinner and found him as good as the last. Last night Sam read prayers and also this morning, and intend to do it henceforth. Certainly we have been most wonderfully protected, and supplied thus far. Nothing is to be seen of the other boats. God speed them and grant that they may be saved. Cloudy all day, which relieves the sun's heat, which otherwise would be almost unendurable. Try to keep in good spirits and we all, particularly Sam, Captain and myself have trust and confidence in God's mercy. This life is very trying and I expect we shall have to reduce our rations still lower. Sam holds up very well and is well though weak. His cough is remarkably improved.

Samuel Ferguson's Journal:

A good breeze blew all night allowing us to head about Northwest or a little better. Took a longitude observation this A.M., but the sun was clouded at noon, so we could make out neither latitude nor longitude. Our chances as we go West increase in regard to being picked up, but each day our scanty fare is so much reduced. Without the fish, turtle, and birds sent us I don't know how we should have got along. The other day I offered to read prayers P.M. and A.M. for the Captain, and last night commenced. The men, though of various nationalities and religions, are very attentive, and always uncovered. May God grant my weak endeavor its issue! Sea much gone down today and altogether a comfortable day. Wind regular Trade, allowing us to head about Northwest. Sun obscured all day most. We want a few good showers to fill up our twice-heavily-drawn-upon cask.* These, however, I hope and trust will be sent in good time. We as yet suffer little from thirst, having as a ration about one half a tumbler a meal. Besides, since the Trades set in it is not so hot and languid. No boobies nor fish today. I am afraid that our chance for fish after this is small, as few here bite at a trolling hook and we have a fresh wind almost all the time. Turtles ditto. Birds I hope for though.

* In dividing up water with the other boats on separation.

THURSDAY, MAY 24

Lat. 14° 18' N. (Long. 114° 20' W.)

Captain Mitchell's Journal:

Fresh Trade and cloudy all this day, showers. Wind Northwest, strong, stood East. Latter part strong from North-Northeast, standing Northwest. All getting very weak, rations insufficient. Fifteen dined on five small oysters apiece (one can). Provisions failing, a few more days and then what, providing we are spared. God care for us.

Henry Ferguson's Journal:

Blew hard all day and raised a heavy sea which makes our position at once very uncomfortable and dangerous. and it looks as if we were going to have an ugly night of it. However, we trust that the God that has protected us from all our dangers so far will continue His gracious protection and in His good time save us. It has been cloudy all day and the wind is very damp for which we are very thankful, for it preserves us from the thirst which our short allowance of water would otherwise occasion. Pray God we may see a ship soon. Our course is about Northwest by North as far as we can tell for the compass sways around every way in this rough weather. Still we are all well yet, God be praised for that. This would have been a most glorious breeze for the *Hornet* if the accident had not happened.

Samuel Ferguson's Journal:

Wind nearly North last night with considerable combings and a little splashing. Made a tack to Eastward, towards morning came out more East and we headed about Northwest all day. P.M. heavy sea up with promise of heavy night. No birds or fish. Can of oysters for dinner which gave five oysters apiece and three spoonfuls of juice, which with an eighth of a biscuit made our allowance, with about a gill of water. Such is our fare. God have mercy upon us all! There is no doubt we are all getting plainly weaker. Our best hope is to Westward in the track of ships and let go the Islands, as we waste twice the time tacking for them. Such is Captain's notion. He bears up well. Oh how I wish I had striven to get the rest of my whiskey! A spoonful of brandy and water has a marked effect upon us all. All evening had a heavy and cobbling sea. Reefed and stood so, making perhaps Northwest by North. A strong breeze.

Mark Twain's Comment:

Five oysters apiece for dinner and three spoonfuls of juice, a gill of water, and a piece of biscuit the size of a silver dollar. That night heavy seas break over the weather side and make everybody wet and uncomfortable, besides requiring constant bailing.

FRIDAY, MAY 25

(Lat. 14° 45′N. Long. 115° 00′W.)

Captain Mitchell's Journal:

This day very rough sea, strong Trade, and cloudy weather. Boat pounding into the sea by the wind. Seems impossible she can live a great while. The hand of God is over us. Provisions getting low, men despondent. It's terrible, Oh God in Thy mercy, send us relief. No observation. Our prospect of being saved is very gloomy. Oh my dear wife and loved ones, pray ever.

Henry Ferguson's Journal:

Last night was very uncomfortable and wet but we passed it in safety and now the sun is up and it warms us up but it did not stay out long and we were unable to get the latitude. Afternoon rough, wet, and windy and there is every prospect of another night like last night was. This cold and wet is very trying and it is nothing but God's Providence that sustains us as well as we are. I fear our chance of reaching Clarion or New Blada* Islands is but small but is as He directs us. Nothing to be seen of the other boats. We must be far ahead and to the windward of them. I fear that the sea and wind may have been too strong for them.

* *New Blada — This mythical island was listed in the 1860 NAVIGATOR in 18° 12' North latitude, by 114° 05' West longitude. New Blada is located in the 1870 NORTH PACIFIC PILOT in 18° 15' North latitude, by 114° 00' West longitude as being VERY DOUBTFUL and probably an erroneous charted position of Clarion Island.*

Samuel Ferguson's Journal:

Last night a very heavy one, under reef all the time till about 4 A.M. Sea breaking over our weather side, making everything wet and uncomfortable; nor was the day any better. I think hardly anyone managed to keep entirely dry. Sun not fully out all day. Tried, but could get no observation. These are splendid Trades for a ship, but too much for our crank craft. Nothing particular happened today. My cramped position makes lying one way any length of time almost impossible and one is sore almost all over. Plenty of flying fish about, but none disposed to come aboard. Passed this P.M. at some distance a spar not near enough to see what it was. Saw also several whales blow. Weather misty with very fine rain which is penetrating. Good prospect of just such another night as last. Great difference in the men in regard to steering and keeping a dry boat. Though our meals are very slight and poor, I don't believe anyone was more ready for them or appreciated them better.

Mark Twain's Comment:

This day "nothing particular happened." Perhaps some of us would have regarded it differently. They saw some whales blow; there were flying-fish skimming the seas, but none came aboard. Misty weather, with fine rain, very penetrating.

SATURDAY, MAY 26

Lat. 15° 50'N. Long. 115° 00'W.

Captain Mitchell's Journal:

We are still preserved. All this day fresh Trade and rough sea. First and middle fine rain and misty. What with seas slopping over, rain, and mist, very wet and uncomfortable. Latter part sunshine, pleasant. A booby and flying fish came on board which makes our dinner for 15 men. I feel very thankful and hope we shall be preserved until taken up.

Henry Ferguson's Journal:

A most dreadfully uncomfortable night wet and cold, a good deal of water splashing over the gunwale now and then. In the night, however, they caught another booby and flying fish which came aboard and we intend devouring them for dinner. God has supplied us with food and lengthened out our provisions most mercifully by birds, turtle, and fish which He has sent us. It has cleared off a good deal and the sun has been out with a bright halo around it. I hope that it will continue clear as our chances of seeing a ship are much better and yesterday's drizzling rain was very unpleasant. Booby and fish very good. Clouded up again before evening, but I hope that we may have an easier night though it looks ugly to windward.

Samuel Ferguson's Journal:

Last night much more comfortable than the one before, though occasionally we took some water. In the 1st watch (watches are divided in 6 hours and 6 hours) a large flying fish came aboard and at about 4 A.M. we caught a booby, which will do for our dinner today. Both fish and flesh we have to go raw after drying or baking in the sun of which we have so far a good hot one. Men grow weaker and I think more despondent, they say very little though. We can't do better in the boat than make eight points particularly as the Trades bring considerable sea which aids to head us off, thus beating is out of the question and it seems our best chance to get in and lie in the track of ships, with the hopes that some one will run near enough our speck to see it. I am afraid for the other two boats for the sea we had Thursday night and Friday was very hard for them. I sincerely hope they stood West and are picked up.

Mark Twain's Comment:

They caught a flying-fish and a booby, but had to eat them raw. "The men say very little." And so, to all the other imaginable and unimaginable horrors, silence is added — the muteness and brooding of constant despair. They hope the other boats stood West and have been picked up. (They will never be heard of again in this world.)

SUNDAY, MAY 27

Lat. 16° 06' N. Long. 117° 24' W.

Captain Mitchell's Journal:

Afternoon pleasant, less sea. Got a chronometer sight putting us in longitude 118° 30'. Can't be right. I judge 115°. First part night very rough. Latter grows smooth, day ending very pleasant. Oh how many thousands are worshipping God this fine day, and how utterly wretched are we. Thankful for the day and our wonderful preservation. Growing very weak. Good sights.

Henry Ferguson's Journal:

Blew hard in the early part of the night so that we put a second reef in our sail, but afterwards it moderated and by morning both wind and sea had gone down considerably and we had our full sail on. It has been blowing fresh Trade all day but it is a good deal calmer and has been clear and bright. Sun indeed very hot. We calculate that with great care we may make our provisions last a week longer and in that time we trust that God will send some vessel to save us. If our chronometer sights are to be depended on in the least it is hopeless to think of reaching any of the Revillagegedo Islands* on the coast and our only chance is being picked up or the bare possibility of making Hendersons** Island, latitude 24°, longitude 128°. The wind has headed us more still West Northwest. Is about the best we can do, God help us. This is far different from the way I hoped to pass Trinity Sunday but God will save us yet if it is His Holy Will.

* *See Editor's Note of May 4 describing the Revillagegedo Islands.*

** *Henderson Island, reported and recorded on some mid-nineteenth century charts in 24° 22′ North latitude by 128° 36′ West longitude, represents a curious and unfortunate cartographical error, for the island actually lies not in the Northern but the Southern hemisphere, a fact reported in THE NORTH PACIFIC PILOT PART II by W.H. Rosser, London, 1870, page 295. Lieutenant M.F. Maury's Wind and Current Chart of 1852 (North Pacific No. 10, Series A) located Henderson (or Elizabeth) Island "as seen by Captain Aulick, USN, of MERMAID" in 24° North. Actually Henderson's location as presently recorded in H.O. No. 166, SAILING DIRECTIONS FOR THE PACIFIC ISLANDS (EASTERN GROUPS), Vol II, 4th edition, Washington, 1933, page 126, is given in 24° 25′ South latitude by 128° 19′ West longitude. Henderson is a coral island about five miles long "raised by some subterraneous convulsion" to an elevation of almost 100 feet. The shrub-covered island is said to have been discovered in 1820 by the boats' crews of the Nantucket whale ship ESSEX, which had been rammed and sunk by an enraged rogue whale in mid-Pacific near the Equator in longitude 119° West. This dramatic event provided Herman Melville's inspiration for MOBY DICK. The ESSEX'S three whaleboats reached Henderson on December 20, 1820 after sailing some 1,500 miles from the point where the whaler went down on November 20. The crew remained on Henderson for several days searching for food and water before heading off again hoping to make Easter Island. Three men elected to remain on the island. They discovered, cut in the bark of a tree, the name THE ELIZABETH according to Mate Owen Chase's account of THE SHIPWRECK OF THE WHALESHIP ESSEX (Reprint, Corinth Books, Inc., New York, 1963, page 71). This explains the alternate name for the island and would seem to disprove the contention that the ESSEX men discovered it. Actually, Chase states that they thought they had landed on Dulcie Island farther East. Both Henderson and Dulcie are considered dependencies of nearby Pitcairn Island of BOUNTY fame. The voyage of the boats of the ESSEX, rivaling those of the BOUNTY and HORNET, was an extraordinary feat of navigation. There were, however, only eight survivors of the original crew of 20. One of the three whaleboats was lost at sea after the boats separated in a storm. Mate Chase's boat was picked up near Juan Fernandez Island on February 18, 1821, and, five days later, Captain Pollard's boat was recovered in the same area but somewhat closer to the coast of Chile. These boats had then been adrift for three months and had covered some 4,500 miles. Advised of their situation, a ship went out and rescued the three self-marooned crewmen on Henderson, picking them up on April 5, 1821. The grim resort of cannibalism followed the death of several of the ESSEX crew and in the captain's boat the cabin boy was shot after drawing lots to see who should give his life for the benefit of the others. Obviously the leadership was not the same as on board the HORNET'S longboat. The 1866 revised edition of Lippincott's GAZETTEER, p. 844, cites Henderson's Island in the South Pacific only where it belongs.*

Samuel Ferguson's Journal:

On 4th Sunday! When we left the ship we reckoned on having about ten days' supplies and now we hope to be able by rigid economy to make them last another week if possible,*** hoping and trusting in the meantime that God will send us some deliverance. Last night sea was comparatively quiet but wind headed us off to about West-Northwest, which has been about our course all day today. Another flying fish aboard last night and another today both smaller ones. No birds. A booby is a great catch and a good large one makes a small dinner for the 15. Tried this A.M. to read the full service to myself with the communion, but found it too much. Am too weak and get sleepy and cannot give strict attention, so I abandoned half till this P.M. I trust God will hear the prayers gone up for us at home today and will graciously answer them by sending us some deliverance. The ship was fired by carelessly drawing some varnish with an open lamp in hand, the barrel of varnish being in the booby hatch, where are stored spare sails, rigging, etc. Orders had been given to have it on deck to open.

*** *There are nineteen days of voyaging ahead yet (Mark Twain).*

Lat. 16° 24'N. (Long. 118° 15'W.)

Captain Mitchell's Journal:

Henderson Isle. 128° (West longitude), 24° (North latitude)* Moderate North-Northeast winds and smooth sea all this day comparatively. Stores small, growing very weak. Thankful for fine weather, want to live as long as possible, hoping to fall in with a ship. Oh my dear Wife and children, if your father has ever given you offence, forgive him as he hopes to be forgiven. Oh could I but see you once more. God have mercy on us.

> *In the 1880 edition of the Pilot Book for the West Coast of Mexico, the following mention is made on page 51:*
> *"Reported Islands and shoals — Numerous shoals and islands have been reported to exist off the coast of Lower California as far as 140° West. Among them are New Island, Maria Laxara Island, Gaspar Rock, Paxaros, Passion, Cooper, and Henderson Islands, with some others. Careful search has been made for them by the United States ships PORTSMOUTH and NARRAGANSETT in the years 1873 to 1875 without finding them or detecting any indications of land near the positions assigned to them."*

Henry Ferguson's Journal:

Passed a great deal more comfortable night as both wind and sea moderated and this morning and afternoon too have been heading up to Northwest. Wind lighter all day than it has been. Some birds around but none came aboard. This calm sea seems as if we ought to see some sail, but none as yet. Beautiful full moon last night or rather nearly full as I believe it fulls to-morrow A.M. Though so near it, I find it impossible to realize death and the judgment as I should. I can't bring my mind to think steadily on it, but I trust that if it comes now or later through the blessed death of the Savior and His merits and mediation my sins may be pardoned. As Sam says I would give anything for a talk with Brathwaite or Dr. Coit.* Sam bears up by God's grace wonderfully, and though he is growing pretty weak in body, is strong in his faith and his trust in God's mercy. We had out the photographs again today and I could not feel but what I should see those dear faces once more. Whatever comes, His will be done.

> *Dr. Henry Augustus Coit, first rector of St. Paul's School, Concord, New Hampshire, a boarding school which Henry had attended, 1859 - 1864.*

Samuel Ferguson's Journal:

Wind light and sea smooth last night so that all hands, I hope, got a good six hours' rest. This A.M. wind freshened enabling us to head about Northwest. A good day for seeing a ship but none to be seen yet. Still feel pretty well but legs very weak. Henry bears up and keeps strength the best of any aboard I think, thank God! My earnest prayer is that he may be saved at any rate, and restored Our only chance is being picked up, and unless we are providentially provided with more provisions in shape of fish or birds which now seem more and more scarce. Do not feel despondent at all for I fully trust that the Almighty will hear our and the Home Prayers and He who suffers not a sparrow to fall sees and cares for us, His creatures. Oh! that I could have a good talk with Brathwaite for I cannot bring myself to view death as I think I should, although I do not at all feel afraid to be taken at any moment, for I fully trust in the merits of my Redeemer.

Mark Twain's Comment:

This day was "a good day for seeing a ship." But none was seen.

TUESDAY, MAY 29

Lat. 16° 44′ N. Long. 119° 20′ W.

Captain Mitchell's Journal:

Very weak today, can hardly stand. Have been favored with smooth sea and fine weather, moderate breezes. Reduced allowance to ¼ biscuit a day hoping to live to be rescued. Have about two quarts bread crumbs left, 1/3 of a ham, and three small tins oysters, 20 gallons water. Oh my God, send us relief!

Henry Ferguson's Journal:

Reduced the number of meals today to two so as to preserve our stores as long as we can, they certainly have been blessed to us. None ever thought when we left the ship that we could stand it more than fifteen days at the most while here we are on the twenty-sixth alive and except for weakness well. God who fed the widow of Larepta has preserved us and I cannot think it is for nothing. It may be in his gracious Providence intended as a longer time for repentance and may He give us grace to use it as such. Going without dinner is very well when you have a good supper to look forward to and last summer I got quite used to it, but here I find you feel pretty hungry. Overcast but thin enough to get the sun. A calm and not so much wind and we are heading more to the Westward. Skipjacks around but none caught. Trust in the Lord Jehovah for in the Lord Jehovah is everlasting strength. Tremendous big sword-fish near the boat chasing a small albacore. Not at all sorry to have him go away as with his sword he was not a pleasant neighbor.

Samuel Ferguson's Journal:

A good breeze last night, not very rough after 9 o'clock. The moon a great benefit to us, sorry it is now on the wane. Today changed to two meals a day, hoping thereby to length out our scanty stores as long as possible. We are all wonderfully well and strong, thanks to God!, and the good fare we had aboard the ship, all the men came hearty and strong. Even those that were down sick are well except poor Peter [Paulson] who had to be left to the 2nd Mate's boat. The two boats I hope are ere this saved, for I fear for them. We have here a man who might have been a Duke* had not political troubles banished him from Denmark. He is one of our best men and I believe a real good man. Have today quite enjoyed a chat with him. The rest, except perhaps Harry (French), seem sort of callous to their condition. All seem attentive to our A.M. and P.M. prayers which Henry, his voice being stronger, reads. Thank God there is no complaining nor swearing aboard, which is a great comfort. Third Mate's disposition I like least, but he is quiet now and does not oppose the Captain. Henry and I have quiet little evening chats which are of great comfort and consolation to us even if on very painful subjects.

* *See Mark Twain's comment for May 30.*

Mark Twain's Comment:

Considering the situation and circumstances, the record for next day, May 29, is one which has a surprise in it for those dull people who think that nothing but medicines and doctors can cure the sick. A little starvation can really do more for the average sick man than can the best medicines and the best doctors. I do not mean a restricted diet; I *mean total abstention from food for one or two days.* I speak from experience; starvation has been my cold and fever doctor for fifteen years, and has accomplished a cure in all instances. The Third Mate told me in Honolulu that the "Portyghee" had lain in his hammock for months, raising his family of abscesses and feeding like a cannibal. We have seen that in spite of dreadful weather, deprivation of sleep, scorching, drenching, and all manner of miseries, thirteen days of starvation "wonderfully recovered" him. There were four sailors down sick when the ship was burned. Twenty-five days of pitiless starvation have followed, and now we have this curious record: *"All the men are hearty and strong; even the ones that were down sick are well,* except poor Peter."

When I wrote an article some months ago urging temporary abstention from food as a remedy for an inactive appetite and for disease, I was accused of jesting, but I was in earnest.

"We are all wonderfully well and strong, comparatively speaking." on this day the starvation regimen drew its belt a couple of buckle-holes tighter: the bread ration was reduced from the usual piece of cracker the size of a silver dollar *to the half of that, and one meal was abolished from the daily three.* This will weaken the men physically, but if there are any diseases of an ordinary sort left in them they will disappear.

The hopeful tone of the diaries is persistent. It is remarkable. Look at the map and see where the boat is: latitude 16° 44', longitude 119° 20'. It is more than two hundred miles West of the Revillagedo Islands, so they are quite out of the question against the Trades, rigged as this boat is. The nearest land available for such a boat is the American Group, *six hundred fifty miles away,* Westward; still, there is no note of surrender, none even of discouragement!

WEDNESDAY, MAY 30

Lat. 17° 17' N. (Long. 121° 00' W.)

Captain Mitchell's Journal:

Broken Trades all this day from North to East, squally and moderate alternately. Misty showers. A good deal of sea breaks into the boat, cold, wet, and very disagreeable. No sleep and very weak. No exercise, blood stagnant. Still we are wonderfully preserved and God is good, in Him we trust.

Henry Ferguson's Journal:

Night tolerably comfortable though it splashed more than was comfortable. Wind and sea moderate. This noon we weathered our course to West, finding that it was impossible to make to the Northward fast enough to give us hope of reaching anything North of us. There is a cluster of islands put down in the *Navigator** simply as such and between the latitudes of 16° and 17°, longitude 133° - 136°, and they are styled in Sam's map the American Group,** doubtful. It seems like a forlorn hope but it is our best chance as our path runs right through the path of both upward and downward ships, and if we can live so long and they are really there, we have tolerable certainty of fetching them, as they are to leeward and we can calculate with confidence on the Trades. God grant that the change may be the means of saving us and that we may be it fall in with some vessel. It is all in His hands and I trust He will favor us. Looking at the moon last night I did not feel as if it were the last time I should see it full and I heartily pray that we may all through His goodness see many more wax and wane.

* *The "Navigator" is, of course, Bowditch's THE NEW AMERICAN PRACTICAL NAVIGATOR, cited in the footnote for May 14 as probably being the Twenty-Ninth edition of 1860. This records on page 375 the "cluster of islands" lying between 16° and 17° North latitude and 133° and 136° West longitude. "A cluster of 5 islands", three of which are labeled New, Roca Coral and Misipi I., are indicated on James Imray's navigational "Chart of the North Pacific Ocean Exhibiting the Eastern Shores of Asia and the Western Coast of North America from the Equator to Behring's Strait" (published London, 1852), a copy of which is in the Library of The Mariners Museum. In addition to those of the "American Group" (although not so labeled), other mythical islands indicated on this chart include Maria Laxara, Coopers and Henderson Island lying Northward of the American Group, and Freshwater, Clouds, Ponafidin, Best, Nublada and Sta. Rosa islands to the Eastward near actual Clarion Island. A final mythical island, unnamed, lies to the Northwest of the American Group in about 19° $30'$ North latitude by 141° $30'$ West longitude. It is labeled on the chart: "Island 40 ft. high, 4 miles long, very barren, seen Dec. 28, 1848." We have plotted the course of the HORNET'S longboat on a zerox copy of this old chart.*

** *No clue has been discovered for the curious naming of this mythical set of islands as the "American Group." However, the following unrelated, but provocative note occurs in Alexander George Findlay's A DIRECTORY FOR THE NAVIGATION OF THE NORTH PACIFIC OCEAN, Third Edition, London, 1886, page 928, in connection with a description of the Central Pacific coral island discovered by Capt. Edmund Fanning in sealer BETSEY, 1798. Fanning Island, carrying its discoverer's name, is located in 3° $50'$ North latitude, by 159° $20'$ West longitude and Findlay states: "It is not improbable that this may be the American Isles stated by Kotzebue to have been discovered by Captain Mather of the AMERICAN in 1814." One named island occupying a comparable position to Bowditch's "cluster of islands" is mythical Bunker Island. As stated above, the 1852 James Imray chart gives names to three of "a cluster of 5 islands." Bunker does not appear on Imray's chart but it is recorded in about 16° $30'$ North latitude by 135° $30'$ West longitude on a Blunt, 1861 "Chart of the General Winds of the Pacific Ocean," bound in Capt. Charles Philippe de Kerhallet's GENERAL EXAMINATION OF THE PACIFIC OCEAN, translated from the French second edition published by E. and G.W. Blunt, New York, 1861. Another Bunker Island is located Westward of the Hawaiian Islands and is seemingly unrelated.*

Samuel Ferguson's Journal:

Last night a comparatively quiet one, though with a good breeze which enabled us to head about North-Northwest showing the result in our latitude today. Shipped little water so all hands did some sleeping. This noon, upon general agreement, we have changed our course to West by North. Our reason is we are just in the latitude of a group of islands, only a long way East of them. Our prevailing wind (Trade) Northeast — our change equally good of seeing vessels and, sailing free, we don't waste time, which as our provisions are very low is a great object. It is a hard scratch and a long 650 miles but, all in all, it is our best go. It is perfectly useless to try to beat [to windward] with this boat so that the other isles* are of no account to us. Our ration yesterday was at 9 (A.M.) a thin slice of ham, say two inches square, and 1/8 biscuit with about a gill of water. At 5 P.M. we had about 1/4 of a cracker with 5 oysters, 1/15 of a can with about a tablespoon and a half of the juice and same allowance of water. This evening we will have to reduce, for our bread is almost gone. We have one can of oysters, about three pounds of raisins, one can of Soup and Boulli and less than one half a ham, and about a quart and a half of biscuit crumbs. May God help us and provide for us. Somehow I feel much encouraged by this change made today.

* *The Revillagiegedo Group*

Mark Twain's Comment:

Fifteen starved men to live on these provisions while they creep and crawl six hundred fifty miles to the American Group. Six hundred fifty miles on a hatful of provisions. Let us be thankful, even after thirty-two years, that they are mercifully ignorant of the fact that it isn't six hundred fifty that they must creep on the hatful, but *twenty-two hundred!*

Isn't the situation romantic enough just as it stands? No. Providence added a startling detail; pulling an oar in that boat, for a common seaman's wages, was a *banished duke* — Danish. We hear no more of him; just that mention, that is all, with the simple remark added that "he is one of our best men" — a high enough compliment for a duke or any other man in those manhood-testing circumstances. With that little glimpse of him at his oar, and that fine word of praise, he vanishes out of our knowledge for all time. For all time, unless he should chance upon this note and reveal himself.

THURSDAY, MAY 31

(Lat. 17° 45′ N. Long. 123° 00′ W.)

Captain Mitchell's Journal:

American Group, gave up Henderson.*
At 1 P.M. this day kept off West for the American Group, cluster of islands, 16° to 17° North, in 133° to 136° West. Moderate Trades, smooth sea, and cloudy weather which greatly relieves our thirst. Two meals a day, 14 raisins and a piece of bread the size of a cent for tea. Morning, a piece of ham and bread the size of a cent each and a gill of water. Oh I am growing so weak. God have mercy and send us despairing ones relief before it's too late. We praise Thy holy name. No observation.

* *See previous Editor's Notes referring to the mythical islands.*

Henry Ferguson's Journal:

Night rather cold, but I managed to get a pretty good rest. Feel very weak today. All well though weak. Sun not been fairly out today which makes us free from the want of water which is a great blessing. God has granted us great help and certainly blessed every mouthful for I never could have believed that we could live and be so healthy with so little. May He send us aid soon while what there is lasts, for it is getting fearfully low. God grant that Sam may not be taken away as he has always been father's stay. He endures and has the most unshaken faith and trust in God. Wind fresh and puffy today and some sea on. Pretty wet in the afternoon as if we were going to have a strong breeze all night. In spite of our dreadful position we found in the morning that the bag had been opened in the night. One would not suppose that anyone claiming the name of man would rob his fellow-sufferers in such a time as this. We have thought before that it went fast, some of the pork went the same way. God forgive them and turn their hearts and may He if it be His will that we should perish and preserve us from embittering our ends.

Samuel Ferguson's Journal:

Very little to chronicle today; last night, cold though not much wet. Made good headway all the full 24 hours. God grant us soon deliverance in the shape of a ship or if not strengthen us to find the islands. This A.M. the bread bag was found open and some bread missing. We hate to suspect anyone of such a rascally act, but such is the case. Two days will certainly finish the remaining morsels. Day obscured till about 3 P.M. when the breeze and sea always seem to increase, but afterwards generally somewhat subside. Have kept an anxious lookout all day for vessels, but have not been rewarded. What should we do without hope and Faith in God! How most miserable we must have been! The Captain lost his glasses so cannot read our Prayer Book as much as I think he would like, though he is not familiar with them. He is a real good man and has been most kind to us, almost fatherly. If it please God that we get to New York again together I hope all at home may get to know and thank him for it. If he had had a longer time to prepare* he says he would probably have brought two of his daughters which now he is devoutly thankful he did not.**

Captain Mitchell took command of the HORNET on January 5, 1866, ten days only before she sailed.

**It makes one shudder yet to think how narrow an escape it was (Mark Twain).*

Mark Twain's Comment:

The last day of May is come. And now there is a disaster to report: think of it, reflect upon it, and try to understand how much it means, when you sit down with your family and pass your eye over your breakfast-table. Yesterday there were three pints of bread-crumbs; this morning the little bag is found open and *some of the crumbs missing.*

The Third Mate told me in Honolulu that in these days the men remembered with bitterness that the "Portyghee" had devoured twenty-two days' rations while he lay waiting to be transferred from the burning ship, and that now they cursed him and swore an oath that if it came to cannibalism he should be the first to suffer for the rest.

FRIDAY, JUNE 1

(Lat. 18° 00' N. Long. 124° 30' W.)

Captain Mitchell's Journal:

Strong squally Trade, very rough high seas, wet and extremely uncomfortable. Hardest day yet, water flying in the boat keeps us continually wet. Can't write, all very weak, particularly myself. Cold and hungry. Great God have us in Thy keeping and preserve us. No observation. Still running for uncertain islands. 30 days in the boat and no sail gladdens us.

Letter written in the back of Captain Mitchell's Journal:

June 1st.
My Dear Wife and Darling Girls and greatly beloved Son:
Could I but see you once more and ask forgiveness of you all for my seeming pettishness at times. God knows how dearly I love you. I hope and trust with the goodness of God you will be able to get along. If I could impart advice to you, what a comfort 'twould be to me before departing hence where there is no return. May peace, plenty, and harmony prevail in your councils, helping and loving one another. Your Father's loss you will all feel, but if it's Thy Father's wish, I am resigned. He knows what is best. Put your trust in Him and make a friend of Jesus our Lord and may your lives be happy and your end peace.

Henry Ferguson's Journal:

God has preserved us to the beginning of another month none of us would have dared hope for when we left the ship and I have great confidence that in His great mercy He will send us deliverance soon. Sea very rough and wind strong all night and all today. But is not so bad now. Last night was cold and uncomfortable, but we all feel tolerably well today. Sun has hardly been out at all. Captain made no attempt to obtain sights not wishing to endanger the instruments. God supports us wonderfully and I feel more and more that He will allow us to see the dear ones we have left at home, but His Holy Will be done. May He keep us all in reason and not permit the passions of men to embitter our ends if He wills that they are to come now. We are going at a pretty swift rate and guess we are certainly making our hundred and twenty miles per day, which ought to bring us to where the Islands are by Monday or Tuesday. Our provisions I think can be made to last that or even longer. God send us aid for we are brought fearfully low.

Samuel Ferguson's Journal:

Last night and today sea very high and cobbling, breaking over and making us all wet and cold. Weather squally and there is no doubt that only careful management with God's care, preserved us both through night and day; and really it is most marvelous how that every morsel that passes our lips is blessed to us. It makes me think daily of the miracle of the loaves and fishes.

Henry, I am thankful, keeps up wonderfully which is a great consolation to me. God grant that he may be spared as well as all of us. I somehow have got great confidence and hope that our afflictions will soon be ended. We are running tho' [?] rapidly across the track of both out and inward bound vessels. and from them our chief hope is a whaler, man-of-war, or some Australian ship. The islands we are steering for are put down in Bowditch, but on my map are said to be doubtful. God grant that they may be there!

Mark Twain's Comment:

Doubtful! It was worse than that. A week later *they sailed straight over them.*

SATURDAY, JUNE 2

Lat. 18° 09'N. (Long. 126° 20'W.)

Captain Mitchell's Journal:

Very high sea all this day and dangerous running. Yet we are miraculously sustained by God's protecting care. Very wet from the sea and very cold so near the water, yet we are all better than could be expected. 30 days today in this boat with two days more supplies of the scantiest measure. 10 raisins apiece and a little piece of bread. The sun shines and God is merciful.

Henry Ferguson's Journal:

Very heavy sea all last night and today, but we have been mercifully preserved from any inconvenience from water. It made the night very hard but we must endure what comes and trust that God will soon give us safety and relief from this awful discomfort and anxiety. Our latitude which was obtained this noon gives us great satisfaction, for we feared that we had been driven to the Southward by the sea. As it is, we can afford to run a point or so more off thus making the sea more aft. Men are getting disheartened terribly. Some of them though, seem to put their trust and reliance on the true Rock of safety. Looking at it as man's eyes would judge our chances of life are terribly small, and are reducing from day to day, but by the grace of God I trust they are great, and that the time of our probation will be short. Short it must be for one end or the other must come soon. God soften the anxiety at Stamford and grant that in His good time we may be restored to them.

Samuel Ferguson's Journal:

Last night much like previous one, squally and cloudy with slight [showers] of rain and a heavy sea. This morning much the same, towards noon, however, sea went down somewhat, and, though it is still high, it is a great deal more comfortable. Sun also was out a good part of the time, which it has not been for some day or two. It is a great blessing as it dries us. The good breeze keeps off thirst wonderfully, so that we really save water on our scanty allowance.

   Have thought much of home and the pleasures both of soul and body we should all have there. God help them in their increasing anxiety for us. We see very few birds now but "Mother Cary's Chickens" and some sea-birds that keep continually darting about just over the tops of the waves, occasionally a few "Boatswains". Can't help thinking of the nice and comfortable time we had aboard the *Hornet* and that presence of mind might have saved her and all this suffering. Nevertheless, God's will be done!

SUNDAY, JUNE 3

Lat. 17° 54′ N. (Long. 128° 30′ W.)

Captain Mitchell's Journal:

Obliged to keep off on account of sea. Very heavy sea all day and very dangerous running. Have spent most of the day in prayer to God and thinking of my beloved family. I must give them all up and commend them to God's mercy. Oh my Father, spare me if it's Thy will, otherwise, prepare me for death.

Henry Ferguson's Journal:

Last Sunday by this time we thought all would be over and still we are alive and not much weaker than then. Certainly He has been very merciful to us and has blessed every crumb of sustenance we have taken. Last night was another very rough one but by His goodness we rode safely through it, without shipping very much water. There is a tremendous sea on for such a small boat and a very strong trade blowing. We pray that He will moderate it and bring us into the haven where we would be. How they are all praying for us at home as they receive the blessed Sacrament. What would I not give to be with them were it but to die with them around. I pray God we may meet all again in safety if not in this world then in Heaven where there will be no more parting. We have left now about 1/3 of a ham, a pan full or so of finely broken biscuit, a few raisins, a can of oysters, one of soup and of bouilli. These with the water we have we hope to make last four or five days and our water still longer. If these islands are there we ought to be among them tomorrow or next day. Read prayers and Litany this A.M.

but found it hard to keep the mind fixed so postponed the Ante Communion till the P.M. Sea is going down somewhat I am thankful to say, wind also more comfortable I think this P.M., but sun not out fully all day.

Samuel Ferguson's Journal:

Heavy sea all night, and from 4 A.M. very wet, breaking over us in frequent gulps, soaking everything aft, particularly. All day the sea has been very high and it is a wonder that we are not swamped. Heaven grant that it may go down this evening! Could not make out to read the full service this A.M., but did the Prayers, Psalms, (both) Epistle and Gospel this P.M. and feel comforted by them. God grant the prayer breathed at home for us may mingle with ours and be answered to us soon for our suspense and condition is getting terrible. Managed this A.M. to crawl more than step forward and was surprised to find I was so weak, legs and knees particularly. Sun has been out so I have managed to dry some things and hope for a better night.

MONDAY, JUNE 4

Lat. 17° 06´ N. Long. 130° 30´ W.

Captain Mitchell's Journal:

We are still preserved by God's mercy. First and middle part of this day very rough and high sea, running before it, wet and cold. Latter part pleasant sunshine and warm. Trying to get dry. Bread and raisins all gone. Everybody very weak and praying for relief. Hope we may fall in with some ship before it's too late. Good sights today.

Henry Ferguson's Journal:

Today has been a fine day with the sun out all the time except for a few passing clouds from time to time. Sea big but better by far than it was and we got dry. If these Islands* are in the place the book puts them, we can't be in a better situation. God in His Mercy grant that we may find them as it is humanly speaking our last hope. Men growing dreadfully discontented and awful grumbling and unpleasant talking is arising. God save us from all strife of men and if we must die now take us Himself and not embitter our bitter death still more. My trust is still firm in Him. But if it is His will that we should die may He soften the anxiety and suffering of our friends and grant them His grace and may He receive us into His Everlasting Kingdom. Eat the last of the raisins and the oysters tonight. Ham and a few bread crumbs and soup all left. God keep us. He has blessed our food to us very long, and has been wonderfully merciful to us.

* *The mythical American Group.*

Samuel Ferguson's Journal:

Shipped hardly any seas last night and today sea has gone down somewhat, although it is still too high for comfort, as we have an occasional reminder that water is wet. Sun out all day so we have had a good drying. Have been trying for the last ten or twelve days to get a pair of drawers dry enough to put on and today at last succeeded. I mention this to show the state in which we have lived. If our chronometer is anywhere near right we ought to see the Islands tomorrow or next day. If they are not there we have only the chance of a few days of a stray ship. Cannot spin out provisions more than five or six days and our strength is failing very fast. Was much surprised to see how much my legs had wasted away, above my knee hardly thicker than my upper arm used to be. Still I trust in God's infinite mercy and feel sure He will do what is best for us. Thirty-two days in an open boat with about ten days fair provisions for thirty-one men to sustain life after division twice is certainly more than human art can accomplish.

TUESDAY, JUNE 5

Lat. 16° 46'N. (Long. 132° 10'W.)

Captain Mitchell's Journal:

First part of this day pleasant with a high rolling sea. Night fine. Latter part cloudy, sea still large, wind light, dryer in the boat than for many days. We are getting very weak. Bread gone, a little piece of ham and a gill of water. A conspiracy formed to murder me. Minds unquiet. God is over all.

Henry Ferguson's Journal:

Day cloudy but calmer, steering West and South. No signs as yet of the Islands. God deliver us, our stores are almost spent and will be entirely if we do not find them soon. Dreadful forebodings. God save us from all such horrors. Some of the men getting to talk a good deal. Nothing to put down. Heart very sad.

Samuel Ferguson's Journal:

Quiet night and pretty comfortable day, though sail and block show signs of failing and need taking down, which latter is something of a job as it requires the shinnying up the mast. We also had bad news from forward, there being discontent and some threatening complaints of unfair allowances, etc., all as unreasonable as foolish. Still it bids us be on our guard. I am getting miserably weak but try to keep up the best I can. God will help us I am sure although we may not all live to be delivered. If we can't find these Islands we can only try to make Northwest and get in the track of Sandwich Islands* bound vessels, living as best we can. God have mercy on us. Today changed to one meal and that about noon with a small ration of water at about 8 or 9 A.M. and 5 or 6 P.M. with a little of course at noon.

* *Hawaaian Islands*

Notes on last pages of Journal of Henry Ferguson:

(S.F.) We can depend on Charlie Iron I think, and Mr. Thomas and Cox, can we not?
(H.F.) I guess so, and very likely on Peter, but there is no telling. Charlie and Cox are certain. There is nothing definite said or hinted as yet, as I understand him [Cox], but starving men are the same as maniacs. It would be well to keep a watch on your pistol so as to have it and

the cartridges safe from theft.

(H.F.) Cox told me last night there is getting to be a good deal of ugly talk among the men against the Captain and us aft. Harry, Jack and Fred especially. They say that the Captain is the cause of all, that he did not try to save the ship at all, nor to get provisions, and even would not let the men put in some they had, and that our allowance aft we are favored. Jack asked Cox the other day if he would starve first or eat flesh. Cox answered he would starve. Jack then told him it would be only killing himself. If we do not find these Islands we would do well to prepare for everything. Harry is the loudest of all.

Oh eternal God who causest both the storm and calm, in whose hand is the power of life and death: we beseech thee to look upon us Thy creatures in our extremity. Spare us. Good Lord, spare Thy people who cry unto Thee for help. Thou who didst feed Thy people in the desert, suffer us not to die with this famine that threatens us. Oh save us Lord or we perish. Spare us for Thy mercy is great. Lord Jesus, who didst command the storm to cease and didst preserve Thy disciples from drowning, help us we beseech Thee, that we being saved by Thy defence may evermore serve Thee and praise Thee as we have never done before. We thank Thee, Oh Lord, for Thy great mercy in keeping us safe for so long, and for blessing our food to us. Grant us still Thy protection and preserve us for Thy great mercy's sake.

Or if it be Thy Holy Will to summon us from this world, give us grace to use the remaining time in preparation for the final judgment. Give us true repentance for our sins, and grant that through the merits of Christ Jesus who died on the Cross to save us, they may be forgiven us. Give us patience and resignation to Thy will and keep us in thy spirit of peace and charity. All which we ask for the sake of Him who suffered hunger, thirst and death for us, who with Thee and the Holy Ghost we worship and glorify, one God world without end — Amen.

Mark Twain's Comment:

They are down to *one* meal a day now, — such as it is, — *and fifteen hundred miles to crawl yet!* And now the horrors deepen. There is talk of murder. And not only that, but worse than that — cannibalism. Now we seem to see why that curious accident happened, so long ago: I mean Cox's return, after he had been far away and out of sight several days in the chief mate's boat. If he had not come back the Captain and the two young passengers would have been slain, now, by these sailors, who have become maniacs through their sufferings.

WEDNESDAY, JUNE 6

Lat. 16° 30' N. Long. 134° 00' W.

Captain Mitchell's Journal:

Another day had been allowed us. First and middle thick and cloudy. Latter very pleasant sky. Good deal of sea and fresh wind. Daily growing weaker. Allowance very small and but three meals left. American Group not there. Must run for Sandwich Islands and trust in God's goodness for food.

Henry Ferguson's Journal:

No signs, that we can call signs, of land. Some sea-weed was passed this morning also something which looked like an old tree. But still no birds. I am beginning to have great doubts of

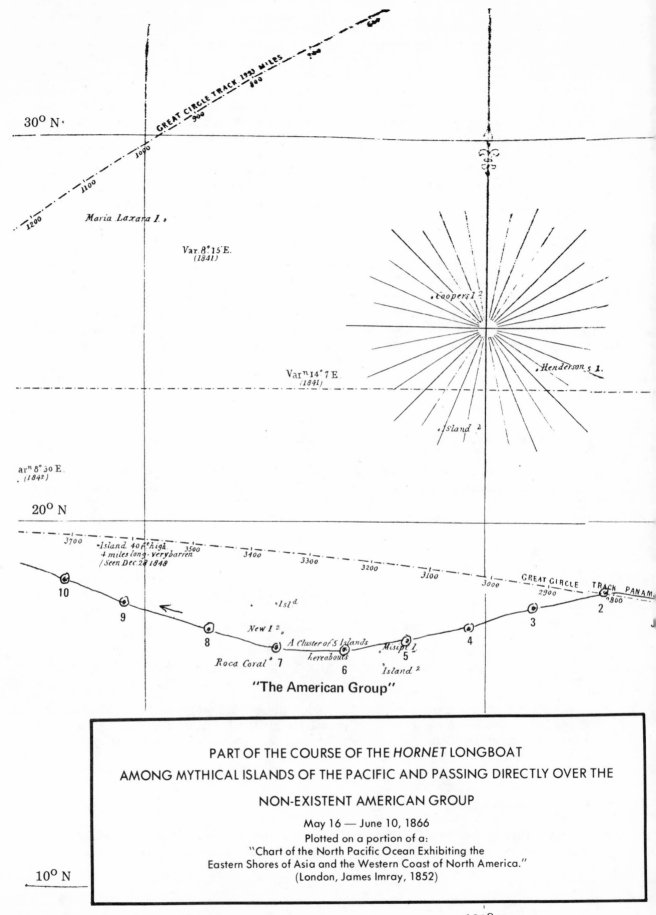

30° N·

GREAT CIRCLE TRACK 1953 MILES

_900_
_800_

_1000_

_1100_

_1200_

Maria Lazara I. ·

Var. 8° 15'E.
_(1841)_

·_Coopers I ?_

Var^n 14° 7 E.
_(1841)_

·_Henderson ₅ 1._

·_Island ?_

ar^n 8° 30 E.
· _(1842)_

20° N

_3700_ _3500_ _3400_ _3300_ _3200_ _3100_ _3000_ GREAT CIRCLE TRACK PANAM.
·_Island 40 f^t high_ _2900_
4 miles long· very barren _2800_
Seen Dec.28 1848

10 ⊙

9 ⊙

← ·_Isl^d_

8 ⊙

New I ? ·

A Cluster of 5 Islands _Misipi I._ 4 ⊙ 3 ⊙ 2 ⊙
Roca Coral · 7 ⊙ _hereabouts_ 5 ⊙

6 ⊙ ·_Island ?_

"The American Group"

PART OF THE COURSE OF THE *HORNET* LONGBOAT

AMONG MYTHICAL ISLANDS OF THE PACIFIC AND PASSING DIRECTLY OVER THE

NON-EXISTENT AMERICAN GROUP

May 16 — June 10, 1866
Plotted on a portion of a:
"Chart of the North Pacific Ocean Exhibiting the
Eastern Shores of Asia and the Western Coast of North America."
(London, James Imray, 1852)

10° N →

140° W

130° W

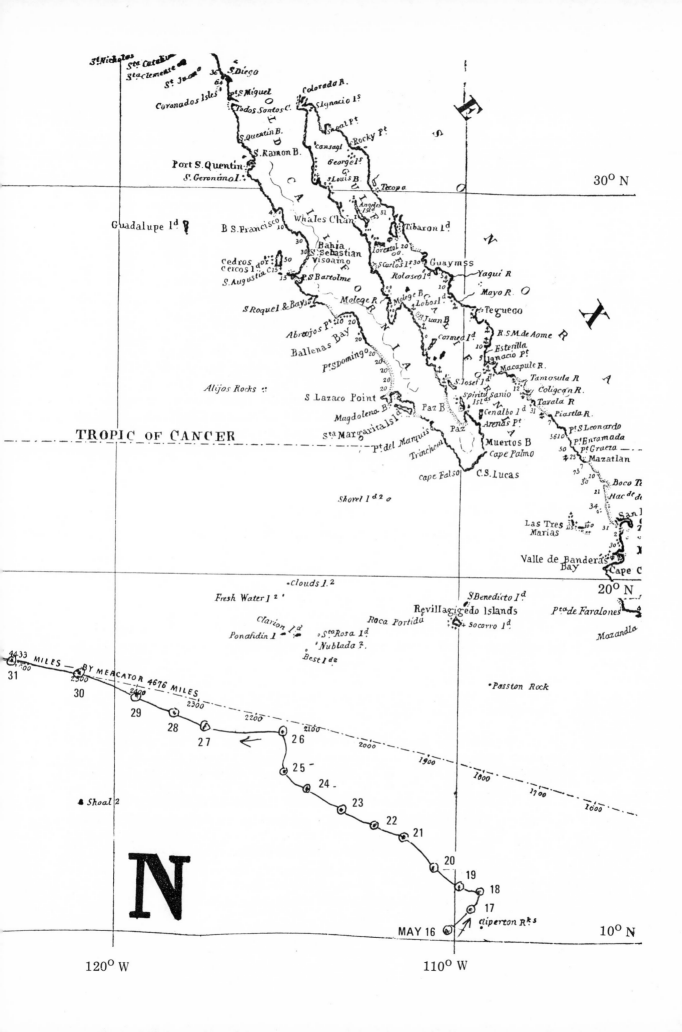

these Islands being here at all. God help us and send us some aid for trouble is nigh at hand. Our stores are next to nothing and though we can make our water last for 8 or 10 days, who can tell what starving men will do? Today it was said to the Captain in all our presence that some of the men would not shrink when a man was dead from using the flesh though would not kill. Horrible! God give us all full use of our reason and spare us from such awful things. May He send deliverance soon. We are, thanks to Him, yet well, but weak. Sam holds out well but is growing weaker and weaker, I fear, as indeed we all are. It has been a beautiful day, with a rain squall in the afternoon. These squalls look as if there might be Islands near. God send they may. If we don't find them soon we shall head for Hawaii and trust that some of us may live to be picked up.

Samuel Ferguson's Journal:

Dry night and wind steady enough to require no change in sail; but this A.M. our attempts to lower found it no go, so first the 3rd Mate tried and got up to the block and fastened a temporary arrangement to reeve the hallyards through but had to come down before finishing, weak and almost fainting. Then Joe tried and after twice ascending fixed it and brought down the block but it was very exhausting work and after which he was good for nothing all day. The clew-iron which we tried to make serve for the broken block works, however, very indifferently and will, I am afraid, soon cut the rope. It is very necessary to get everything connected with the sail in good easy running order before we get too weak to do anything with it.

THURSDAY, JUNE 7

Lat. 16° 36' N. Long. 136° 00' W.

Captain Mitchell's Journal:

Five weeks in the boat, provisions all gone but one small can. A little water left. Beautiful June day. Running all day hoping to reach Sandwich Islands. Failing fast, everybody very weak, a day or two more and all will be over. Oh God have mercy on us and forgive us our sins.

Henry Ferguson's Journal:

No signs of land at all and we are heading for Hawaii as our last chance trusting in God's Providence. If we are not picked up by the Island traders we may manage to reach the Islands. It will be an awful stretch for us as weak as we are now to go without food. But who knows what a day may bring? We are, we calculate, a thousand miles from it and can manage to keep something to eat little as it will be till Sunday when I think we must use the last of our provisions. Images of food and niceties are ever recurring to our minds and we think with remorse of how much we have wasted when we had plenty. If I only had what Toby lives on I would do well and the pigs mess would supply us all. How different it is at College today. All enjoying themselves. The Class of '66 bidding their farewells. Little did I think last year that I would pass the next Class Day in this manner. God send us all strength to endure and support it. May He preserve our reason is my ceaseless prayer.

Samuel Ferguson's Journal:

Tonight pretty wet and uncomfortable. Today shows us pretty certainly that the Islands are not here, although we have had some signs that look like them. At noon we decided to abandon looking any further for them and tonight haul a little more Northerly so as to get in the way of Sandwich Island vessels, which fortunately come down pretty well this way, say to 19° or 20° latitude, to get the benefit of the Trades. Of course all the Westing we have made is gain and I hope that the chronometer is wrong in our favor for I don't see how any such delicate instrument can keep good time with the constant jarring and thumping we get from the sea. With the strong Trade we have I hope that with God's help and sustaining power a week from Sunday will put us in sight of the Isles, if we are not saved before that by being picked up.

Mark Twain's Comment:

It is twelve hundred miles to the Sandwich Islands; the provisions are virtually exhausted, but not the perishing diarist's pluck.

Seaman Frederick Clough Reminiscenses:*

We slept in all sorts of positions, lying in water, wet through for weeks, numb and cramped, weak and chilled by wind and spray, yet often dreaming of Christmas dinners and of most beautiful things. I remember looking at a rosy sunset one evening after a storm. It was at a time when hunger had pulled me down until I was fearfully weak and delirious, but when I fell asleep I dreamt of turkeys on feast tables, and in happy dreams I seemed to be enjoying a meal fit for a king.

* *Recorded by Legh H. Irvine in "The Lone Cruise of the HORNET Men." WIDE WORLD, September, 1900.*

FRIDAY, JUNE 8

(Lat. 17° 15' N. Long. 138° 00' W.)

Captain Mitchell's Journal:

1,000 miles from Sandwich Islands.* Still alive but very very weak. Another beautiful day. Sea very high. Still we are wonderfully preserved by God's mercy. Grant us contented grateful hearts, and peace in Thee our God. No sights. Men quiet and all seem resigned. A better feeling prevails.

* *Apparently written in another hand, probably added at a later date.*

Henry Ferguson's Journal:

Beautiful day as could be and the wind is favorable. What a delightful day anywhere else. I think all the time how pleasant it must be at home. God send that we may again see it. I felt encouraged all yesterday and today, and have full confidence that He who has preserved us such a wonderful time will yet spare us. He has given us great help thus far and the way our provisions have lasted really seems miraculous. May He who fed Elijah in the famine and supported his people in the wilderness feed us. Our water is our great reliance and we cannot be thankful enough for it. Sam bears wonderfully and keeps cheerful. God who ever pities those who trust has given him His strength, and I cannot think but that He will spare both him and us. Opened the soup can and took one half today. Small enough for fifteen men's food for an entire day, but more than we will have next week, unless we get fish or birds. Half tomorrow and a morsel of him on Sunday will end our stores. God help us.

Samuel Ferguson's Journal:

My cough troubled me a good deal last night which kept me from almost any sleep. Still I make out pretty well and ought not to complain. Yesterday the 3rd Mate mended up the block and this P.M. the sail, after some difficulty, was got down and Harry got up to the top of the mast and rove the halliards through after some difficulty so that it now works easy and well, thank God! This getting up the mast is no easy matter at any time with the sea we have and is very exhausting in our state now. We could only reward him by an extra ration of water. Have made good time and course today. Heading her up, through, makes us aft and all in fact more wet which, however, can't be helped, and writing is a pretty precarious thing to do at any time. Our meal today for the fifteen consists of one half can of "soup and boulli," other half reserved for tomorrow. Henry, I am thankful to say, still keeps up grandly, and is a great favorite. God grant he may be spared!

SATURDAY, JUNE 9

Lat. 17° 52'N. (Long. 140° 20' W.)

Captain Mitchell's Journal:

We still live. Divided the last of a tin of soup and broth. High sea and fresh Trades, running for Sandwich Islands. Some of the men will be able to reach there, they are young and strong. I never shall except for the great mercy of my Heavenly Father.

Henry Ferguson's Journal:

No entry.

Samuel Ferguson's Journal:

Finished today, I may say, our whole stock of provisions.* We have left the lower end of a ham bone with some of the outer rind and skin on. In regard to water, though, we have I guess at the allowance we go perhaps 10 days supply, this with what nourishment we can get from boot-legs and such chewable matter, we hope to weather it out till we can reach the Sandwich Islands, or getting in the track of vessels there to be picked up. My hope is in the latter for in all human probability I cannot stand the other. Still we have been marvellously protected and God, I hope, will preserve us all in His own good time and way. Men are getting weaker, but are still quiet and orderly.

* *Six days to sail yet, nevertheless. (Mark Twain).*

SUNDAY, JUNE 10

Lat. 18° 36′ N. Long. 142° 30′ W.

Captain Mitchell's Journal:

Another beautiful June Sabbath finds us still alive in this boat. Oh may the day be blessed and sanctified unto us to the salvation of our souls as nearer approach to heaven. How much we think of dear ones at home this sacred day and their privileges. We are fast starving to death. God have mercy on our souls.

Henry Ferguson's Journal:

Another Sunday and yet we are spared and in health. God has been very merciful to us and I trust that if we can manage to spin our life for five or six days more we may reach Hawaii. Our lives are in His hands and if He sees but to save us, He will. If not, His Will be done. Our ham-bone has given us a taste of good today and we have left a little meat on the bone still for tomorrow. Certainly never was there such a sweet knuckle bone or one which was so thoroughly appreciated. Read the service and heartily prayed that the time is not far off when we can return thanks to God in His Holy Church. I do not know as I feel any worse than I did last Sunday notwithstanding the reduction of diet; and I trust that we may all have strength given us from above to sustain the suffering and hardship of the coming week. We estimate that we are about 700 miles from the Islands and I suppose our average is about 120 miles. If anything, over that, so that our hopes have some foundation of reason. God grant that we may all live to reach land. "From plague, pestilence, and famine, from battle and murder, and from sudden death, Good Lord deliver us."

Samuel Ferguson's Journal:

A pretty good night last night with some wettings and again another beautiful Sunday. I cannot but think how we should all enjoy it at home and what a contrast there is! Oh how terrible their suspense must begin to be! God grant it may be relieved before very long and He certainly seems to be with us in everything we do and has preserved this boat wonderfully. Since we left the ship we have sailed considerably over 3,000 miles, which, taking on consideration our stock of provisions, is about unprecedented.

As yet I don't feel the stint of food so much as I do water. Henry who is naturally a large water-drinker can save his one half allowance from time to time when I cannot. My throat may have something to do with that, however.

Mark Twain's Comment:

Nothing is now left which by any flattery can be called food. But they must manage somehow for five days more, for at noon they have still eight hundred miles to go. It is a race for life now.

This is no time for comments or other interruptions from me — every moment is valuable. I will take up the boy brother's diary at this point, and clear the seas before it and let it fly.

MONDAY, JUNE 11

Lat. 19° 23' N. (Long. 145° 00' W.

Captain Mitchell's Journal:

A lovely June day. Everything that is possible to eat is eaten. Living on three gills water per day. I am growing very weak indeed. Don't feel that I can possibly last to the islands unless by some special grace of God who has been very merciful to us. My head troubles me today for the first. I trust and pray that my conversion is truly sincere and that my sins may be forgiven.

Henry Ferguson's Journal:

Pleasant today and sea gone down, quite calm. Wind lighter with squalls in the afternoon which increased it, and we have been going pretty fast all day and have every hope that God will allow us to reach shore if we do not find a trader first. We are heading West by North and hope that we will fall in with some of them. Eat the meat and rind of the ham-bone and have the bone and the greasy cloth left to eat tomorrow. God send us some birds or fish and let us not perish of hunger or be brought to the dreadful alternative of human flesh! As I feel now I don't think anything could persuade me, but can't tell what you will do when reduced by hunger and crazy. I hope and pray we can make out to reach them before we get to this strait, but we have one or two pretty desperate men aboard although they are quiet enough now. They must be dreadfully anxious at home. God soften it to them and grant we may be spared to see them again. Sam bears it well and is supported by God's grace wonderfully. It is my firm trust and belief that we are going to be saved and he has kept up so long that I think he will endure as long as most of us.

Samuel Ferguson's Journal:

Early part of last night squally and stormy or I should say splashing.

Mark Twain's Comment:

It was at this time discovered that the crazed sailors had gotten the delusion that the Captain had a million dollars in gold concealed aft, and they were conspiring to kill him and the two passengers and seize it.

TUESDAY, JUNE 12

Lat. 19° 52' N. (Long. 147° 20' W.)

Captain Mitchell's Journal:

Still permitted to live and write. This is my birthday. God grant it may be to me a new birth day for the soul, washed and made clean for the Kingdom of Heaven. Nothing to eat, sucking rags and leather, hoping to be preserved to reach the islands which may God in His great mercy grant. We have been spared so long, 40 days today, that we dare think we may arrive. God has been very merciful to us.

- 164 -

Memorandum in the back of Captain Mitchell's Journal:

Again I am still spared. It's the 12th. of June, a lovely day as my birthdays have ever been. I pray God it may be a birthday of the soul born into Christ. Oh darling wife and children, I think if I am ever permitted to see you again, I shall try to be more of a dutiful father than I have ever been. No parent could love his children more, but I feel that I have neglected my duty in not leading you to Christ. Should this ever reach you girls and Harry, *do not fail* of making Jesus your friend, *now* early in life. You can always rely upon Him steadfast and sure. I trust and pray that my sins are pardoned and that we shall all meet in heaven at last. You never can realize what a trial this has been. And still by God's great mercy preserved forty days today on the ocean with not stores enough to last a week, and sailed over 3,000 miles in an open boat with 15 men crowded into her. The ship was burned very carelessly by the Mate. Oh how much suffering it has caused. We are very nearly starved. It's with great difficulty I can stand. Growing weak fast, sands will soon be run. God bless you all now and forever and may you all be happy in this world and the world to come.

Henry Ferguson's Journal:

Fine day with a squall in the afternoon. Wind hauling a good deal to the East and we run dead ahead of it. Good hopes, but the prospects of hunger are awful. Eat ham-bone today.

Samuel Ferguson's Journal:

No entry.

WEDNESDAY, JUNE 13

Lat. 20° 10' N. Long. 149° 50' W.

Captain Mitchell's Journal:

Still preserved by God's wonderful mercy. Beautiful weather and fair wind. Naught to eat this day. Reduced allowance of water to two gills hoping to survive until we reach the islands. Oh very very weak and so reduced, cannot write more.

Henry Ferguson's Journal:

Sea calm and wind light today. It has been a most beautiful day but the heat or rather the force of the sun has been very oppressive. Getting to feel very weak but trust that we will all get through all right. God grant that our chronometer may not be far out of the way and that three or at the most four days will see us in safety. I cannot but feel that we are going to be saved since God has defended us from the dangers of the sea and kept us in health so long. Water is, I grieve to say, getting very low. We have reduced our allowance and only take a gill at night and morning which is the least we seem to be able to do with when we have no food. A flying fish came aboard last night. We divided him and so had a taste today. The ham rags are not gone yet and bootlegs are quite palatable we find when we get the salt out of them. A little smoke I think does a little good, but I don't know. God help us and grant we may reach shore in safety. Squall coming up astern as I write.

Henry Ferguson journal for June 15 reporting sighting land.

Actual size

Samuel Ferguson's Journal:

No entry.

THURSDAY, JUNE 14

(Lat. 20° 00'N. Long. 152° 00'W.)

Captain Mitchell's Journal:

Six weeks in the boat today. Still running, nothing to eat, and water for one day more, yet I feel better than I could expect. Too weak to write. God has been very merciful. We may yet be preserved.

Henry Ferguson's Journal:

Most lovely rainbow last evening, perfect bow with color most vivid and supplementary bow very distinct. Certainly it is a good sign. Saw new moon, God has spared us wonderfully to see it. I never expected it. It made us feel much better and gives us hopes. Hunger does not pain us so much, but we are dreadful weak. Our water is getting frightfully low. God grant we may see land soon. Nothing to eat, but feel better than I did yesterday.

Samuel Ferguson's Journal:

Very weak but very hopeful. Good wind and everything very promising.

FRIDAY, JUNE 15

Lat. 19° 55'N. (Long. 154° 30'W.)

Captain Mitchell's Journal:

At 10:30 A.M. made certain of land. Saw indications of land but dare not say it for fear of disappointment. Landed on Hawaii at 4 P.M. a famished starved set of men after being in the boat over 43 days 8 hours. Not a man could walk. All taken out and carried up by the kind Kanakas who try to outvie each other in doing all they can to lessen our misery. Now comes the trial whether or not we can be built up after such a trial. No passage of bowels for 23 days.

Henry Ferguson's Journal:

God be forever praised for his infinite mercy to us! Land seen today at 10:30 to the West-ward. Rapidly neared and soon were sure of it. Made out a settlement on the shore and ran in for it, in afternoon came close and were shown where to go by a native. Managed to make out to get near right among a dreadful surf, or sharp coral and volcanic rocks when two noble Kanarkas swam to us and aided us to guide the boat into a little bight where we were most joyfully received by two white men and the Kanakas who live here. They treated us splendid-

- 167 -

ly, aided us and carried us up the bank and brought us there water, poi, bananas, green cocoanuts, but the white men, Mr. Jones and his steward took care and prevented those who would have eaten too much from doing so. Everybody overjoyed to see us and all sympathy expressed in faces, deed, and words. We were then helped up to the house and help we needed. Mr. Jones has a Kanaka wife and except his steward is the only white man here. He treated us splendidly. Gave us first about a teaspoonful of some spirits in water and then to each a cup of hot tea with a little bread. Takes every care of us. Gave us later another cup of tea and bread the same and then let us go to rest. We landed at about 4:30. It is the happiest day of my life and God in His infinite mercy has heard our prayer. Nothing hurt in the boat. All dreadfully reduced, but hope that we will soon pick up under this kind treatment. Beautiful place as ever was seen, a little Paradise and the natives seem as simple and innocent. The priest, a young Belgian, happened in after we got to the house and we had him offer thanks. Everybody is so kind. Words can't tell.

Samuel Ferguson's Journal:

Good night's run. About 9 A.M. discovered the joyful sight of land.
Saved at about 4 P.M. almost gone. Met with most marvellous kindness from everybody.
Place named Laupahoehoe.* Agent of place named Mr. Jones from L.I., N.Y.

* *The first edition of THE HAWAIIAN GUIDE BOOK FOR TRAVELERS by Henry M. Whitney (Honolulu, 1875, reprinted in facsimile by Charles E. Tuttle Co., 1970) quotes a description of Laupahoehoe village in the Hilo District of the Island of Hawaii as follows: "Laupahoehoe is a mere leaf of basaltic lava pushed out into the sea from the narrow valley, which formed the pathway for the last volcanic throe of Maunakea. We have no doubt that the name of the village is derived from the shape of the lava point on which it is situated, Lau-pa-hoe-hoe, meaning a LEAF OF LAVA . . . Except at Hilo Bay, the coast is composed of bold cliffs from a hundred to upwards of 1000 feet high; these are higher on the North and the pali [cliff], at Laupahoehoe, is a remarkable one. Suddenly the traveler rides on to a point where the road ends on the face of a cliff above a beach where three rows of big, combing breakers constantly beat against the shore . . . Close to the sea, with a narrow sand fringe on its more sheltered side, in a coconut grove, lies Laupahoehoe village."*

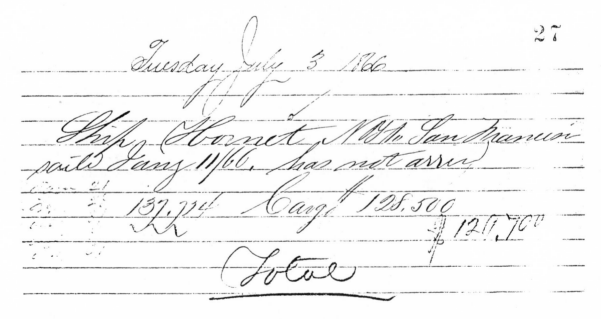

Atlantic Mutual Insurance Company's register notation of the Hornet *being overdue as of July 3, 1866.*

PART V—SALVATION— REPORTING THE DISASTER

Two 1875 photographs of Laupahoehoe, Island of Hawaii. Courtesy Mr. Henry L. Ferguson

MONDAY, JUNE 18

Letter from Captain Mitchell to A. Caldwell, Esq. United States Consul, Honolulu.*

Laupahoehoe, Hawaii
Monday, June 18, 1866

By the mail of today I am just able to inform you of the loss (by fire at sea) of the American ship *Hornet*, under my command, on the 3rd of May last, in lat. 2⁰ N., long. 112⁰ 30′W., bound from New York for San Francisco. In the providence of God I was permitted to land at this place, on the afternoon of the 15th inst., after being 43 days in the boat with 2 passengers, 11 men and Third Officer (15 in all), all in a starving condition. The Consul at Hilo has already kindly and promptly relieved me of the men, which I trust will add much to my recovery,** I am very weak and shall require some days of quiet rest to recover some vitality before moving from here. We were obliged to leave the ship in haste, the first officer taking eight of the crew in one quarter boat, the second officer and six men going in the other quarter boat. The boats were together nineteen days before separating, at which time we divided what few remaining stores we had and parted company. I trust they may have been picked up and not left to the sufferings we endured. Annexed I furnish the names of those in the boat with me: Mr. Samuel Ferguson and Mr. Henry Ferguson, passengers; J.S. Thomas, Third Officer; and the following Seamen: Henry Morris, Joseph Williams, Peter Smith, C.H. Kaartman, Antonio Possene, John Ferris, Frederick Clough, Neal Turner, Thomas J. Tate, James Cox, John Campbell.

---

* *THE PACIFIC COMMERCIAL ADVERTISER, Honolulu, June 29, 1866, headlined, "Loss of the HORNET."*

** *Third Mate Thomas and the HORNET'S seamen were sent from Hilo to Honolulu on the clipper brigantine NAHIENAENA.*

MONDAY, JUNE 18

Letter from Captain Mitchell to his agents:

Laupahoehoe, Hawaii
Monday, June 18, 1866

George Howes & Co.,
(San Francisco)
Gents.:

By the mail of today I am just able to inform you of the loss by fire at sea, of the American ship *Hornet*, under my command, on the 3d. of May last, in latitude 2⁰ North, longitude 112⁰ 30′West, bound from New York for San Francisco. In the providence of God I was permitted to land at this place on the 15th. of June, after being forty-three days in the boat, with two passengers, eleven men, and the Third Officer, (fifteen in all,) all in a starving and destitute condition. The Consul at Hilo has already relieved me of the men, which I trust will add much to my speedy recovery. I am very weak, and shall require some days of quiet rest to recover some vitality, before moving from here. We were obliged to leave the ship in haste, the First Officer taking eight of the crew in one quarter boat, and the Second Officer six men in the other quarter boat. The boats were together nineteen (19) days before separating at which time we divided what few remaining stores we had left and parted company. I trust they may have been picked up, and not left to the sufferings we endured. Annexed I furnish the names of those in the boat with me: Mr. Samuel Ferguson, Mr. Henry Ferguson New York passengers; J.S. Thomas, Third Officer; Henry Morris, Joseph Williams, Peter Smith, C.H. Kaartman, Antonio Possene, John Ferris, Thomas J. Tate, James Cox, John Campbell, Frederick Clough, Neal Turner, seamen.

It is with great exertion I have written this much, for my brain, as well as body, is very weak. The passengers are still with me, much reduced, and require care and rest. Trusting a few days quiet and the kind hands into which we have fallen will soon restore our strength sufficient to reach your city, I remain, respectfully, etc.,

(Signed) Josiah A. Mitchell

MEMORANDUM in the back of Captain Mitchell's Journal: *Reproduced on page 136.*

Men in Mate's Boat:
Samuel F. Hardy, Mate,
Henry Chisling, Steward,
Joseph A. Washington, Cook,
William Laing, Seaman, New York,
George Whitworth, Seaman, New York,
William Lintern, Seaman, New York,
Joseph Frank, Seaman, Spain,
Joseph Collagen, Seaman, Spain,
Charles Beale, Seaman, New York.

2nd. Mate's Boat:
John H. Parr, Master, North Shields (England),
B. Lawson, Carpenter, Sweden
Jachim Bekuke, Hamburg, [Joachim Betinke]
John Noldt, Hamburg,
A.J. Anderson, Sweden,
James A. Mathson, Denmark,
Peter Paulson, Denmark.

MONDAY, JUNE 18

CALIFORNIA NEWSPAPER EXTRACT:

THE LOSS OF THE *HORNET.* —

The entire loss of the American ship *Hornet*, bound from New York to San Francisco, has already been alluded to in our columns. An affecting incident in connection with this loss is related by Mr. Howes.* An old man, whose son was one of the crew of the lost ship, had repeatedly called at the office of the consignees to ask for tidings of her and gone away disappointed. On the day of the arrival of the news of the loss, he came in as the letter of the Captain** was being read, and stood by the side of the reader too deeply anxious to trust his voice to ask a question, the while with suppressed breath, glancing eagerly down the page. At last his eye fell on the name of his son among the saved, and with the exclamation, "Thank God, my son is spared to me!" fainted from excess of emotion. The letter, which contains all that is known of the shipwreck and subsequent sufferings of the crew, is as follows: [quoted above]

* *of George Howes & Company, San Francisco, consignees of the HORNET.*

** *Captain Mitchell's letter from Laupahoehoe of June 18, 1866.*

Copy of Henry's Letter:

> Laupahoehoe
> June 18th., 1866

Dear Father:

   You will have learned by telegraph of our arrival and most merciful preservation but thinking that you would like to hear more particulars I will try as much as my head will allow me to make use of the chance, so that the packet that carries the telegram may also take this to the States. It is of course entirely useless to attempt to say anything in regard to our feelings so I will just put down a short sketch and when we have recovered our strength write more fully. It approaches nearer to a miracle than anything I ever heard of and in everything we have been most wonderfully protected by God's mighty arm. We had a most delightful passage in the poor *Hornet* everybody vieing with each other in showing us kindness and Capt. Mitchell being kinder than words can express. The weather favored us and we crossed the line 25 days from New York. The first night was the worst in the whole passage. It was an ugly Southeast gale with snow and rain which drove us back from the offing we had obtained in the day to thirty fathom water when providentially it shifted to the West and discomfort and sea sickness were the only evil result. From the Line to fifty South on the Atlantic side was a slow time but we reached that latitude on the 17 March and were wonderfully favored rounding the Cape having a fair wind all the time and making the passage from fifty to fifty (which is generally accomplished in 18 or 20 days) in only 9. From there we had fine weather, one tolerable Southwester perhaps excepted, all the way to the Line except that it was provokingly calm and rather slow. However, the kindness and fatherly care of the Captain made it pleasant to us and when we crossed the equator on the 30th. of April we were expecting in three more pleasant weeks to arrive in San Francisco. But on the 3rd of May early in the morning the Mate of the ship had occasion to draw some varnish (which contrary to orders was between decks).

He recklessly went with an open lamp, it ignited, and in a few minutes the ship was in flames. There was no chance of saving her, the flames got such headway, so we all had to take to the boats of which fortunately there were three, Sam and I went with the Captain first into one of the quarter boats and, when he arranged matters, into the longboat. We had when we left the ship I suppose provisions and water for the full thirty-one of us for about ten or twelve days consisting of pork, 4 hams, some hard bread, cans of meat, and ½ box raisins. We kept all three boats together from the third to the nineteenth steering East of North in Doldrums and dreadful weather all the time. Frightful nights with thunder, lightning, and drenching rain, and scorching sun by day. However, it was the rain we caught in them that preserved our lives.

By the end of this time we found it was impossible to continue towing the boats so on the 19th we separated from the Mate, dividing stores and water *pro rata*, he having nine in his boat, the Second Mate, seven and we fourteen. On the Sunday night following we took the "Trades" and, as they came pretty stiff, found we would have to part company with the Second Mate also, so divided with him the remaining stores and took one of his men out of his boat.

We then parted and as we were faster and also could lay to the windward closer than they, soon lost sight. Poor men. We hope and pray that they have been picked up but if they were not in the first three or four days after we separated I fear they are gone as there arose a very heavy sea which I do not think they could have stood. We were all of us then heading for Clarion Island, Lat. 18° 12′, Longitude 114° West, but the "Trades" instead of coming from the Eastward came nearly North and were accompanied by such a sea that it would have been suicide to attempt to beat our boat which was like a bowl against it. So on the 30th. having spun out our provisions wonderfully with great care and with the fish and birds we caught,

Two modern views of Laupahoehoe showing the reefs through which longboat sailed and Betty Ferguson McCance looking over longboat landing place 100 years after the event. Tom McCance photos, 1966.

we changed our course to West running as a last and forlorn hope for a cluster of islands mentioned in the epitome and laid down in the map of Sam's (which was the only one we had) as doubtful. We ran a week for them and found they were not there and with a hope that, by God's providence, some of us at least might linger in the bottom of the boat, on Thursday the 7th of this month we shaped our course for Hawaii having left of our provisions for fifteen men for 1000 miles a little more than the knuckle of ham and one can of soup and bouilli, nothing else. God favored us with wind and kept us for over a week on this while it lasted and for four days on nothing but a couple of gills of water and such nourishment as could be extracted from greasy rags and boot leather. Friday noon we were gladdened with the sight of land and by 4:30 P.M. landed at this little settlement of natives. There is one white man, Mr. Jones, who has treated us with more kindness than I ever supposed a man could and spares not every trouble for our own good. We were all very much exhausted and could hardly move and are still here (Sam, Captain and myself) though the men have been sent to the Consul's agent. We are all very weak but I think are improving fast and intend to go to Hilo when we have recovered strength with rest and repose here where the people are so kind to us. Sam's cough improved a good deal during the voyage but was not entirely gone when the accident happened. Thank God I think it is no worse than when the ship burned but he is weak and will, as well as all, need much rest and recruiting. I am afraid to write more. Thank God for us. God bless you all.

Your loving Son
(Signed) Henry Ferguson

P.S. Sam has stood it wonderfully by God's grace and I trust will soon regarn his strength, which he had picked up a great deal aboard ship. I never saw such trust and faith as were his when we were in the boat - H.F.

MONDAY, JUNE 18

Copy of Samuel's Letter:

Dear Home Ones —

Henry has written so fully I will not try to add anything till next mail as I have to write to Mr. LeGrain to ask him to send this telegram [telegram sent July 15th.] You will see by the papers the mode of communication is so hard from these islands and it is useless to make a long story now. Henry's youth and vitality and trust have kept him up wonderfully and he will pick up very fast. You cannot imagine what a miraculous deliverance we have had and how thankful we are and should be.

Yours, Saml. F--

Copy of Letter to Mr. LeGrain written in the back of Samuel Ferguson's Journal:

Mr. Le Grain. Dear Sir:

Please dispatch the enclosed telegraph to Messrs. J. & S. Ferguson, 25 Pine Street, New York, as soon as possible and also please honor any draft up to $500 I may draw. My father has probably communicated with you in regard to this matter long ere this.

Yours sincerely
S. Ferguson

(The Telegram)

To   Messrs Ferguson
     New York

We are saved; in good hands, and doing well.

                         Samuel
Will proceed to San Francisco as prudence allows and report progress.

Mark Twain's Letter No. 14 to the Sacramento *Daily Union*, Postscript.*
(Published July 16, 1866)

                                        Honolulu, June 22, 1866

A letter arrived here yesterday morning giving a meager account of the arrival on the island of Hawaii of nineteen [15] poor starving wretches, who had been buffeting a stormy sea in an open boat for forty-three days! Their ship, the *Hornet*, from New York, with a quantity of kerosene on board, had taken fire and burned in latitude 2^O North and longitude 135° West. Think of their sufferings for forty-three days and nights, exposed to the scorching heat of the center of the torrid zone, and at the mercy of a ceaseless storm! When they had been entirely out of provisions for a day or two and the cravings of hunger became insupportable, they yielded to the shipwrecked mariner's final and fearful alternative, and solemnly drew lots to determine who of their number should die to furnish food for his comrades** — and then the morning mists lifted and they saw land. They are being cared for at Sanpohoihoi [Laupahoehoe], a little seaside station I spent a night at two weeks ago. This boatload was in charge of the Captain of the *Hornet*. He reports that the remainder of the persons in his ship (twenty in number) left her in two boats, under command of the first and second mates, and the three boats kept company until the night of the nineteenth day, when they got separated. No further particulars have arrived here yet, and no confirmation of the above sad story.

---

* *Quoted in full in MARK TWAIN'S LETTERS FROM HAWAII, edited by A. Grove Day (New York, 1966), pages 135 - 136. A truncated version is in Albert Bigelow Paine's LETTERS OF MARK TWAIN (2 vols. New York, 1917), pages 113 - 114).*

** *Fortunately the plan to engage in cannibalism never reached this stage.*

Mark Twain's Letter to Mrs. Jane Clemens and Mrs. Moffet in St. Louis*

                                        Honolulu, June 27, 1866

. . . I got the whole story from the Third Mate and two of the sailors. If my account gets to the *Sacramento Union* first it will be *published* first all over the U.S., France, England, Russia, and Germany — all over the world, I may say. You will see it. Mr. Burlingame** went with me all the time, and helped me question the men — throwing away invitations to dinner with the princes and foreign dignitaries, and neglecting all sorts of things to accommodate me . . .

---

* *Paine, LETTERS, page 108. He notes: Twain laid up with saddle boils, carried on a stretcher to the hospital for interview "securing material for the most important piece of serious writing he had thus far performed." (Same, pages 113-114)*

** *Anson Burlingame, United States Minister to China, who with General Van Valkenburgh, United States Minister to Japan, was making a fourteen-day stopover visit in Hawaii en route to the Orient. Of Burlingame Mark Twain wrote: he "is a man who would be esteemed, respected, and popular anywhere, no matter whether he were among Christians or cannibals." See Henry Ferguson's Journal for July 4.*

Mark Twain as a young man. Photo from Mark Twain memorial, Hartford.

SACRAMENTO DAILY UNION
JULY 19, 1866

LETTER FROM HONOLULU.

(CORRESPONDENCE OF THE UNION.)

**BURNING OF THE CLIPPER SHIP
HORNET AT SEA.**

Detailed Account of the Sufferings of Officers and Crew, as given by the Third Officer and Members of the Crew.

Honolulu, June 25, 1866.

In the postscript to a letter which I wrote two or three days ago, and sent by the ship *Live Yankee*,* I gave you the substance of a letter received here. from Hilo by Walker, Allen & Co., informing them that a boat containing fifteen men, in a helpless and starving condition, had

---

* *The wooden bark Live Yankee, 338 tons, was built at Bath, Maine in 1854, and was owned by J. J. Marks & Co., San Francisco.*

drifted ashore at Laupahoehoe, Island of Hawaii, and that they had belonged to the clipper ship *Hornet*, Mitchell master, and had been afloat on the ocean since the burning of that vessel, about one hundred miles north of the equator, on the 3d of May — forty-three days.

The third mate and ten of the seamen have arrived here and are now in the hospital. Captain Mitchell, one seaman named Antonio Possene, and two passengers (Samuel and Henry Ferguson, of New York city, young gentlemen aged respectively 28 and 18) are still at Hilo, but are expected here within the week.

In the Captain's modest epitome of this terrible romance, which you have probably published, you detect the fine old hero through it. It reads like Grant.

Courtesy California State Library

The Third Mate.

I have talked with the seamen and with John S. Thomas, third mate, but their accounts are so nearly alike in all substantial points, that I will merely give the officer's statement and weave into it such matters as the men mentioned in the way of incidents, experiences, emotions, etc. Thomas is a very intelligent and a very cool and self-possessed young man, and seems to have kept a pretty accurate log of his remarkable voyage in his head. He told his story, of three hours length, in a plain, straightforward way, and with no attempt at display and no straining after effect. Wherever any incident may be noted in this paper where any individual has betrayed any emotion, or enthusiasm, or has departed from strict, stoical self-possession, or had a solitary thought that was not an utterly unpoetical and essentially practical one, remember that Thomas, the third mate, was not that person. He has been eleven days on shore, and already looks sufficiently sound and healthy to pass almost anywhere without being taken for an invalid. He has the marks of a hard experience about him though, when one looks closely. He is very much sunburned and weather-beaten, and looks thirty-two years old. He is only twenty-four, however, and has been a sailor fifteen years. He was born in Richmond, Maine, and still considers that place his home.

Sailing of the *"Hornet"* — Pacific Railroad Iron.

The following is the substance of what Thomas said: The *Hornet* left New York on the 15th of January last, unusually well manned, fitted and provisioned — as fast and as handsome a clipper ship as ever sailed out of that port. She had a general cargo — a little of everything; a large quantity of kerosene oil in barrels; several hundred cases of candles; also four hundred tons Pacific Railroad iron and three engines. The third mate thinks they were dock engines, and one of the seamen thought they were locomotives. Had no gales and no bad weather; nothing but fine sailing weather, and she went along steadily and well — fast, very fast, in fact. Had uncommonly good weather off Cape Horn; he had been around that Cape seven times — each way — and had never seen such fine weather there before. On the 12th of April, in latitude, say, 35° south and longitude 95° west, signaled a Prussian bark; she set Prussian ensign, and the *Hornet* responded with her name, expressed by means of Merritt's system of signals. She was sailing west — probably bound for Australia. This was the last vessel ever seen by the *Hornet's* people until they floated ashore at Hawaii in the long boat — a space of sixty-four days.

The Ship on Fire.

At seven o'clock on the morning of the 3d of May, the chief mate and two men started down into the hold to draw some "bright varnish" from a cask. The captain told him to bring the cask on deck — that it was dangerous to have it where it was, in the hold. The mate, instead of obeying the order, proceeded to draw a can full of the varnish first. He had an "open light" in his hand, and the liquid took fire; the can was dropped, the officer in his consternation neglected to close the bung, and in a few seconds the fiery torrent had run in every direction, under bales of rope, cases of candles, barrels of kerosene, and all sorts of freight, and tongues of flame were shooting upward through every aperture and crevice toward the deck.

The ship was moving along under easy sail, the watch on duty were idling here and there in such shade as they could find, and the listlessness and repose of morning in the tropics was upon the vessel and her belongings. But as six bells chimed, the cry of "Fire!" rang through the ship, and woke every man to life and action. And following the fearful warning, and almost as fleetly, came the fire itself. It sprang through hatchways, seized upon chairs, table, cordage, anything, everything — and almost before the bewildered men could realize what the trouble was and what was to be done the cabin was a hell of angry flames. The mainmast was on fire — its rigging was burnt asunder! One man said all this had happened within eighteen or twenty minutes after the first alarm — two others say in ten minutes. All say that one hour after the alarm, the main and mizzenmasts were burned in two and fell overboard.

Captain Mitchell ordered the three boats to be launched instantly, which was done — and so hurriedly that the longboat (the one he left the vessel in himself) had a hole as large as a man's head stove in her bottom. A blanket was stuffed into the opening and fastened to its place. Not a single thing was saved, except such food and other articles as lay about the cabin and could be quickly seized and thrown on deck. Thomas was sent into the longboat to receive its proportion of these things, and, being barefooted at the time, and bareheaded, and having no clothing on save an undershirt and pantaloons, of course he never got a chance afterward to add to his dress. He lost everything he had, including his log-book, which he had faithfully kept from the first. Forty minutes after the fire alarm the provisions and passengers were on board the three boats, and they rowed away from the ship — and to some distance, too, for the heat was very great. Twenty minutes afterward the two masts I have mentioned, with their rigging and their broad sheets of canvas wreathed in flames, crashed into the sea.

All night long the thirty-one unfortunates sat in their frail boats and watched the gallant ship burn; and felt as men feel when they see a tried friend perishing and are powerless to help him. The sea was illuminated for miles around, and the clouds above were tinged with a ruddy hue; the faces of the men glowed in the strong light as they shaded their eyes with their hands and peered out anxiously upon the wild picture, and the gunwales of the boats and the idle oars shone like polished gold.

At five o'clock on the morning after the disaster, in latitude 2° 20′ north, longitude 112° 8′ west, the ship went down, and the crew of the *Hornet* were alone on the great deep, or, as one of the seamen expressed it. "We felt as if somebody or something had gone away — as if we hadn't any home any more."

Captain Mitchell divided his boat's crew into two watches and gave the third mate charge of one and took the other himself. He had saved a studding sail from the ship, and out of this the men fashioned a rude sail with their knives; they hoisted it, and taking the first and second mates' boats in tow, they bore away upon the ship's course (northwest) and kept in the track of vessels bound to or from San Francisco, in the hope of being picked up.

Their Water, Provisions, Etc.

I have said that in the few minutes time allowed him, Captain Mitchell was only able to seize upon the few articles of food and other necessaries that happened to lie about the cabin. Here is the list: Four hams, seven pieces of salt pork (each piece weighed about four pounds), one box of raisins, 100 pounds of bread (about one barrel), twelve two-pound cans of oysters, clams and assorted meats; six buckets of raw potatoes (which rotted so fast they got but little benefit from them), a keg with four pounds of butter in it, twelve gallons of water in a forty-gallon tierce or "scuttle-butt," four one-gallon demijohns full of water, three bottles of brandy, the property of passengers; some pipes, matches and a hundred pounds of tobacco; had no medicines. That was all these poor fellows had to live on for forty-three days — the whole thirty-one of them!

Each boat had a compass, a quadrant, a copy of Bowditch's *Navigator* and a nautical almanac, and the captain's and chief mate's boats had chronometers.

Rations

Of course, all hands were put on short allowance at once. The day they set sail from the ship each man was allowed a small morsel of salt pork — or a little piece of potato, if he preferred it — and half a sea biscuit three times a day. To understand how very light this ration of bread was, it is only necessary to know that it takes seven of these sea biscuits to weigh a pound. The first two days they only allowed one gill of water a day to each man; but for nearly a fortnight after that the weather was lowering and stormy, and frequent rain squalls occurred. The rain was caught in canvas, and whenever there was a shower the forty-gallon cask and every other vessel that would hold water was filled — even all the boots that were water-tight were pressed into this service, except such as the matches and tobacco were deposited in to keep dry. So for fourteen days. There were luxurious occasions when there was plenty of water to drink. But after that how they suffered the agonies of thirst for four long weeks!

Hoping against Hope.

For seven days the boats sailed on, and the starving men eat their fragment of biscuit and their morsel of raw pork in the morning, and hungrily counted the tedious hours until noon and night should bring their repetitions of it. And in the long intervals they looked mutely into each other's faces, or turned their wistful eyes across the wild sea in search of the succoring sail that was never to come.

"Didn't you ·talk?" I asked one of the men.

"No; we were too down-hearted — that is, the first week or more. We didn't talk — we only looked at each other and over the ocean."

And thought, I suppose. Thought of home — of shelter from storms — of food, and drink, and rest.

The hope of being picked up hung to them constantly — was ever present to them, and in their thoughts, like hunger. And in the Captain's mind was the hope of making the Clarion Islands, and he clung to it many a day.

The nights were very dark. They had no lantern and could not see the compass, and there were no stars to steer by. Thomas said, of the boat, "She handled easy, and we steered by the feel of the wind in our faces and the heave of the sea." Dark, and dismal, and lonesome work was that! Sometimes they got a fleeting glimpse of the sailor's friend, the north star, and then they lighted a match and hastened anxiously to see if their compass was faithful to them — for it had to be placed close to an iron ringbolt in the stern, and they were afraid, during those first nights, that this might cause it to vary. It proved true to them, however.

Sumptuous Fare.

On the fifth day a notable incident occurred. They caught a dolphin! and while their enthusiasm was still at its highest over their stroke of good fortune, they captured another. They made a trifling fire in a tin plate and warmed the prizes — to cook them was not possible — and divided them equitably among all hands and eat them.

On the sixth day two more dolphins were caught.

Two more were caught on the seventh day, and also a small bonita, and they began to believe they were always going to live in this extravagant way; but it was not to be; these were their last dolphins, and they never could get another bonita, though they saw them and longed for them often afterward.

Rations Reduced.

On the eighth day the rations were reduced about one-half. Thus — breakfast, one-fourth of a biscuit, an ounce of ham and a gill of water to each man; dinner, same quantity of bread and water, and four oysters or clams; supper, water and bread the same, and twelve large raisins or fourteen small ones, to a man. Also, during the first twelve or fifteen days, each man had one spoonful of brandy a day, then it gave out.

This day, as one of the men was gazing across the dull waste of waters as usual, he saw a small, dark object rising and falling upon the waves. He called attention to it, and in a moment every eye was bent upon it in intensest interest. When the boat had approached a little nearer, it was discovered that it was a small green turtle, fast asleep. Every noise was hushed as they crept upon the unconscious slumberer. Directions were given and hopes and fears expressed in guarded whispers. At the fateful moment — a moment of tremendous consequence to these famishing men — the expert selected for the high and responsible office stretched forth his hand, while his excited comrades bated their breath and trembled for the success of the enterprise, and seized the turtle by the hind leg and handed him aboard! His delicate flesh was carefully divided among the party and eagerly devoured — after being "warmed" like the dolphins which went before him.

The Boats Separate.

After the eighth day I have ten days unaccounted for — no notes of them save that the men say they had their two or three ounces of food and their gill of water three times a day — and then the same weary watching for a saving sail by day and by night, and the same sad "Hope deferred that maketh the heart sick," was their monotonous experience. They talked more, however, and the Captain labored without ceasing to keep them cheerful. (They have always a word of praise for the "old man.")

The eighteenth day was a memorable one to the wanderers on the lonely sea. On that day the boats parted company. The Captain said that separate from each other there were three chances for the saving of some of the party where there could be but one chance if they kept together.

The magnanimity and utter unselfishness of Captain Mitchell (and through his example, the same conduct in his men) throughout this distressing voyage, are among its most amazing features. No disposition was ever shown by the strong to impose upon the weak, and no greediness, no desire on the part of any to get more than his just share of food, was ever evinced. On the contrary, they were thoughtful of each other and always ready to care for and assist each other to the utmost of their ability. When the time came to part company, Captain Mitchell and his crew, although theirs was much the more numerous party (fifteen men to nine and seven respectively in the other boats), took only one-third of the meager amount of provisions still left, and passed over the other two-thirds to be divided up between the other crews; these men could starve, if need be, but they seem not to have known how to be mean.

After the division the Captain had left for his boat's share two-thirds of the ham, one-fourth of a box of raisins, half a bucket of biscuit crumbs, fourteen gallons of water, three cans of "soup-and-bully." (That last expression of the third mate's occurred frequently during his narrative,

and bothered me so painfully with its mysterious incomprehensibility, that at length I begged him to explain to me what this dark and dreadful "soup-and-bully" might be. With the Consul's assistance he finally made me understand the French dish known as "soup bouillon" is put up in cans like preserved meats, and the American sailor is under the impression that its name is a sort of general title which describes any description of edible whatever which is hermetically sealed in a tin vessel, and with that high contempt for trifling conventionalities which distinguishes his class, he has seen fit to modify the pronunciation into "soup-and-bully" — Mark.)

The Captain told the mates he was still going to try to make the Clarion Isles, and that they could imitate his example if they thought best, but he wished them to freely follow the dictates of their own judgment in the matter. At eleven o'clock in the forenoon the boats were all cast loose from each other, and then, as friends part from friends whom they expect to meet no more in life, all hands hailed with a fervent "God bless you, boys; Good-bye!" and the two cherished sails drifted away and disappeared from the longing gaze that followed them so sorrowfully.

Another Capture.

On the afternoon of this eventful eighteenth day two "boobies" were caught — a bird about as large as a duck, but all bone and feathers — not as much meat as there is on a pigeon — not nearly so much, the men say. They eat them raw — bones, entrails and everything — no single morsel was wasted; they were carefully apportioned among the fifteen men. No fire could be built for cooking purposes — the wind was so strong and the sea ran so high that it was all a man could do to light his pipe.

A Good Friend Gone.

At even tide the wanderers missed a cheerful spirit — a plucky, strong-hearted fellow, who never drooped his head or lost his grip — a staunch and true good friend, who was always at his post in storm or calm, in rain or shine — who scorned to say die, and yet was never afraid to die — a little trim and taut old rooster, he was, who starved with the rest, but came on watch in the stern-sheets promptly every day at four in the morning and six in the evening for eighteen days and crowed like a maniac! Right well they named him Richard of the Lion Heart! One of the men said with honest feeling: "As true as I'm a man, Mr. Mark Twain, if that rooster was here to-day and any man dared to abuse the bird, I'd break his neck!" Richard was esteemed by all and by all his rights were respected. He received his little ration of bread crumbs every time the men were fed, and, like them, he bore up bravely and never grumbled and never gave way to despair. As long as he was strong enough, he stood in the sternsheets or mounted the gunwale as regularly as his watch came round, and crowed his two-hour talk, and when at last he grew feeble in the legs and had to stay below, his heart was still stout and he slapped about in the water on the bottom of the boat and crowed as bravely as ever! He felt that under circumstances like these America expects every rooster to do his duty, and he did it. But is it not to the high honor of that boat's crew of starving men, that, tortured day and night by the pangs of hunger as they were, they refused to appease them with the blood of their humble comrade? Richard was transferred to the chief mate's boat and sailed away on the eighteenth day.

Religious Services.

The third mate does not remember distinctly, but thinks morning and evening prayers were begun on the nineteenth day. They were conducted by one of the young Fergusons, because the Captain could not read the prayer-book without his spectacles, and they had been burned with the ship. And even after this date, at the rising of the sun, the storm-tossed mariners reverently bowed their heads while prayers went up for "they that are helpless and far at sea."

An Incident.

On the morning of the twenty-first day, while some of the crew were dozing on the thwarts and others were buried in reflection, one of the men suddenly sprang to his feet and cried, "A sail! a sail!" Of course, sluggish blood bounded then and eager eyes were turned to seek the welcome vision. But disappointment was their portion, as usual. It was only the chief mate's boat drifting across their path after three days absence. In a short time the two parties were abreast each other and in hailing distance. They talked twenty minutes; and the mate reported "all well" and then sailed away, and they never saw him afterward.

Further Reduction of Rations.

On the twenty-fourth day Captain Mitchell took an observation and found that he was in latitude 16° north and longitude 117° west — about 1,000 miles from where his vessel was burned. The hope he had cherished so long that he would be able to make the Clarion Isles deserted him at last; he could only go before the wind, and he was now obliged to attempt the best thing the southeast trades could do for him — blow him to the "American group" or to the Sandwich Islands — and therefore he reluctantly and with many misgivings turned his prow towards those distant archipelagoes. Not many mouthfuls of food were left, and these must be economized. The third mate said that under this new programme of proceedings "we could see that we were living too high; we had got to let up on them raisins, or the soup-and-bullies, one, because it stood to reason that we warn't going to make land soon, and so they wouldn't last." It was a matter which had few humorous features about it to them, and yet a smile is almost pardonable at this idea, so gravely expressed, of "living high" on fourteen raisins at a meal.

The rations remained the same as fixed on the eighth day, except that only two meals a day were allowed, and occasionally the raisins and oysters were left out.

What these men suffered during the next three weeks no mortal man may hope to describe. Their stomachs and intestines felt to the grasp like a couple of small tough balls, and the gnawing hunger pains and the dreadful thirst that was consuming them in these burning latitudes became almost insupportable. And yet, as the men say, the Captain said funny things and talked cheerful talk until he got them to conversing freely, and then they used to spend hours together describing delicious dinners they had eaten at home, and earnestly planning interminable and preposterous bills of fare for dinners they were going to eat on shore, if they ever lived through their troubles to do it, poor fellows. The Captain said plain bread and butter would be good enough for him all the days of his life, if he could only get it.

But the saddest things were the dreams they had. An unusually intelligent young sailor named Cox said: "In those long days and nights we dreamed all the time — not that we ever slept, I don't mean — no, we only sort of dozed — three-fourths of the faculties awake and the other fourth benumbed into the counterfeit of a slumber; oh, no — some of us never slept for twenty-three days, and no man ever saw the Captain asleep for upward of thirty. But we barely dozed that way and dreamed — and always of such feasts! bread, and fowls, and meat — everything a man could think of, piled upon long tables, and smoking hot! And we sat down and seized upon the first dish in our reach, like ravenous wolves, and carried it to our lips, and — and then we woke up and found the same starving comrades about us, and the vacant sky and the desolate sea!"

These things are terrible even to think of.

Rations Still Further Reduced.

It even startles me to come across that significant heading so often in my notebook, notwithstanding I have grown so familiar with its sound by talking so much with these unfortunate men.

On the twenty-eighth day the rations were: One teaspoonful of bread crumbs and about an ounce of ham for the morning meal; a spoonful of bread crumbs alone for the evening meal, and one gill of water three times a day! A kitten would perish eventually under such sustenance.

At this point the third mate's mind reverted painfully to an incident of the early stages of their sufferings. He said there were two between decks, on board the *Hornet*, who had been lying there sick and helpless for he didn't know how long; but when the ship took fire they turned out as lively as any one under the spur of the excitement. One was a "Portyghee," he said, and always of a hungry disposition; when all the provisions that could be got had been brought aft and deposited near the wheel to be lowered into the boats; "that sick Portyghee watched his chance, and when nobody was looking he harnessed the provisions and eat up nearly a quarter of a bar'l of bread before the old man caught him, and he had more than two notions to put his light out." The third mate dwelt upon this circumstance as upon a wrong he could not fully forgive, and intimated that the Portyghee stole bread enough, if economized in twenty-eighth-day rations, to have run the long-boat party three months.

They Capture a Prize.

Four little flying fish, the size of the sardines of these latter days, flew into the boat on the night of the twenty-eighth day. They were divided among all hands and devoured raw. On the twenty-ninth day they caught another, and divided it into fifteen pieces, less than a teaspoonful apiece.

On the thirtieth day they caught a third flying fish and gave it to the revered old Captain — a fish of the same poor little proportions as the others — four inches long — a present a king might be proud of under such circumstances — a present whose value, in the eyes of the men who offered it, was not to be found in the Bank of England — yea, whose vaults were not able to contain it! The old Captain refused to take it; the men insisted; the Captain said no — he would take his fifteenth - - they must take the remainder. They said in substance, though not in words, that they would see him in Jericho first! So the Captain had to eat the fish.

I believe I have done the third mate some little wrong in the beginning of this letter. I have said he was as self-possessed as a statue — that he never betrayed emotion or enthusiasm. He never did except when he spoke of "the old man." It always thawed through his ice then. The men were the same way; the Captain is their hero — their true and faithful friend, whom they delight to honor. I said to one of these infatuated skeletons, "But you wouldn't go quite so far as to die for him?" A snap of the finger — "As quick as that! — I wouldn't be alive now if it hadn't been for him." We pursued the subject no further.

Rations Still Further Reduced.

I still claim the public's indulgence and belief. At least Thomas and his men do through me. About the thirty-second day the bread gave entirely out. There was nothing left, now, but mere odds and ends of their stock of provisions. Five days afterward, on the thirty-seventh day — latitude 16° 30′ north, and longitude 170° west — kept off for the "American group" — "which don't exist and never will, I suppose," said the third mate. Ran directly over the ground said to be occupied by these islands — that is, between latitude 16° and 17° north, and longitude 133° to 136° west. Ran over the imaginary islands and got into 136° west, and then the Captain made a dash for Hawaii, resolving that he would go till he fetched land, or at any rate as long as he and his men survived.

The Last Ration!

On Monday, the thirty-eighth day after the disaster, "we had nothing left," said the third mate, "but a pound and a half of ham — the bone was a good deal the heaviest part of it — and one soup-and-bully tin." These things were divided among the fifteen men, and they ate it all — two ounces of food to each man. I do not count the ham bone, as that was saved for next day. For some time, now, the poor wretches had been cutting their old boots into small pieces and eating them. They would also pound wet rags to a sort of pulp and eat them.

Starvation Fare.

On the thirty-ninth day the ham bone was divided up into rations, and scraped with knives and eaten. I said: "You say

the two sick men remained sick all through, and after awhile two or three had to be relieved from standing watch; how did you get along without medicines!"

The reply was: "Oh, we couldn't have kept them if we'd had them; if we'd had boxes of pills, or anything like that, we'd have eaten them. It was just as well — we couldn't have kept them, and we couldn't have given them to the sick men alone — we'd have shared them around all alike, I guess." It was said rather in jest, but it was a pretty true jest, no doubt.

After apportioning the ham bone, the Captain cut the canvas cover that had been around the ham into fifteen equal pieces, and each man took his portion. This was the last division of food the Captain made. The men broke up the small oaken butter tub and divided the staves among themselves, and gnawed them up. The shell of the little green turtle, heretofore mentioned, was scraped with knives and eaten to the last shaving. The third mate chewed pieces of boots and spit them out, but eat nothing except the soft straps of two pairs of boots — eat three on the thirty-ninth day and saved one for the fortieth.

The Awful Alternative.

The men seem to have thought in their minds of the shipwrecked mariner's last dreadful resort — cannibalism; but they do not appear to have conversed about it. They only thought of the casting lots and killing one of their number as a possibility; but even when they were eating rags, and bone, and boots, and shell, and hard oak wood, they seem to have still had a notion that it was remote. They felt that some one of the company must die soon — which one they well knew; and during the last three or four days of their terrible voyage they were patiently but hungrily waiting for him. I wonder if the subject of these anticipations knew what they were thinking of? He must have known it — he must have felt it. They had even calculated how long he would last; they said to themselves, but not to each other, I think they said, "He will die Saturday — and then!"

There was one exception to the spirit of delicacy I have mentioned — a Frenchman, who kept an eye of strong personal interest upon the sinking man and noted his failing strength with untiring care and some degree of cheerfulness. He frequently said to Thomas: "I think he will go off pretty soon, now sir. And then we'll eat him!" This is very sad.

Thomas and also several of the men state that the sick "Portyghee," during the five days that they were entirely out of provisions, actually eat two silk handkerchiefs and a couple of cotton shirts, besides his share of the boots, and bones, and lumber.

The Captain's Birthday.

Captain Mitchell was fifty-six years old on the 12th of June — the fortieth day after the burning of the ship and the third day before the boat's crew reached land. He said it looked somewhat is if it might be the last one he was going to enjoy. He had no birthday feast except some bits of ham-canvas — no luxury but this, and no substantials save the leather and oaken bucket staves.

Speaking of the leather diet, one of the men told me he was obliged to eat a pair of boots which were so old and rotten that they were full of holes; and then he smiled gently and said he didn't know, though, but what the holes tasted about as good as the balance of the boot. This man was still very feeble, and after saying this he went to bed.

Land Ho!

At eleven o'clock on the 15th of June, after suffering all that men may suffer and live for forty-three days, in an open boat, on a scorching tropical sea, one of the men feebly shouted the glad tidings, "Land ho!" The "watch below" were lying in the bottom of the boat. What do you suppose they did? They said they had been cruelly disappointed over and over again, and they dreaded to risk another experience of the kind — they could not bear it — they lay still where they were. They said they would not trust to an appearance that might not be land after all. They would wait.

Shortly it was proven beyond question that they were almost to land. Then there was joy in the party. One man is said to have swooned away. Another said the sight of the green hills was better to him than a day's rations, a strange figure for a man to use who had been fasting for forty days and forty nights.

The land was the island of Hawaii, and they were off Laupahoehoe and could see nothing in shore but breakers. I was there a week or two ago and it is a very dangerous place. When they got pretty close to shore they saw cabins, but no human beings. They thought they would lower the sail and try to work in with the oars. They cut the ropes and the sail came down, and then they found they were not strong enough to ship the oars. They driften helplessly toward the breakers, but looked listlessly on and cared not a straw for the violent death which seemed about to overtake them after all their manful struggles, their privations and their terrible sufferings. They said "it was good to see the green fields again." It was all they cared for. The "green fields" were a haven of rest for the weary wayfarers; it was sufficient; they were satisfied; it was nothing to them that death stood in their pathway; they had long been familiar to him; he had no terrors for them.

Two of Captain Spencer's natives saw the boat, knew by the appearance of things that it was in trouble, and dashed through the surf and swam out to it. When they climbed aboard there were only five yards of space between the poor sufferers and a sudden and violent death. Fifteen minutes afterward the boat was beached upon the shore and a crowd of natives (who are the very incarnation of generosity, unselfishness and hospitality) were around the strangers dumping bananas, melons, taro, poi — anything and everything they could scrape together that could be eaten — on the ground by the cart-load; and if Mr. Jones, of the station, had not hurried down with his steward, they would soon have killed the starving men with kindness. As it was, the sick "Portyghee" really eat six bananas before Jones could get hold of him and stop him. This is a fact. And so are the stories of his previous exploits. Jones and the Kanaka girls and men took the mariners in their arms like so many children and carried them up to the house, where they received kind and judicious attention until Sunday evening, when two whale-boats came from Hilo, Jones furnished a third, and they were taken in these to the town just named, arriving there at two o'clock Monday morning.

Remarks

Each of the young Fergusons kept a journal from the day the ship sailed from New York until they got on land once more at Hawaii. The Captain also kept a log every day he was adrift. These logs, by the Captain's direction, were to be kept up faithfully as long as any of the crew were alive, and the last survivor was to put them in a bottle, when he succumbed, and lash the bottle to the inside of the boat. The Captain gave a bottle to each officer of the other boats, with orders to follow his example. The old gentleman was always thoughtful.

The hardest berth in that boat, I think, must have been that of provision-keeper. This office was performed by the Captain and the third mate; of course they were always hungry. They always had access to the food, and yet must not gratify their craving appetites.

The young Fergusons are very highly spoken of by all the boat's crew, as patient, enduring, manly and kind-hearted gentle-men. The Captain gave them a watch to themselves — it was the duty of each to bail the water out of the boat three hours a day. Their home is in Stamford, Connecti-cut, but their father's place of business is New York.

In the chief mate's boat was a passenger — a gentlemanly young fellow of twenty years, named William Liang, son of a stock-broker in New York.*

The Chief mate, Samuel Hardy, lived at Chatham, Massachusetts; second mate be-longed in Shields, England; the cook, George Washington (negro), was in the chief mate's boat, and also the steward (negro); the carpenter was in the second mate's boat.

* *Laing was really a member of the crew, who was going to sea for experience.*

Captain Mitchell

To this man's good sense, cool judg-ment, perfect discipline, close attention to the smallest particulars which could con-duce to the welfare of his crew or render their ultimate rescue more probable, that boat's crew owe their lives. He has shown brain and ability that make him worthy to command the finest frigate in the United States, and a genuine unassuming heroism that entitle him to a Congressional medal. I suppose some of the citizens of San Francisco who know how to appreciate this kind of a man will not let him go on hungry forever after he gets there. In the above remarks I am only echoing the ex-pressed opinions of numbers of persons here who have never seen Captain Mitchell, but who judge him by his works — among others Hon. Anson Burlingame and our Minister to Japan, both of whom have called at the hospital several times and held long conversations with the men. Burlingame speaks in terms of the most un-qualified praise of Captain Mitchell's high and distinguished abilities as evinced at every point throughout his wonderful voy-age.

The Sick.

Captain Mitchell, one sailor, and the two Fergusons are still at Hilo. The two first mentioned are pretty feeble, from what I can learn. The Captain's sense of responsi-bility kept him strong and awake all through the voyage; but as soon as he landed, and that fearful strain upon his faculties was removed, he was prostrated — became the feeblest of the boat's company.

The seamen here are doing remarkably well, considering all things. They already walk about the hospital a little; and very stiff-legged, because of the long inaction their muscles have experienced.

When they came ashore at Hawaii no man in the party had had any movement of his bowels for eighteen days, several not for twenty-five or thirty, one not for thirty-seven, and one not for forty-four days. As soon as any of these men can travel they will be sent to San Francisco.

I have written this lengthy letter in a

great hurry in order to get it off by the bark *Milton Badger*,* if the thing be possible, and I may have made a good many mistakes, but I hardly think so. All the statistical information in it comes from Thomas, and he may have made mistakes, because he tells his story entirely from memory, and although he has naturally a most excellent one, it might well be pardoned for inaccuracies concerning events which transpired during a series of weeks that never saw his mind strongly fixed upon any thought save the weary longing for food and water. But the log-books of the Captain and the two passengers will tell the terrible romance from the first day to the last in faithful detail, and these I shall forward by the next mail if I am permitted to copy them.

* *The Schooner Milton Badger, 248 tons, was built in 1863 at Madison, Conn., and was owned by Capt. Miller of New Haven.*

MARK TWAIN.

Harper's Weekly woodcut of Sept. 29, 1866 showing Hornet *burning.
This full page woodcut accompanied a story based on Mark Twain's*
Sacramento Union *report of July 19.*

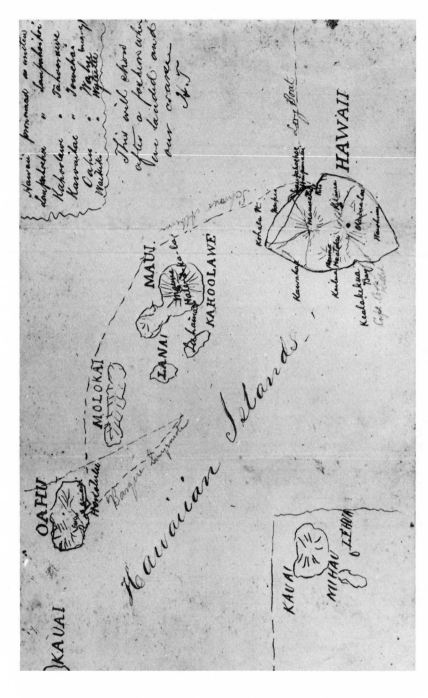

Map of Hawaiian Islands drawn by Henry Ferguson in his journal showing route Hilo to Honolulu.

PART VI—READJUSTMENT

SATURDAY, JUNE 16

Captain Mitchell's Journal:

Sent word by a gentleman to Consul at Hilo of our famished and destitute condition. Want medical assistance. Some of the men very bad today and in great pain. I feel about as yesterday, resigned, cannot sleep. The island seems to rock like the boat. My head confused.

Henry Ferguson's Journal:

These kind people gave us a delightful bed and night's rest, but we were too happy to sleep. The Captain had a little room and the same to Sam and me and bid the men sleep in the sitting room. We enjoyed the night but really feared that we might wake up and find ourselves in the boat again. Got up and washed to waist, got some clean clothes from Mr. Jones who has a small store here and we were lucky enough to save most of our money. Several times in the night they would look in to see if everything went on well with us. There came along an English traveller named Gaston who was on his way to Hilo. He will carry the news there to the consul. They treat us just as kindly as is possible and are doing everything in their power for our health and comfort. Some of the men are pretty bad suffering from the rags and boot-leather. I had a good deal of pain and nearly fainted tonight, but the purgative medicines they had given me have done the work. Sam and the Captain are better. I wish we could get these men off soon, as some of them already are horribly ungrateful. God be praised for conducting us to this little spot which seems like a Paradise to us. One of the men is very low with an abscess or something of that nature with which he was suffering before even we left the ship. Charles the steward here knows something of surgery and has doctored and cut him some and he is rather better.

Samuel Ferguson's Journal:

Suffered considerably.*

* *Crossed Out.*

SUNDAY, JUNE 17

Captain Mitchell's Journal:

Enjoyed a calm quiet sleep last night, the first I have known for a long time. A good passage this morning. Feel a great deal better today. A beautiful quiet holy day and have much to be thankful for. Brain troubles me some and I am very weak, yet I feel in hopes now that in the hands of these kind people I may recover. Men doing well.

Henry Ferguson's Journal:

Early this morning came persons from Hilo bringing nourishing food and boats to take the men thither, they will leave this evening. Sam, Captain and I stay here for a time to recruit with the quiet after they leave. It will be a relief to get rid of them as they are a tremendous source of anxiety both to the Captain and us, and our kind host. They are with some exceptions an ungrateful set of dogs. Natives and some white men came in to see us, one big Englishman tormenting us exceedingly with well meant but ill timed attentions. Feel all much better today. Kindnesses of our host unceasing. He has a native wife who speaks no English but whose kindness is unceasing as is that of all. Men got off after sunset very well. They are all doing well and even the very sick one is much better. This place is called Laupahoehoe. Can we ever be grateful enough to God for his infinite mercy.

Samuel Ferguson's Journal:

Men sent on at night in 3 whale boats to Hilo.

MONDAY, JUNE 18

Captain Mitchell's Journal:

All the men started for Hilo at seven o'clock last night, a great relief to me. The Consul [was] very kind to send so promptly for them. I am very weak today. No vitality, no blood, no moisture on my skin yet. Need medical aid to restore me. Hope after a day or two quiet, shall be able to get to Hilo. No sleep.

Henry Ferguson's Journal:

All better still today, though my health improves more rapidly than that of Samuel or Captain. They are well and are recovering their strength fully as well as could be expected. Medical treatment is I think necessary nevertheless, and as soon as they are strong enough we will go to Hilo where there is a good physician. Kindness unceasing from all. Very pleasant and quiet now the men are gone. Did up the job of writing today by the mail which passes through here tonight. I found that it tired me less than I expected but Sam only attempted a little. He coughs more than in the boat but I hope that it is only caused by the weakness. Boat came back from Hilo bringing news of safe arrival there of all the men, and bringing some provision. Also received from Consul at Hilo by mail tonight a letter saying they had arrived and some provisions that he had sent us.

Samuel Ferguson's Journal:

Improving but very weak and emaciated, weigh 81 pounds. Heard of men's safe arrival at Hilo from Consul there. Sent letter to Mr. Le Grain at San Francisco and telegraphed to New York. Henry wrote. I put in a slip.

TUESDAY, JUNE 19

Captain Mitchell's Journal:

Got a letter from Consul at Hilo. Men all arrived safe. Expressed great sympathy, desired me to command his services for anything I might want. Very kind indeed. Sent me little comforts. Wrote Consul at Honolulu to forward news [at the] first opportunity to San Francisco.

Brain troubles me today. Must be very quiet and careful. Nature is trying hard to resume her functioning. Wish I could consult a physician. No sleep. Have little better use of my legs. Everybody kind.

Henry Ferguson's Journal:

All gradually improving. I am much better. Sam's cough is I think better, but he worries about me which is not good for him. There is no stint in these good people's kindness. All walked down to the water side.

Samuel Ferguson's Journal:

Quiet day, gradually improving, can sleep very little though. Henry improves and has got quite strong.

WEDNESDAY, JUNE 20

Captain Mitchell's Journal:

Went to the dear old boat after dinner. Much affected. Longest walk yet, perhaps thirty rods. Bad night, no sleep, nervous, trouble with brain. Body gains faster than head. Kind letter from Captain Spencer at Hilo. Shall go there soon as able. Hope it will be soon. Eat too much here, diet bad.

Henry Ferguson's Journal:

The French bishop of Honolulu came here on his way thither accompanied by a priest from Hilo and brought a most kindhearted and wholesouled letter from Capt. Spencer proffering hospitality, which we will accept as Sam and Captain need medical care — Sam for head and body, and Captain for head. Boat with Frenchmen came in from Hilo at night to see after buying the longboat. Very cautious about telling his business. Captain sent letter to Captain Spencer to Hilo accepting his kind offer, and we probably will go up Friday night if well enough to stand the voyage.

Samuel Ferguson's Journal:

Captain had a most wholesouled letter from Captain Spencer of Hilo where we intend to repair on Friday if weather permits. He and I want medical treatment.

THURSDAY, JUNE 21

Captain Mitchell's Journal:

Pretty well today, symptoms good. Slept well last night. Senses and muscles seem to be relaxing the terrible tension that has so long held them. Head troubles me yet. Bargained for the boat to a Frenchman for $200 as she lies.

Henry Ferguson's Journal:

Captain and Sam had better night's rests and are better today. Sam in better spirits but his cough renders him nervous and anxious. He is gaining strength though faster than he thinks. Captain sold the boat to the men who came last night for $200. Some natives also wish to buy it and will try to get the bargain with the Hilo men and snap at their's. Hot but good breeze. Feel the warmth more now, than when my stomach was empty. Squally in afternoon so that we were unable to sit on the porch or to walk after dinner.

Samuel Ferguson's Journal:

Had a more quiet night last night than have had yet. My cough seems to have come back very badly, but hope strengthening up will take it away. Captain sold the boat today for $200 to a Hilo Frenchman. Henry has got almost quite as well as when he left the ship. Captain is also pretty well, better that is, stronger bodily than mentally. The present intention is to leave here tomorrow night if Capt. Spencer sends the boat and the weather suits for Hilo and remain his guest some little time and then work our ways on to Honolulu and San Francisco. Felt very weak and miserable all day. Really the worst I have felt, etc.

FRIDAY, JUNE 22

Captain Mitchell's Journal:

Consul at Hilo sent a boat for us. At 5 P.M. left the kind people at Laupahoehoe. May they never want for friends. Dying men never received such kind attention before. Arrived at Hilo at 12:30 midnight, wet with rain and cold. Received most kindly and well provided for. Retired at 2 A.M.

Memorandum in the back of Captain Mitchell's Journal:

Names at Laupahoehoe:

Charles Bartlett, John J. Jones, Mrs. J. Jones and sister. To the above I owe a debt that can never be paid on this earth for their exceeding kindness and attention to me in the weakened condition I was in when I first landed.

Henry Ferguson's Journal:

Boat arrived this morning from Capt. Spencer. New whale boat with good crew. Packed up and paid Mr. Jones for the outfit we got at his store, which he was unwilling to take, but did so as he saw we wanted it. Sam had a good night and is stronger and better today, and I think will stand the trip tonight very well. Captain well. I feel perfectly restored, Thank God, though my head is very weak and does not allow me to use it very much. I hope I cause Sam no uneasiness now on that score. Left Laupahoehoe at about 5 P.M. Sad parting with them. I hope we may have an opportunity of seeing them again, for it is to them, next to God that we owe our life, and the degree of health we have. We have a nice boat and strong crew and expect a pleasant six hours row along this lovely coast.

Samuel Ferguson's Journal:

Capt. Spencer's boat arrived about 9 A.M. this day, so most of the day has been spent in getting ready to leave, which is unexpressibly overcoming and hard as these simple people have been every kindness itself, putting themselves out for us and giving us everything needful.

We arrived safely at Hilo at about 12:30 having had to row all the way. Found no one expecting us at Capt. Spencer's so late, but he was soon up and made us as comfortable as could be and all but myself had a good night of it. Sorry to say I coughed and choked terribly.

SATURDAY, JUNE 23

Captain Mitchell's Journal:

Walked more today than any day yet, tired. Slept little last night. Got up early. Charming, lovely spot. People began to call early, doctor, Consul, and all the gentlemen in the place tendering their sympathies and hospitalities. Surely we are more than blessed. Have felt pretty well today considering the excitement.

Henry Ferguson's Journal:

Arrived at Hilo about 12:30, after a tolerable easy trip up. It was delightful till we came to the point about 10 miles from here when it came on to rain. While it was light it was the most beautiful row I ever had. One cannot describe the beauties or rather the magnificence. Sam bore the trip well but is very tired this morning from the result of the excitement and the walk from the beach to Capt. Spencer's. He has received us very kindly and so has everyone we have met.

Dr. Wetmore in this A.M. Like him very much. Said Sam's lungs were unimpaired and encouraged him, I think, greatly. He is much better this P.M. but has not gone to the table today. This is the loveliest place I ever was in. Balmy air, tropical trees and plants with most luxuriant foliage of various shades of green. Flowers in great variety.

Samuel Ferguson's Journal:

Guests of Capt. Spencer who is exceedingly kind and hospitable and does everything for us imaginable. I am still very weak and my cough troubles me much.

The climate pleasant and fruits of all kinds abundant. Capt. North and wife very kind also. Dr. Whittemore [Wetmore] and wife, the former (Dr. W) being a Connecticut man though I am afraid a pretty mean doctor and very much behind the age.

SUNDAY, JUNE 24

Captain Mitchell's Journal:

We read service, talked, and enjoyed the day very much to ourselves. Doctor gave me a pill to take upon retiring. Slept splendidly. Feel pretty well today, all but my head which is still giddy. Lovely day and loveliest spot on earth. I have never seen such a paradise as this little Hilo. And the kindness and sympathy of all towards us. Truly we are blessed.

SUNDAY, JUNE 24, 1866.

We dressed—service talk'd & Enjoyed the day very much. Doctor gave me a pill to take upon retiring. Slept splendidly, feel pretty well to day, all but my head which is still giddy. Lonely day, and loveliest spot on earth, I have never seen, such a paradise as this little Hilo. And the kindness & sympathy of all towards us. Truly we are blessed.

MONDAY 25

Took another pill last night, slept finely. Some Am Gentlemen from Honolulu going to the Crater call'd, very pleasant talk, they left. 3 york mate 1st just come from San F. Gave us much news. Walk'd to the Consuls, had a pleasant call. fine family. Afternoon Schr. onl. for Honolulu bringing late papers from the States. read more than my head would bear & went to bed tired. —

TUESDAY 26

Read too much last night, not so well to day. Head very giddy. Called on Mrs Fick an American Lady whose husband is in the Election. pleasant call — borrowed some thread & needles to sew buttons on my trousers. Doctor called. One of my arms nearly paralyzed very little use of the hand. rainy day, in the house all day. Everybody exceedingly kind. Many came to see me.

Capt. Mitchell's journal for June 24—26.

Actual Size

Henry Ferguson's Journal:

Went to service in the Church. Service began with a hymn from Portsmouth Collection, then some Scripture was read, then another hymn was sung, then a prayer, then a sermon, then another prayer; hymn again, ending up with Old Hundred, "Praise God from whom." There is a resident Missionary here but he happened to be absent at present and the doctor officiated, that is read the Bible and sermon and gave out the hymns. Sam and Captain did not venture. Sam improving fast. Rests better and coughs a good deal less. Is still weak but I trust will soon pick up. Hilo is recommended by all as an excellent place for the cure of any bronchial or pulmonary affectation. Find my throat a little sore today. Read out loud Evening Service to them at night, but I fear tired it. This is the loveliest of places I ever saw, and though hot, one can almost always have a breeze and is not scorched as at home. Everybody kind as possible.

Samuel Ferguson's Journal:

Still guests of Capt. Spencer. Various persons call and offer services.

MONDAY, JUNE 25

Captain Mitchell's Journal:

Took another pill last night, slept finely. Some American gentlemen from Honolulu going to the Crater called. Very pleasant talk. They left New York March 1st, just came from San Francisco. Gave us much news. Walked to the Consul's, had a pleasant call, fine family. Afternoon, schooner arrived from Honolulu bringing late papers from the States. Read more than my head would bear and went to bed tired.

Henry Ferguson's Journal:

Throat a little sore and tooth troublesome, otherwise I feel very well and strong. Last night two young American gentlemen who are traveling with [Anson] Burlingame came here and to Capt. Spencer's. They came in to see us in the morning and brought us the latest news. They started off for the Volcano of Kilanca at about 8 and after they have seen that wonder of the world hope by hard riding to reach Kana in time to catch the steamer on Wednesday. Went down and called on the Consul's wife this morning and went walking to see the men in the afternoon, also to the beach to see the schooner, the *Alberin** come in. She brought papers from Honolulu up to the 10th and from San Francisco to the 6th. Sam took a ride with Dr. Wetmore. Beautiful day. Sam is, I am glad to say, improving fast and I trust will get quite strong soon. The Captain is careless and uses his head reading the papers more than is good for him.

* *"The fine schooner ALBERIN, Clark, Master, 160 tons per register" plied among the Hawaiian Islands according to Honolulu shipping advertisements placed by the Hawaiian Steam and General Inter Island Navigation Company.*

Written in back of Samuel Ferguson's Journal on page for Dec. 30.

A.E. Laing, 18 Broad St., New York
J.A. Mitchell, Freeport, Maine U.S.
J. & S. Ferguson, 35 Pine St., New York, U.S.

James Cox, care Wellington & Cox, 74 Broad St. or 327 West 34th. St., N.Y.
Joe Washington, Mrs. Mary Lyons c/o Mrs. Cone, No. 2 Catherine Lane, N.Y. Cook colored.
Capt. Josiah Hardy, Chatham, Mass.
Ira Winner, Union St., Portland, Me. (Water St.)
Joe Williams, New Bedford, Mass., c/o Thomas Green
Amos Clough, c/o Adams Blinn & Co., San Francisco, Calif.
Niel Turner, c/o John Coffee, Port Chester, Westchester Co., N.Y.
Carl Henrich Kaartman, gebiren Augustenburg
James Tait, last known quartermaster MORNING STAR, New Orleans Line.

Samuel Ferguson's Journal:

At Hilo. Think I get stronger but cough very bad and disturbs sleep at night.

TUESDAY, JUNE 26

Captain Mitchell's Journal:

Read too much last night, not so well today. Head very giddy. Called on Mrs. Fish, an American lady whose husband is in the Arctic. Pleasant call. Borrowed some thread and needles to sew buttons on my dungarees. Doctor called. One of my arms nearly paralyzed, very little use of the hand. Rainy day, in the house all day. Everybody exceedingly kind. Boys came to see me.

Henry Ferguson's Journal:

Went down town and spent the morning in Consul's office reading the papers. Got some Chl-potash for my throat which is pretty sore. Came on the rain from the sea at about . . . .
[sentence never completed]

Samuel Ferguson's Journal:

Same till 29th.

WEDNESDAY, JUNE 27

Captain Mitchell's Journal:

Beautiful day, gaining fast as we could expect under the best and kindest of attentions and every comfort and luxury that is possible to have. Introduced to Mr. Cohen and Mr. Lyman, old residents from the Foreign Missions Society. Stayed in house all day.

Henry Ferguson's Journal:

No entry.

Samuel Ferguson's Journal:

No entry.

THURSDAY, JUNE 28

Captain Mitchell's Journal:

Got up at daylight. Bathe all over. Feel very well this morning. Nice cool blowing air. This is certainly the Eden of the world. If Susan* was only here, she would never desire to leave. In all my travels I have never found so desirable a place in climate, productions, and everything else. It is a perfect little paradise.

* Captain Mitchell's wife.

Henry Ferguson's Journal:

No entry.

Samuel Ferguson's Journal:

No entry.

FRIDAY, JUNE 29

Captain Mitchell's Journal:

Warm, sultry day. Tried to write a little. Head somewhat giddy. I feel that I am gaining strength daily, but my body gains faster than my brain. Everybody in the place proffers their kindness and attentions, and of all the places I have ever seen on the earth, this comes the nearest to Paradise. Truly our lives have fallen in pleasant places.

Henry Ferguson's Journal:

Sam did not have a very good night, and I am sorry to say does not seem to be as well today. Capt. and I are well.

Samuel Ferguson's Journal:

Went today to stay with Rev. Mr. Cohen, an old established missionary, who was very kind as was his wife who was his regular helpmate. Had been sent out by the Am. Board, 34 years ago, and had a great deal of experiences to tell. Was rather ego but otherwise very pleasant.

SATURDAY, JUNE 30

Captain Mitchell's Journal:

Hot and sultry. Walked too much in the morning, felt tired. Mr. Ferguson has not been so well the last two days. Poor fellow, I fear he will never reach home. Afternoon, rode four miles horseback to a sugar estate. Enjoyed it very much, tired, but on whole felt better for it. Evening, Mr. Ferguson went to Mr. Cohen's. Will remain there until we leave.

Henry Ferguson's Journal:

Another bad night for Sam and he is very tired for want of sleep. Mr. Cohen this morning gave us an invitation to go to his house where Sam would have better care. He went, but wished me to stay with Capt. Spencer. We went over at about 4:30 and I stayed to dinner and till about 8 with him, when I left him in good kind hands and in better spirits than he had been in for some time. Change always benefits him. Mr. Cohen's family consists of himself, wife, daughter of about the age 18, and two young ladies of about the same age, schoolmates of hers. I think he will be very comfortable there, and a woman's care will be a great thing for him besides having new and cheerful faces around him. I wanted to go with him bad enough, but when he puts his foot down even when, well you might as well attempt to lift Mauna Loa as it, and now he takes queer fancies. Took a ride to sugar plantation. Most beautiful view over the bay and surrounding country.

Samuel Ferguson's Journal:

Still at Mr. Cohen's. Henry and Captain walking around generally. Nothing to chronicle.

SUNDAY, JULY 1

Captain Mitchell's Journal:

Beautiful day. In the morning attended the native church. Mr. Cohen preached in the Kanaka tongue. Full attendance, singing very good, Plymouth tunes. Afternoon, attended service again in English to the few American families. Mr. Cohen preached, full attendance, many children. Monthly concert in the evening.

Henry Ferguson's Journal:

Sam had a good night with refreshing sleep, and seems much better and brighter today. He will, I have no doubt improve at Mr. Cohen's, and I wish he could stay till the next schooner if he continues to do so. Thought of going to native service in afternoon. Heard an address to the children one hour long by watch. Did not feel very well today, but am getting straight now. I think my ride jogged me up a little. Beautiful day. If they only knew at home that we were safe and in such kind hands what a relief it would be. However, they will hear soon, I hope, for the news has most probably left Oahu for San Francisco and it will be telegraphed immediately.

Samuel Ferguson's Journal:

Wanted to go to P.M. English service, but did not feel able. Stayed home and read and walked about.

MONDAY, JULY 2

Captain Mitchell's Journal:

Stayed home all day, read and wrote. Settled Consul's bill, picked up traps, and got ready to leave for Honolulu. Made some calls on those who had shown us so much kindness. Went to bed tired and fell asleep immediately for a wonder and slept well.

Henry Ferguson's Journal:

No entry.

Samuel Ferguson's Journal:

Capt. Clarke of *Alberin* gave notice of her going to sail for Honolulu tomorrow, so this evening I leave Mr. Cohen's for old quarters and get ready to go aboard. Have as companions on voyage the Governess of Hawaii and suite, also Mrs. Pierce, Capt. Worth, the Consul's sister.

TUESDAY, JULY 3

Captain Mitchell's Journal:

Got breakfast at 7 o'clock. Called on Consul. Embarked at 9 A.M. on Schooner *Alberin* for Honolulu. Left Hilo with streaming eyes, bidding farewell to so many new friends that had heaped upon us so many obligations and shown us so much sympathy. God bless and reward them.

Henry Ferguson's Journal:

Left Hilo at about 10 in the schooner *Alberin*, Capt. Clark, for Honolulu, and went out of the bay easily with a light breeze. Took a good strong Trade when we got a little way out and have been travelling on nicely all day. Sam looks brighter I think, but his cough troubles him terribly and is painful. I hope that Dr. Ford will help his trouble when we get to Honolulu. Beautiful sail along the Island. Great crowd aboard. The Governess of Hawaii and suite. She is a mighty ugly, fat, Kanaka woman of about 300 lbs. tonnage. Tolerable accommodations aboard and nice meals.

Samuel Ferguson's Journal:

Got off at about 10:30 A.M. and soon struck a good wind and had a good run for a start. Boat got adrift when two Kanakas jumped in and swam to it, bring it up very soon, they are regular amphibians.

The Governess is a person and would weigh I should think fully 300. She and suite all stayed on deck all the time and eat Poi and their own victuals. Mrs. Pierce sick very soon after starting and retired. Wind made me cough considerable.

Capt. Clarke treated us with a number of airs on the accordion which, played as well as he played it, sounded first rate. It was a real treat to hear some of own familiar tunes.

WEDNESDAY, JULY 4

Captain Mitchell's Journal:

Passed the length of Hawaii, East and West, Maui, Lanai, and at daylight abreast of Molokai. A very beautiful sail, new beauties appearing every minute. It will be a solemn 4th. for my dear family. Arrived at Honolulu at 4 P.M. Went to the American House. Accepted the invitation of Mr. Whitney, Editor of *Advertiser*, to tarry with him for a day or two. Very nice family.

Henry Ferguson's Journal:

Sailed along the Islands and arrived at Honolulu Bay at about 4. Came up to the American Hotel where Sam and I got a room, but the Captain went with a gentleman who offered accommodation. Burlingame* Von Valkenburg, and Co. here yet. Sam coughs a good deal, but will I guess be comfortable here. When these Embassies leave Mr. Kerchoff has promised us better rooms, looking *manka*.

* *Anson Burlingame (1820-1870), a U.S. Congressman and diplomat completed a brilliant career as United States Minister to Peking. He was returning to China with General Van Valkenberg at the very moment the HORNET survivors were brought to the hospital at Honolulu and he was of immeasurable assistance to Mark Twain in aiding him to obtain their story.*

Samuel Ferguson's Journal:

Had a medium night. Again a fine day, still a good breeze. Schooner doing very prettily and going pretty fast. Arrived in Honolulu at about 4:30 to 5 and was kindly sent by some gent in his carriage up to the American where we found Minister Burlingame and suite, also General Van Valkenburg, the first going to China, the latter Japan — both very kind and cordial invitation given us to make the Embassy our residence if we went across the water. Managed to get rooms in a cottage till they sailed which was Saturday when we moved to very good ones at the hotel, the proprietor of which was very kind indeed. Capt. M[itchell] accepts an invitation to stay with a private family. Mr. Whitney, Editor of the Honolulu *Advertiser*. Was met by a message from Weed to go directly to his house, but was too forlorn to do so, beside I want quiet and attendance at home.

THURSDAY, JULY 5

Captain Mitchell's Journal:

Got up early. Bath, clean clothes, breakfast, prayers, rode down town. Saw the Consul and some of the men. Introduced to several gentlemen, Mr. Burlingame, the Minister to China, also to General Vonbal Kenberg, [Von Valkenberg], Minister to Japan and suite. Paid me a very high compliment which I felt undeserved for all was God's mercy. It was on the moral power of government of the men.

Henry Ferguson's Journal:

Went down to the Doctor's and he prescribed to Sam, the use of whiskey both as an expect-

A mid-nineteenth century view of Honolulu with Diamond Head in the distance was painted by an unidentified Chinese artist. Courtesy the Mariners Museum.

orant and also as a strengthener and stimulant, to live on nourishing good hearty food and plenty of it, and every morning to take an egg and beat it up in milk and whiskey. I hope that on this he may soon improve and I pray God he may. Find it pretty hot here in the daytime, but tolerably cool at night.

Samuel Ferguson's Journal:

Passed a pretty miserable night, but found the fare at the hotel more suitable to my wants than I have yet had it. Saw Dr. Ford, the best doctor who prescribed plenty of good wholesome food with eggs lightly done and a glass of whiskey, sugar and water constantly at hand, the latter being strengthening as well as a first rate expectorant which I much need. Very little passes worthy of note. The men that are here are all well but Niel and Charley. They are at the hospital, but will go to San Francisco by some of the first sailing vessels.

This P.M. called upon Weed and wife - the latter a native of Tahiti, Soc[iety] Islands, of an olive color and quite light. They are both very pressing, but I had the doctor's opinion to urge. It is like the "shadow of a Great Rock in a barren land" to fine home away out here.

FRIDAY, JULY 6

Captain Mitchell's Journal:

Hot day, walked more than I ought. Shopped a little, came home at 5 P.M., took a bath. Head not so well at night. This is a fine, well governed, affectionate family. Mr. and Mrs. Whitney understand each other perfectly. They are very religious, as most all the residents of the Islands are.

Henry Ferguson's Journal:

No entry.

Samuel Ferguson's Journal:

Tired most to death by various visitors and well wishers. Tried to keep quiet.

Very little that I know or heard to chronicle. I am too weak to do anything but take a short walk. Find the air here very hot though at night there seems to be a breeze from the mountains which is really the Trades. This is even (back of the town) a more volcanic looking place than Hilo.

SATURDAY, JULY 7

Captain Mitchell's Journal:

Still at Mr. Whitney's. Went down town today and out to the hospital to see the men, all want money. Mr. Burlingame and General Von Valkenburgh departed today. They were very kind to me, said if I ever came to China I must make their house my home. Said I was one of the great men of the age and flattered me a good deal. Bought a suit of clothes, $30.00.

Henry Ferguson's Journal:

Legations left and we got into our new rooms. Sam rather better but still very weak indeed.

Samuel Ferguson's Journal:

No entries until July 19.

SUNDAY, JULY 8

Captain Mitchell's Journal:

Attended church morning and evening this day with the family. Called down to see the Messrs. Ferguson at the American Hotel. Don't think I shall leave here until I take passage. Write wife. Went to bed at 10, slept well. Feel that I am gaining. Had an introduction to Judge Allen formerly of Bangor and a pleasant chat.

Henry Ferguson's Journal:

Went to English church in A.M. Sam and I took a walk in the evening and called on Mrs. Pierce.

MONDAY, JULY 9

Captain Mitchell's Journal:

Walked to town this day and back at night. Very tired, find I am still weak in the legs as well as in the head. Everybody very kind and if I do not thrive certainly it is not the fault of the kind people upon whom my lot is cast. Mr. F. [Sam] is not improving. Fear he will never be any better. Several callers in the evening.

Henry Ferguson's Journal:

Sam had a tolerable night's rest and says he feels he is better. I hope and trust he will improve and get strong and that I may not have to leave him sick on this island in the hands of strangers. He is much set to have me go home immediately and I don't know but that it may be the best, though it will break my heart to do it. He and I took a walk this evening, the longest he has had yet. My trust is great that the good living and exercise when he gets so he can take it will pick him up, but the doctor says it is consumption and he has been fearfully reduced by our exposure and famine.

TUESDAY, JULY 10

Captain Mitchell's Journal:

Walked to town this morning. Sat for pictures. Was presented with a purse containing $310 in gold collected for me. I felt like a criminal upon receiving it, was completely overcome. The first time in my life I was ever in such a situation. Could not refuse it. There is some true charity in the world yet. Engaged to dine out on Thursday between 3 and 4.

Henry Ferguson's Journal:

Sam went down to Dr. Ford's this morning and he advised his leaving Honolulu and going to California so he will go with the Captain and myself in the *Smyrniote** most probably. God grant that the change may be for the best and that he may find some place in California where he will regain his strength and make headway against his dreadful disease. His cough seems easier than it was, but he still expectorates largely. However, I should say that he was better than when he came here. He has never had the two other concomitants of consumption — night sweats and blood spitting, and I hope that the trouble has not gone so far but that it may be arrested.

* *"The A1 Clipper Bark SMYRNIOTE, C.J. Lovett, commander" was built at Duxbury, Massachusetts, in 1859 and measured 397 tons. She sailed in regular packet service between Hawaii and California.*

WEDNESDAY, JULY 11

Captain Mitchell's Journal:

Wrote letters until 10 A.M. Went down town and found the ship gone and took no mail. Dinner party at the house, several ladies and gentlemen, Reverend Mr. Rising who is to be one of our fellow passengers over to San Francisco. Have not felt so well as usual today. Slept but little last night.

Henry Ferguson's Journal:

No entries until July 19.

THURSDAY, JULY 12

Captain Mitchell's Journal:

Slept well and feel better for it. Engaged out to dine today. Wish I could avoid these dinner parties. Dined with Mr. Avers, pleasant time. Got home at 8 P.M. Sick in the night. Must be more careful. Went to bed at 10 P.M. Mr. Whitney and wife out in the evening. Saw the men all off this day.

FRIDAY, JULY 13

Captain Mitchell's Journal:

Walked to town and back this day. Visited Parliament House. Lunched at American Hotel. Fergusons about the same. Had pictures taken together for Hilo friends. Also got copies of

Photo of Capt. Mitchell and the two Ferguson boys taken in Honolulu July 13, 1866.

Laupahoehoe. Paid for all, $14.00. Bought night shirts and handkerchiefs which I hope will carry me through to San Francisco. Came home early and read.

SATURDAY, JULY 14

Captain Mitchell's Journal:

Wrote owners for the first time, also wife. To go by *Comet** on Tuesday. Hope we shall get off by Wednesday. Loafed all the rest of the day and read until my head ached. Walked to the American House in the evening and back. Went to bed tired.

* *The San Francisco bark COMET measured 361 tons. She had been built at Pembroke in 1852 and was then owned by McRuer & Merrill of San Francisco.*

SUNDAY, JULY 15

Captain Mitchell's Journal:

One month today since we landed at Laupahoehoe, a starving set of men. We are all yet living. How much we have to thank God for. Attended Bethel in the morning. In the evening went to Mr. Cerwin's. Heard a native preacher, very eloquent.

MONDAY, JULY 16

Captain Mitchell's Journal:

Dull day, time begins to hang heavy. *Smyrniote* delayed, passed the day visiting Parliament House, calling on friends, etc. People all so kind, especially Mr. and Mrs. Whitney. They are

Record of the loss of the Hornet - *from Atlantic Mutual Insurance Company records.*

true Christians. Many call to see me and I am certainly thriving well. All I desire is to get my letters from home and know how my dear family are getting along.

TUESDAY, JULY 17

Captain Mitchell's Journal:

Still waiting for ship. Dined out today in company with Prince William and others of the Royal Pedigree. Day passed without anything worthy of remark. Tedious waiting for *Smyrniote*. They say she will sail tomorrow without fail. Hope the *Ethan Allen** will arrive.

* *The wood bark ETHAN ALLAN, 397 tons, was built in 1859 at East Boston, Mass., for E. Snow & Co. H.P. Snow, master.*

WEDNESDAY, JULY 18

Captain Mitchell's Journal:

Still delayed and *Ethan Allen* not come. Shall have to go to sea, I fear, without news. Mrs. Whitney insists upon doing a great deal to get me ready. Called on the minister today, Mr. McBride, good talk. Sent Mr. Ferguson $25.00.

Bark Smyrniote *on which Captain Mitchell, the two Fergusons and Mark Twain returned to San Francisco - Peabody Museum painting.*

THURSDAY, JULY 19

Captain Mitchell's Journal:

Got everything to depart early this morning. Mr. and Mrs. Whitney very kind indeed, urging upon me in such a way as [to] make denial impossible. At 4:30 left the dock and proceeded to sea. Fresh Trade from Northeast. About twenty passengers on board, pleasant people. Most all the ladies sick. End of harbor log.

Henry Ferguson's Journal:

Hoped to leave Honolulu and did so in the afternoon at about 4:30. The *Comet* got off about two hours ahead of us and made good use of his time as when we got outside of the reef she was out of sight. Very glad to get off as I think Honolulu climate very bad for Sam. Sent whiskey aboard in A.M. and found the eggs had been sent by Weed. Said goodbye to Mrs. Weed at her house. Weed, Pierce and Mr. Post came down to see us off. Sam tolerably well and also glad to get off. Great crowd of passengers and their friends on starting. There will not be so many of them to be seen tomorrow, as it is there were present at the dinner table tonight only Sam, Mr. Rising, Capt. Mitchell and myself out of the entire sixteen. Fine Trade and we have been going along past the land nicely. Before it was too dark we could see Lanai and Molokai as well as Oahu. Will run pretty near Lanai and then tack to the Northward past Oahu. Saw the *Comet* on the other tack at sunset.

Samuel Ferguson's Journal:

Started on the *Smyrniote* at about 5:30 P.M. for San Francisco. *Comet* sailed two hours before. Many bets as to which gets to S.F. first. We have perhaps one of the best staterooms, but the bark is small and we have a full set of passengers with an over full complement of babies. The number I believe, not counting the latter, sixteen, four of which were at first meal. H[enry], Captain M[itchell], and I being three. Mark Twain suffering other than seasickness, however.

Made a good start and saw the *Comet* before night on the other tack. During the night tacked and stood North by West, but was becalmed part of the time. Saw the last of the islands in the afternoon of next day. Ship a very nice one, though very small after the *Hornet*. Cabin of course uncomfortable for gents.

FRIDAY, JULY 20

Captain Mitchell's Journal:

At 4:30 P.M. sea account. Cast off from wharf, stood out on port tack. At 8 tacked. At 12 close under Oahu. Boat out clear making one tack. *Comet* in company. Continued on starboard tack, wind Northeast to East-Northeast, moderate. Island just in sight. Found my mangoes all right. Latitude observed, 22° 20′. *Comet* not in sight.

Henry Ferguson's Journal:

Today is I suppose the real time from which to date the commencement of the passage. We have had a good trade all day and have long since taken our farewell look at Oahu. We ran a little too far under Lanai and got caught in a calm for a couple of hours but then (11 P.M. Thursday) got a good breeze and passed the East point of Oahu all right though we must have been only about a mile from it. Sam has had a good appetite to his meals but did not sleep extra well last night. However, I hope that he will gain in that and in all other respects. Ladies, children, some of the men passengers very sick although there could not be finer weather, and the sea as flat as a board. Neither Sam or myself troubled. Would have been very much disgusted with myself if I had been. Course from West to North by West, sometimes even East of North.

Samuel Ferguson's Journal:

Staterooms very small and hot though each has a "Bull's Eye."* Everything so far looks calm though, which is a blessing. Have made a very good start and have a good strong T'ade which heads us, however, a little to the West of North. We have not quite as much cargo in as desirable and make more leeway. Lady passengers still continue sick, some quite so Babies sick and crying making being in the cabin anything but delightful.

A Bull's Eye is a piece of thick glass set flush in the deck to let light below.

SATURDAY, JULY 21

Lat. 24° 50' N. Long. 157° 31' W. Dist. 179 miles

Captain Mitchell's Journal:

Fresh Trade all day with an occasional squall. Wind about East-Northeast, heading North. Passengers getting over seasickness. Children bawling, etc. Sea smooth. My room mate Reverend Mr. Rising of Sacramento.

Henry Ferguson's Journal:

3 A.M. gave us a pretty smart squall that made things boil for an hour or two. Then it departed and left a calm behind it which did not last long however, and by six there sprung up a good breeze which has been increasing till now she is going 9 knots close hauled with the royals off her. She is not very fast, don't make the good use of her opportunities that the poor *Hornet* did. Sam had rather a better night and has not coughed as much today. I think this is going to do him good. It has been a splendid day, fresh Trade all the time but sea very calm. Lady passengers with one exception pretty miserable still. But still we had three at dinner which as Ed would say must have been accomplished by a triumph of mind over matter. From noon to noon ran 179 miles.

Samuel Ferguson's Journal:

No entries, save for noting daily positions, appear hereafter.

SUNDAY, JULY 22

Lat. 28° 12'N. Long. 157° 42'W. Dist. 200 miles

Captain Mitchell's Journal:

Strong Trade and squally all this day. Wing about E.N.E. Ladies sick. Mr. Rising unable to hold service. Fine day but somewhat rough. Read *Independents* furnished by Mrs. Whitney.

MONDAY, JULY 23

Lat. 31° 34'N. Long. 157° 30'W. Dist. 202 miles

Captain Mitchell's Journal:

Strong Trades all this day from E.N.E. Mr. Rising better today. Unable to preach yesterday. Blow good breeze and let's fly!

TUESDAY, JULY 24

Lat. 34° 31'N. Long. 157° 40'W. Dist. 180 miles

Captain Mitchell's Journal:

Fresh Trades or rather Northeast by North winds all this day. Weather getting cool and thick clothes comfortable. Passengers all getting well and children troublesome. Now we want a Westerly wind.

WEDNESDAY, JULY 25

Lat. 37° 18'N. Long. 158° 06'W. Dist. 170 miles

Captain Mitchell's Journal:

Moderate East-Northeast winds all this day. Occasionally headed off to the Westward a point or two. Passengers are well, social, and agreeable. Now for a change of wind!

THURSDAY, JULY 26

Lat. 38° 53'N. Long. 158° 24'W. Dist. 100 miles

Captain Mitchell's Journal:

Moderate winds, smooth sea, and pleasant weather. Wind Northeast all the first part. Middle very light. Latter part, calm.

FRIDAY, JULY 27

Lat. 38° 55' N. Long. 157° 37' W. Dist. 38 miles

Captain Mitchell's Journal:

Light airs and calms all this day. Not well today.

SATURDAY, JULY 28

Lat. 38° 46' N. Long. 156° 36' W. Dist. 48 miles

Captain Mitchell's Journal:

Light baffling airs and calms all this day. Very little progress.

SUNDAY, JULY 29

Lat. 38° 43' N. Long. 154° 55' W. Dist. 80 miles

Captain Mitchell's Journal:

Moderate winds all this day, fine weather, and smooth sea. Wind West. Services on board to-day, the Reverend Mr. Rising officiating.

MONDAY, JULY 30

Lat. 38° 46' N. Long. 154° 03' W. Dist. 51 miles

Captain Mitchell's Journal:

First part light breeze from North. Middle and latter calm.

Letter from Mark Twain to Mrs. Jane Clemens and Mrs. Moffet in St. Louis*

On Board Ship *Smyrniote*
At Sea, July 30, 1866

Dear Mother and Sister:

. . . We left the Sandwich Islands eight or ten days — or twelve days ago . . .

Ever since we got becalmed — five days — I have been copying the diary of one of the young Fergusons (the two boys who starved and suffered, with thirteen others, in an open boat at sea for forty-three days, lately, after their ship, the *Hornet*, was burned on the equator). Both these boys and Captain Mitchell are passengers with us. I am copying the diary to publish in *Harper's Magazine*, if I have time to fix it up properly when I get to San Francisco . . .

* *Paine, LETTERS, pages 115-116.*

TUESDAY, JULY 31

No position recorded.

Captain Mitchell's Journal:

Light airs and calms all this day.

WEDNESDAY, AUGUST 1

Lat. 38° 50' N. Long. 150° 56' W. Dist. 100 miles

Captain Mitchell's Journal:

Light breezes from South all this day.

Henry Ferguson's Journal:

Breeze better today. Our distance run by observation was 100 miles. I hope we won't have any more calm now — till we get to San Francisco.

THURSDAY, AUGUST 2

Lat. 38° 50' N. Long. 147° 59' W. Dist. 138 miles

Captain Mitchell's Journal:

Moderate breezes and fine weather all this day. Wind Southwest. Mr. Rising and Mr. Clements (alias Mark Twain) busy writing.

Samuel Ferguson's Journal: Entry written by Henry Ferguson in Greek. (Translation:)*

The wind is stronger today, and we are grateful for it. We have made on our course seven knots and even nine. Samuel is the same as he was yesterday. He slept briefly. It is a beautiful day and we think the wind will increase in strength. We sailed — from noon yesterday to noon today. The wind is off the starboard quarter.

FRIDAY, AUGUST 3

Lat. 38° 56' N. Long. 145° 13' W. Dist. 130 miles

Captain Mitchell's Journal:

Very light winds from Southwest and South all day. Sea smooth, passengers impatient.

Henry Ferguson's Journal: Entry written in Greek (Translation:)*

Today the wind dropped and now it is almost calm, it also veered forward, which is too bad. Samuel slept better and appears better today and took an afternoon nap. We could not make better than a knot's progress. Can do nothing, however. It is very tedious. Henry Ferguson, Stamford, on board *Smyrniote*.

Overcast and it seems about to blow. The wind has increased. 11 P.M.

SATURDAY, AUGUST 4

Lat. 39° 12'N. Long. 143° 59'W. Dist. 63 miles

Captain Mitchell's Journal:

Very light winds all day and variable. Latter part cloudy and every appearance of a change.

Henry Ferguson's Journal: Entry written in Greek. (Translation:)*

Today the wind was all right in the morning, but has now dropped off to almost calm.

* *The passages appearing in Greek in the Ferguson Brothers' diaries were both written by Henry, seemingly merely to amuse himself. They were kindly translated by Dr. George J. Ryan, assistant professor of ancient languages at the College of William and Mary, Williamsburg, Virginia, at the request of the editor. Dr. Ryan commented that this was "obviously the Greek of a student who remembers only imperfectly" and who had no dictionary around to lean on. Dr. Ryan could find "no ulterior motive" for the Ferguson boy to be writing in an ancient language. Time was evidently hanging heavily upon Henry's hands and "he simply amused himself by trying to write his journal in Greek." "It is not a bad job for a college student" is Dr. Ryan's summary.*

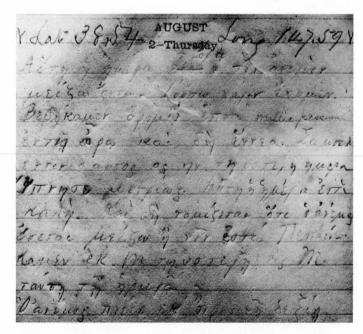

Henry Ferguson's journal entry written in Greek Aug. 2, 1866.

SUNDAY, AUGUST 5

Lat. 39° 54´ N. Long. 142° 13´ W. Dist. 80 miles

Captain Mitchell's Journal:

Light head winds all this day and fair weather. A bark in sight to leeward, supposed the *Comet* that left Honolulu same day as ourselves. Mr. Rising preached again today from part of same text as last Sunday.

MONDAY, AUGUST 6

Lat. 40° 24´ N. Long. 140° 00´ W. Dist. 55 miles

Captain Mitchell's Journal:

Light airs, baffling, and calms all this day. Dull dull work this. Passengers no life and I am getting impatient. *Comet* just in sight South of us.

Henry Ferguson's Journal:

Comet seen.

TUESDAY, AUGUST 7

Lat. 40° 44´ N. Long. 140° 21´ W.

Captain Mitchell's Journal:

Calm all the afternoon. Middle and latter part very light airs from South. A brig in company, colors flying. Sea smooth and weather fine. *Comet* not in sight.

Henry Ferguson's Journal:

French brig *Pioneer*.
Comet in distance.

WEDNESDAY, AUGUST 8

Lat. 40° 24´ N. Long. 137° 55´ W. Dist. 110 miles

Captain Mitchell's Journal:

Moderate breeze all this day. Bark and brig in company. Cloudy weather and cool wind, South-Southwest.

THURSDAY, AUGUST 9

Lat. 39° 45' N. Long. 133° 38' W. Dist. 195 miles

Captain Mitchell's Journal:

Steady fresh breeze all this day from South-Southwest. Clear and cloudy alternately. Brig still in company.

FRIDAY, AUGUST 10

Lat. 39° 23' N. Long. 130° 58' W. Dist. 122 miles

Captain Mitchell's Journal:

Begins moderate from Southwest. Middle part hauls to West. Foggy, drizzling, and cold. Ends pleasant at Southwest, breeze light and sea smooth.

SATURDAY, AUGUST 11

Lat. 39° 00' N. Long. 128° 42' W. Dist. 105 miles

Captain Mitchell's Journal:

Light baffling airs, squalls, calms, rain, and fog make up the day. No great progress. Another Sabbath to be passed on board. Tedious passage.

SUNDAY, AUGUST 12

Lat. 38° 34' N. Long. 126° 33' W. Dist. 98 miles

Captain Mitchell's Journal:

Very light breeze from Northwest to North, smooth sea and fine weather. Services by Mr. Rising from Parable of the Prodigal Son.

MONDAY, AUGUST 13

Captain Mitchell's Journal:

Arrived at San Francisco at 4 P.M. Went to the Occidental. Harry* came up in the evening. Went to his room and passed the night with him. Slept but little.

* *Captain Mitchell's son.*

Henry Ferguson's Journal:

Made land at about 9 A.M. Took pilot off the Heads and came into the wharf at 5:30 P.M. Went to Occidental. Met Mr. Harter. He told us that all our friends were well, which is a great relief to our anxiety. Landed in along with the *Comet*, thus beating her by two hours. Will go to Alameda tomorrow.

(No further entries in Henry Ferguson's Journal)

EXTRACTS FROM CAPTAIN MITCHELL'S JOURNAL

AUGUST 14 through DECEMBER 31, 1866

Aug. 14
   Called on Mr. Hawes today and telegraphed owners. Bought a suit of clothes from top to toe. Remained at the Occidental Hotel. Clothes cost $70.00. Sat up until one o'clock reading letters from home.

Aug. 15
   Head troubled me very much this day — more than ever. Kept quiet as possible all day — caused probably by reading letters late at night. Passed the night with Harry.

Aug. 16
   Pretty well today, extended protest. Walked a good deal looking up crew. Felt no bad effects from it.

Aug. 17
   Wrote Wife and Messrs. Lawrence, Giles & Co.
   Paid board at Occidental Hotel $14.00
   Passage from Honolulu 65.00
                                                                          $79.00

Aug. 18
   Extended Protest - etc — Walked about seeing old friends.

Aug. 19
   Went to Episcopal Church and lunched with Mr. Pennell. Evening called at Alf's and Mr. Tracy's.

Aug. 20
   Monday found Ellen Gaynor. Evening at home with Harry.

Aug. 21
   Passed evening at Mr. Low's.

Aug. 22
   Wandered about as usual Paid Fred Clough his proportion of Boat sold at Honolulu — 4.37.

Aug. 23
   Busy all day doing nothing.

Aug. 24

Bought another suit of clothes this day for	$25.00
Trunk $25 — Duster 3.50	28.50
Under clothes	5.00
Collars, cravat, &c	4.25
	$62.75

Aug. 25

Took the cars at 8:30 for San Jose, where we dined, then took a team and drove to Warm Springs, Santa Clara, fine drive. Found Mr. Ferguson and Brother about the same. Very glad to see me. Fare to San Jose and incidentals 2.00.

Aug. 26

Beautiful day — took a warm sulphur bath. Felt first rate, wish I could take one every day. Left at 2:30 P.M. Arrived at San Jose at 6 P.M. Supped at Auserias House. Went to Church in the evening.

Fare to San Jose for two		$ 5.00
Bill at Springs		7.00
At Auserias House		5.00
		$17.00
	Extra	2.00
		$19.00

Aug. 27

Arrived at San Francisco at 9 A.M. Saw Captain Burgess of *David Crocket*.* Good passage, 114 days.

* *The fast American clipper ship DAVID CROCKETT was built at Mystic, Connecticut, in 1853 and measured 1546 tons.*

Aug. 28

Smyrniote sailed at 12 noon. Sent pictures and glass to Honolulu. Saw them all off for Honolulu. Wish I could go there and live. How happy my wife would be there. It may be yet.

Aug. 29

Busy making calls and getting ready to leave by steamer tomorrow. Have received great kindness from all while here.

Gave Harry in gold	$160.00
Fare to New York	232.00
	$392.00

Aug. 30

Paid bill at Mrs. B's - 11 days - $22.00. Bid poor Harry goodby again and other friends.

At 11, cast off from wharf on steamer *Golden City*,* Captain Lappidge, and proceeded to sea. Very foggy weather all day. Reverend Mr. Rising on board.

* *The Pacific Mail Steamship Company's wooden sidewheel steamer GOLDEN CITY plied a regular run from San Francisco to Panama. She was expressly built for this service by William H. Webb of New York in 1863, measuring 3373 tons and was 343 feet long, by 45 beam, by 23 deep. She was lost in 1870.*

Sept. 1
Very light winds and calm, hazy weather, smooth sea. Ship's run, 267 miles. Small number of passengers on board. Don't feel very well, been sick since I came from the Springs. Went to bed early and slept fine.

Sept. 6
Landed at Acapulco at 8 this morning. Sailed again, 1 P.M. Did not go ashore. Many did.

Sept. 12
Arrived at Panama at 5 A.M. Left at 7. Arrived Aspinwall at 10. Left at 2 P.M. for New York on steamer *New York*.* Latter part rough, all seasick, no fun.

* *The wooden sidewheel steamer NEW YORK was built in 1864 for Cornelius Vanderbilt and transferred to the Pacific Mail Steamship Company. She was operated between New York and Aspinwall on the Atlantic side of the Isthmus of Panama, synchronizing her service with the San Francisco to Panama steamer GOLDEN CITY. Slightly smaller, the NEW YORK was 2217 tons and 292 feet long, by 41.7 beam, by 26.5 deep.*

Sept. 19
Arrived at New York at 4 P.M., 20 days from San Francisco.

Sept. 20
Wrote Wife and Harry. Heard from home, my poor wife sick which accounts for my not getting letters.

Sept. 22
Got into town at 12 noon. Settled all bills in the City, also account with Mr. Lawrence, receiving $2,045.70 balance due me. Disappointed in not getting away tonight.

Sept. 23
Left New York at 5 P.M. Railroad. Arrived in Boston at 2 A.M. Monday.

Sept. 25
Arrived home at 2 P.M. Wife much sicker than I expected.

Sept. 28
Wrote Mr. McChesney, U.S. Consul at New Castle-on-Tyne in reference to Mr. Parr, Second Officer. Poor wife not so well.

Oct. 4
Wife still very comfortable and appears better, but no strength. Does not seem to me to gain. Girls came home from Toledo.

Oct. 5
Letter from Mr. Ferguson announcing Samuel's death [on October 1]. Poor boys. Henry I shall ever remember. My poor wife still quite comfortable but does not gain strength.

Oct. 6
Went over to Pennell's Yard. A good ship on the stocks.

Oct. 22

My dear wife still lingers, suffers at times beyond description and times exceedingly happy and joyful. Much in the spiritual and so anxious to go and yet so drawn to earth. At times face perfectly radiant. No particle of nourishment.

Oct. 31

Poor wife released from her sufferings at 2:30 A.M.

Nov. 1

Sad day, relieving mind by constant application to divers things. O my own dear wife, why am I so stricken and left when as you said we ought all to rejoice. God strengthen and comfort us all. Cannot write, mind not in a fit state.

Dec. 21

Hove down with a sort of billious squall, called Dr. Norton. Pretty well shook up aloft. The old craft wants to be kept in good weather and smooth seas.

Dec. 31

Settled every outstanding bill to my knowledge and commence the world square this next year. Thus ends this eventful year.

Modern view of Captain Mitchell's house at Freeport, Maine.
Photographed by Alexander C. Brown, 1973.

PART VII—

MARK TWAIN'S DÉBUT
AS A LITERARY PERSON

FORTY—THREE DAYS IN AN OPEN BOAT

Compiled from Personal Diaries, by Mark Swain*

(From *Harper's New Monthly Magazine*, Vol. xxxiv, December, 1866, pp. 104-113)

The superb clipper-ship *Hornet*, Captain Josiah Mitchell, sailed out of New York harbor about the first week in January, 1866, bound for San Francisco. She had a quick passage around the Horn, and experienced no ill luck of any kind until just after crossing the equator, upward bound, in the Pacific. Then, on the morning of the 3d of May, she took fire and was burned up, and the crew and passengers, with ten days' provisions saved from the vessel, found themselves adrift in three open boats.

Each boat had a compass, a quadrant, a copy of Bowditch's Navigator, and a Nautical Almanac, and the Captain's and chief mate's boats had chronometers. There were 31 men, all told. The Captain took an account of stock, with the following result: four hams, nearly thirty pounds of salt pork, half-box of raisins, one hundred pounds of bread, twelve two-pound cans of oysters, clams, and assorted meats, a keg containing four pounds of butter, twelve gallons of water in a forty-gallon "scuttle-butt," four one-gallon demijohns full of water, three bottles of brandy (the property of passengers), some pipes, matches, and a hundred pounds of tobacco. No medicines. Of course the whole party had to go on short rations at once.

The Captain kept a "log," and so did each of the two passengers, Samuel and Henry Ferguson, ages 28 and 18 respectively — young gentlemen making their first sea voyage. The plain, matter-of-fact journal of the older Ferguson was as interesting to me as a novel, notwithstanding I knew all the circumstances of the desperate voyage in the open boat before I read it. I give it entire, adding extracts from the other logs occasionally. A perusal of the diary for the 2d of May will introduce the reader to the cheerful, home-like ship, before she takes her final leave of the stage:

> Note: At this point Mark Twain quoted directly from the Journals. The quotations together with Mark Twain's comments have already appeared in their proper sequence in Part Four of the narrative and are not repeated here.

They have told their story, and in their own language. I hardly know which to admire most — the steady persistence and faithfulness with which they kept up their journals through such a weary time, or the unwavering hopefulness they showed from first to last, in the face of the seeming hopelessness of rescue.

They wanted to "doctor" the diaries a little, but it did not appear to me that any amendations were necessary; a careful and elegantly composed log-book, gotten up in the midst of thirst, starvation, and a stormy sea, would seem so strikingly unnatural that its genuineness might reasonably be questioned.

The men were so carefully nursed where they landed (at Laupahoehoe, on the island of Hawaii) that all except one seaman were able to walk about within ten days afterward. Yet in some cases there had been no action of their bowels for twenty and thirty days, and in one case for forty-four days!

With ten days' provisions Captain Mitchell performed this extraordinary voyage of forty-three days and eight hours in an open boat (sailing 4000 miles in reality and 3360 by direct courses), and brought every man safe to land. Each individual day of those six weeks bears

* This is how Mark Twain's name actually appeared, to his considerable annoyance and disgust. See page 224.

its testimony to his watchfulness, his prudence, his cool courage, his foresight, perseverance, and fidelity to his duty, and his rare intelligence. In him are the elements of greatness.

This strange voyage, in its entirety, is an eloquent witness of the watchful presence of an all-powerful Providence, and as such its record carries with it a lesson that cannot be valueless. This presence was distinctly manifested on two occasions at least. Henry mentions the fact of the island on the last day. It was getting late. They had to make land that day or perish. They struck boldly for the shore, and when they had got pretty well in they lowered the sail, and afterward, not liking the appearance of the reef, tried to hoist it again and retreat, but they were too feeble to accomplish it, and beheld themselves drifting helplessly upon the rocks after all their toils and hardships. And it was all the better. They swept through an almost imperceptible opening in the coral reef and were saved. There was not another place within thirty-five miles where they could have got to the land or found a human habitation. Every where else a precipice more than a thousand feet high comes down like a wall to the sea, with forty fathoms water at its base, and not even bordered by a strip of ground wide enough for a man to stand upon. The other case is that of Cox. The mate's boat had bidden the Captain's good-by and departed, but came back directly and the Captain was requested to receive a man. Cox came on board, and was the only man who warned the Captain and the passengers afterward, when the conspirators had sworn their lives away.

Before closing, a few words ought to be said about the conspiracy. The Captain says that for many days he had known that a murderous discontent was brewing by the distraught air of some of the men and the guilty look of others, and so he staid on guard — slept no more — kept his hatchet hid and close at hand.

At this time the famishing, ravenous men were cutting boots, handkerchiefs, and shirts into bits and eating them. They had done so for days. They were even eating the staves of the butter-cask. They were wild with hunger. They were in a manner insane, and in the judgment of no just and merciful man responsible for their words or deeds. They afterward dreaded, in Honolulu, that the Captain and passengers would take legal measures against them because of their murderous conspiracy; but their fears were without foundation. These gentlemen well understood the case, and only pitied the men. They insisted for some time that I should leave out all mention of the conspiracy from their published journals. That the men were frenzied is shown by the fact that they told Cox, in a whispered conference at night, that the Captain had all the ship's money in the boat — "a million dollars in gold and silver!" — just about enough to sink such a craft. They were to watch until such time as the Captain might become worn out and fall asleep, and then kill him and the passengers. They were afraid of Ferguson's pistol and the Captain's hatchet, and laid many a plan for getting hold of these weapons. They told Cox they would divide the money with him if he kept quiet and helped, but they would kill him if he exposed them. He refused to join the conspiracy, and they said he should die; and so, after that, day after day and night after night, he did not go to sleep, but kept watch upon them in fear for his life. The Captain and passengers remained under arms, and watched also, but talked pleasantly, and gave no sign that they knew what was in the men's minds. The Captain spoke now and then of his strength holding out being a necessity, since only he could use the chart and the quadrant and find the land.

By way of conclusion it may be well enough to say that up to the present time no tidings have been received of the poor fellows in the missing boats. It seems almost idle, now to hope that they are saved.

Honolulu, Sandwich Islands
July 2, 1866

MY DÉBUT AS A LITERARY PERSON

By Mark Twain (Formerly "Mike Swain")

(From *The Century Magazine*, Vol. 59, No. 1, November, 1899, pp. 76-88. This was reprinted in *The Man That Corrupted Hadleyburg and Other Stories and Essays*, by Mark Twain. Collected Works, Harper & Brothers, New York, 1901)

In those early days I had already published one little thing ("The Jumping Frog") in an Eastern paper, but I did not consider that that counted. In my view, a person who published things in a mere newspaper could not properly claim recognition as a Literary Person: he must rise away above that; he must appear in a magazine. He would then be a Literary Person; also, he would be famous — right away. These two ambitions were strong upon me. This was in 1866. I prepared my contribution, and then looked around for the best magazine to go up to glory in. I selected the most important one in New York. The contribution was accepted. I signed it "Mark Twain"; for that name had some currency on the Pacific coast, and it was my idea to spread it all over the world, now, at this one jump. The article appeared in the December number, and I sat up a month waiting for the January number; for that one would contain the year's list of contributors, my name would be in it, and I should be famous and could give the banquet I was meditating.

I did not give the banquet. I had not written the "Mark Twain" distinctly; it was a fresh name to Eastern printers, and they put it "Mike Swain" or "MacSwain," I do not remember which.* At any rate, I was not celebrated, and I did not give the banquet. I was a Literary Person, but that was all — a buried one; buried alive.

My article was about the burning of the clipper-ship *Hornet* on the line, May 3, 1866. There were thirty-one men on board at the time, and I was in Honolulu when the fifteen lean and ghostly survivors arrived there after a voyage of forty-three days in an open boat, through the blazing tropics, on ten days' rations of food. A very remarkable trip, but it was conducted by a captain who was a remarkable man, otherwise there would have been no survivors. He was a New-Englander of the best sea-going stock of the old capable times — Captain Josiah Mitchell.

I was in the islands to write letters for the weekly edition of the Sacramento *Union*, a rich and influential daily journal which hadn't any use for them, but could afford to spend twenty dollars a week for nothing. The proprietors were lovable and well-believed men: long ago dead, no doubt, but in me there is at least one person who still holds them in grafeful remembrance; for I dearly wanted to see the islands, and they listened to me and gave me the opportunity when there was but slender likelihood that it could profit them in any way.

I had been in the islands several months when the survivors arrived. I was laid up in my room at the time, and unable to walk. Here was a great occasion to serve my journal, and I not able to take advantage of it. Necessarily I was in deep trouble. But by good luck his Excellency Anson Burlingame** was there at the time, on his way to take up his post in China, where he did such good work for the United States. He came and put me on a stretcher and had me carried to the hospital where the shipwrecked men were, and I never needed to ask a question. He attended to all of that himself, and I had nothing to do but make the notes. It was like him to take that trouble. He was a great man and a great American, and it was in his fine nature to come down from his high office and do a friendly turn whenever he could.

* *Actually Mark Swain. HARPER'S MONTHLY MAGAZINE, Nov. 1866.*

** *See footnote for Henry Ferguson's Journal of July 4.*

We got through with this work at six in the evening. I took no dinner, for there was no time to spare if I would beat the other correspondents. I spent four hours arranging the notes in their proper order, then wrote all night and beyond it; with this result: that I had a very long and detailed account of the *Hornet* episode ready at nine in the morning, while the correspondents of the San Francisco journals had nothing but a brief outline report — for they didn't sit up. The now-and-then schooner* was to sail for San Francisco about nine; when I reached the dock she was free forward and was just casting off her stern-line. My fat envelop was thrown by a strong hand, and fell on board all right, and my victory was a safe thing. All in due time the ship reached San Francisco, but it was my complete report which made the stir and was telegraphed to the New York papers, by Mr. Cash; he was in charge of the Pacific bureau of the New York *Herald* at the time.

When I returned to California by and by, I went up to Sacramento and presented a bill for general correspondence at twenty dollars a week. It was paid. Then I presented a bill for "special" service on the *Hornet* matter of three columns of solid nonpareil at a *hundred dollars a column.* The cashier didn't faint, but he came rather near it. He sent for the proprietors, and they came and never uttered a protest. They only laughed in their jolly fashion, and said it was robbery, but no matter; it was a grand "scoop" (the bill or my *Hornet* report, I didn't know which); "pay it. It's all right." The best men that ever owned a newspaper.

The *Hornet* survivors reached the Sandwich Islands the 15th of June. They were mere skinny skeletons; their clothes hung limp about them and fitted them no better than a flag fits the flagstaff in a calm. But they were well nursed in the hospital; the people of Honolulu kept them supplied with all the dainties they could need; they gathered strength fast, and were presently nearly as good as new. Within a fortnight the most of them took ship for San Francisco; that is if my dates have not gone astray in my memory. I went in the same ship, a sailing-vessel.** Captain Mitchell of the *Hornet* was along; also the only passengers the *Hornet* had carried. These were two young gentlemen from Stamford, Connecticut — brothers: Samuel Ferguson, aged twenty-eight, a graduate of Trinity College, Hartford, and Henry Ferguson, aged eighteen, a student of the same college, and now at this present writing a professor there, a post which he has held for many years. He is fifty years old this year (1898). Samuel had been wasting away with consumption for some years, and the long voyage around the Horn had been advised as offering a last hope for him. The *Hornet* was a clipper of the first class and a fast sailer; the young men's quarters were roomy and comfortable, and were well stocked with books, and also with canned meats and fruits to help out the ship-fare with; and when the ship cleared from New York harbor in the first week of January there was promise that she would make quick and pleasant work of the fourteen or fifteen thousand miles in front of her. As soon as the cold latitudes were left behind and the vessel entered summer weather, the voyage became a holiday picnic. The ship flew Southward under a cloud of sail which needed no attention, no modifying or change of any kind, for days together. The young men read, strolled the ample deck, rested and drowsed in the shade of the canvas, took their meals with the captain; and when the day was done they played dummy whist with him till bedtime. After the snow and ice and tempests of the Horn, the ship bowled Northward into summer weather again, and the trip was a picnic once more.

Until the early morning of the 3d of May. Computed position of the ship 112° $10'$ West longitude; latitude 2° above the equator; no wind, no sea — dead calm; temperature of the atmosphere, tropical, blistering, unimaginable by one who has not been roasted in it. There was a cry of fire. An unfaithful sailor had disobeyed the rules and gone into the booby-hatch

* *The MILTON BADGER.*

** *The bark SMYRNIOTE.*

with an open light to draw some varnish from a cask. The proper result followed, and the vessel's hours were numbered.

There was not much time to spare, but the captain made the most of it. The three boats were launched — longboat and two quarterboats. That the time was very short and the hurry and excitement considerable is indicated by the fact that in launching the boats a hole was stove in the side of one of them by some sort of collision, and an oar driven through the side of another. The captain's first care was to have four sick sailors brought up and placed on deck out of harm's way — among them a "Portyghee." This man had not done a day's work on the voyage, but had lain in his hammock four months nursing an abscess. When we were taking notes in the Honolulu hospital and a sailor told this to Mr. Burlingame, the third mate, who was lying near, raised his head with an effort, and in a weak voice made this correction — with solemnity and feeling:

"*Raising* abscesses! He had a family of them. He done it to keep from standing his watch."

Any provisions that lay handy were gathered up by the men and the two passengers and brought and dumped on the deck where the "Portyghee" lay; then they ran for more. The sailor who was telling this to Mr. Burlingame added:

"We pulled together thirty-two days' rations for the thirty-one men that way."
The third mate lifted his head again and made another correction — with bitterness:

"The Portyghee et twenty-two of them while he was soldiering there and nobody noticing. A damned hound."

The fire spread with great rapidity. The smoke and flame drove the men back, and they had to stop their incomplete work of fetching provisions, and take to the boats with only ten days' rations secured.

Each boat had a compass, a quadrant, a copy of Bowditch's "Navigator," and a nautical almanac, and the captain's and chief mate's boats had chronometers. There were thirty-one men all told. The captain took an account of stock, with the following result: four hams, nearly thirty pounds of salt pork, half-box of raisins, one hundred pounds of bread, twelve two-pound cans of oysters, clams, and assorted meats, a keg containing water in a forty-gallon "scuttle-butt," four bottles of brandy (the property of passengers), some pipes, matches, and a hundred pounds of tobacco. No medicines. Of course the whole party had to go on short rations at once.

The captain and the two passengers kept diaries. On our voyage to San Francisco we ran into a calm in the middle of the Pacific, and did not move a rod during fourteen days; this gave me a chance to copy the diaries. Samuel Ferguson's in the fullest; I will draw up it now. When the following paragraph was written the ship was about one hundred and twenty days out from port, and all hands were putting in the lazy time about as usual, as no one was forecasting disaster.

Note: As in the previous article, Mark Twain here quotes directly from the logs of the Captain and the Ferguson brothers and his comments have already appeared in proper sequence in the text and are not repeated here. The present narrative is continued with Mark Twain's summary.

It is an amazing adventure. There is nothing of its sort in history that surpasses it in impossibilities made possible. In one extraordinary detail — the survival of *every person* in the boat — it probably stands alone in the history of adventures of its kind. Usually merely a part of a boat's company survive — officers, mainly, and other educated and tenderly reared men, unused to hardship and heavy labor; the untrained, roughly reared hard workers succumb. But in this case even the rudest and roughest stood the privations and miseries of the voyage almost as well as did the college-bred young brothers and the captain. I mean, physically. The minds of most of the sailors broke down in the fourth week and went to temporary ruin, but physically the endurance exhibited was astonishing. Those men did not survive by any merit of their own, of course, but by merit of the character and intelligence of the captain; they lived by the mastery of his spirit. Without him they would have been children without a nurse; they would have exhausted their provisions in a week, and their pluck would not have lasted even as long as the provisions.

The boat came near to being wrecked at the last. As it approached the shore the sail was let go, and came down with a run; then the captain saw that he was drifting swiftly toward an ugly reef, and an effort was made to hoist the sail again: but it could not be done; the men's strength was wholly exhausted; they could not even pull an oar. They were helpless, and death imminent. It was then that they were discovered by the two Kanakas who achieved the rescue. They swam out and manned the boat and piloted her through a narrow and hardly noticeable break in the reef — the only break in it in a stretch of thirty-five miles! The spot where the landing was made was the only one in that stretch where footing could have been found on the shore; everywhere else precipices came sheer down into forty fathoms of water. Also, in all that stretch this was the only spot where anybody lived.

Within ten days after the landing all the men but one were up and creeping about. Properly, they ought to have killed themselves with the "food" of the last few days — some of them, at any rate — men who had freighted their stomachs with strips of leather from old boots and with chips from the butter-cask; a freightage which they did not get rid of by digestion, but by other means. The captain and the two passengers did not eat strips and chips, as the sailors, but *scraped* the boot-leather and the wood, and made a pulp of the scrapings by moistening them with water. The third mate told me that the boots were old and full of holes; then added thoughtfully, "but the holes digested the best". Speaking of digestion, here is a remarkable thing, and worth noting; during this strange voyage, and for a while afterward on shore, the bowels of some of the men virtually ceased from their functions; in some cases there was no action for twenty and thirty days, and in one case for forty-four! Sleeping also came to be rare. Yet the men did very well without it. During many days the captain did not sleep at all — twenty-one, I think, on one stretch.

When the landing was made, all the men were successfully protected from overeating except the "Portyghee"; he escaped the watch and ate an incredible number of bananas: a hundred and fifty-two, the third mate said, but this was undoubtedly an exaggeration; I think it was a hundred and fifty-one. He was already nearly full of leather; it was hanging out of his ears. (I do not state this on the third mate's authority, for we have seen what sort of person he was; I state it on my own.) The "Portyghee" ought to have died, of course, and even now it seems a pity that he didn't; but he got well, and as early as any of them; and all full of leather, too, the way he was, and butter-timber and handkerchiefs and bananas. Some of the men did eat handkerchiefs in those last days, also socks; and he was one of them.

It is to the credit of the men that they did not kill the rooster that crowed so gallantly mornings. He lived eighteen days, and then stood up and stretched his neck and made a brave, weak effort to do his duty once more, and died in the act. It is a picturesque detail; and so is that rainbow, too, — the only one seen in the forty-three days — raising its triumphal arch in the skies for the sturdy fighters to sail under to victory and rescue.

With ten days' provisions Captain Josiah Mitchell performed this memorable voyage of forty-three days and eight hours in an open boat, sailing four thousand miles in reality and thirty-three hundred and sixty by direct courses, and brought every man safe to land. A bright, simple-hearted, unassuming, plucky, and most companionable man. I walked the deck with him twenty-eight days, — when I was not copying diaries, — and I remember him with reverent honor. If he is alive he is eighty-six years old now.*

If I remember rightly, Samuel Ferguson died soon after we reached San Francisco.** I do not think he lived to see him home again; his disease had doubtless doomed him when he left it.

For a time it was hoped that the two quarter-boats would presently be heard of, but this hope suffered disappointment. They went down with all on board, no doubt, not even sparing that knightly chief mate.

The authors of the diaries wanted to smooth them up a little before allowing me to copy them, but there was no occasion for that, and I persuaded them out of it. These diaries are finely modest and unaffected, and with unconscious and unintentional art they rise toward the climax with graduated and gathering force and swing and dramatic intensity; they sweep you along with a cumulative rush, and when the cry rings out at last, "Land in sight!" your heart is in your mouth, and for a moment you think it is you that have been saved. The last two paragraphs are not improvable by anybody's art; they are literary gold; and their very pauses and uncompleted sentences have in them an eloquence not reachable by any words.

The interest of this story is unquenchable; it is of the sort that time cannot decay. I have not looked at the diaries for thirty-two years, but I find that they have lost nothing in that time. Lost? They have gained; for by some subtle law all tragic human experiences gain in pathos by the perspective of time. We realize this when in Naples we stand musing over the poor Pompeian mother, lost in the historic storm of volcanic ashes eighteen centuries ago, who lies with her child gripped close to her breast, trying to save it, and whose despair and grief have been preserved for us by the fiery envelop which took her life but eternalized her form and features. She moves us, she haunts us, she stays in our thoughts for many days, we do not know why, for she is nothing to us, she has been nothing to anyone for eighteen centuries; whereas of the like case today we should say, "Poor thing! it is pitiful," and forget it in an hour.

* *Captain Mitchell died in New York, July 23, 1876 at the age of 64.*
** *Samuel Ferguson died at Santa Clara, October 1, 1866.*

Volcanic Islands — woodcut from The Ocean, *1856.*

AFTERWORD

AFTERWORD

Although the Ferguson Brothers stopped writing in their journals once the bark *Smyrniote* had delivered them safely to San Francisco on August 13, Captain Mitchell continued to keep up his diary, faithfully recording at least a line or two right through to the end of the year 1866. From these entries we learn that, when he returned to his home in Freeport, Maine, on September 25, he found desperately ill his beloved wife, Susan, who he had mentioned so frequently. After much suffering, Mrs. Mitchell died only a little more than a month later, on October 31, effectively wiping out the captain's dream of taking her back with him to retire in Hawaii. On August 28, before leaving San Francisco, he had written that he wanted to go to the islands to live — "how happy my wife would be there," he said — residing on board what Mark Twain had feelingly characterized as "the loveliest fleet of islands that lies anchored in any ocean."

In due time, then, Captain Mitchell went back to sea once more — in a variety of vessels and for voyages of varying duration. He got married again in 1874 to Katie Thing, but this new tie did not keep him long ashore. Apparently his last command was the *Ellen Austin*, an 1812-ton ship built at Damarascotta, Maine, in 1854 and owned by Spofford and Tileston. On August 1, 1875, he wrote from San Francisco that the ship was lying in the stream all ready to take off with a full crew of 28 for Callao and the guano ports of Peru, thence 'round the Horn and on to London.

"A long, perplexing and hard voyage for me with my poor health to undertake and were it not for fear the owners might be displeased and think me ungrateful and attribute my leaving

Capt. J.A. Mitchell later life photo from Mrs. C.L. Tilden.

- 230 -

to other causes, I should assuredly leave — for I am weak and more miserable, and feeble, than is known to any but myself.*

The foreword prepared for the privately printed version of Captain Mitchell's 1866 Diary states: "His health, however, which had never been robust since his terrible experience in 1866, now failed completely and he was obliged to give up his command and return by steamer to New York. His failing strength barely enabled him to reach the home of a relative in New York where his daughters Florence and May and his wife of less than a year [actually two years] reached him in time for a greeting and farewell."

Death came on July 23, 1876 in his sixty-fourth year and he was buried in Freeport.

The precious *Hornet* diary then became in turn the possession of his children — his son Harrison W. Mitchell ("Harry" in the diary) and, upon his death, his daughters Florence Hudson of Niles and Lily Tilden of Alameda, California, thence to the former's daughter, Mrs. Chester Hudson Hatch of Auburn, California.

Regrettably, Samuel Ferguson never lived to see home again. Perishing with consumption all along, the fearful privations of the boat voyage proved insurmountable. Only a month and a half after arriving in California, he died at Santa Clara on October 1, 1866. His body was returned to a grieving family for burial in St. John's Parish adjoining St. Andrew's Church, 27 Washington Avenue, Stamford, Connecticut. In due course his journal was handed down to a nephew, Henry L. Ferguson, the son of another brother, Walton Ferguson.

Henry Ferguson, a sophomore at Trinity College in Hartford when he interrupted his academic career to accompany his brother Samuel on the *Hornet* voyage, returned home and resumed his studies. Making up for lost time, he managed to graduate with his Class of 1868. His experiences at sea contributed in large part to a later decision to enter the Episcopal ministry and he began the study of Theology at the Barkeley Divinity School in 1869. He was ordained Deacon in 1872 and became a Priest a year later. Then ensued the rectorship of various parishes in New Hampshire followed by a period of travel and study abroad.

In 1863 the young clergyman-scholar was chosen Northam Professor of History and Political Science at Trinity and the remainder of his long and useful career was dedicated to education. He gave up his active 23-year Trinity professorship in 1906 to become the third Rector of St. Paul's School in Concord, New Hampshire, from which he had graduated over forty years earlier. He returned to Hartford in 1911 and to less strenuous academic work at Trinity which in 1900 had awarded him the degree of Doctor of Laws.

Henry Ferguson, widely revered as a man of God and a man of letters, died in his 69th year at his Hartford home at 123 Vernon Street, March 30, 1917. He was survived by his wife Emma, three sons and a daughter. Burial was held on Palm Sunday, April 1, 1917, in the churchyard of St. Paul's School.**

Mark Twain, by that time the nation's foremost literary lion, moved to Hartford in the 1870's living in a house at 351 Farmington Avenue, now preserved as his memorial. Here he renewed his acquaintance with Henry Ferguson, both belonging to Hartford's literary society, the Monday Evening Club. The little circle of friends bound together by common association with the *Hornet* disaster was further reduced when Mark Twain died on April 21, 1910. As stated, Dr. Ferguson followed him seven years later.

---

* *Quoted in Epilogue of William Roos, THE HORNET LONGBOAT, Boston, 1940, page 239.*

** *Hartford Daily COURANT, Saturday, March 31, 1917; St. Paul's School HORAE SCHOLASTICAE (Vol. 50, No. 7), May 5, 1917, pp. 158-162.*
  Trinity College BULLETIN: Necrology records kindly provided by Peter J. Knapp, Reference Librarian, Trinity College Library.

The Rev. Henry Ferguson, LL.D., Rector of St. Paul's School.
Official School portrait, Courtesy the Library.

The journal which Mark Twain had copied by hand so industriously on board the *Smyrniote* then was carefully preserved by his son, Samuel Ferguson [II]. He had it privately printed in 1924, including also parts taken from Samuel Ferguson's Journal. Three years later, Mr. Ferguson borrowed Captain Mitchell's diary from his daughter, Mrs. Hudson, and also had it privately printed.

The last known survivor of the *Hornet's* company, former seaman Frederick Clough, lived to the ripe old age of eighty, succumbing in 1926 at San Francisco where he had long resided. Apparently Captain Mitchell kept in occasional touch with former members of the *Hornet's* crew. In any event, Clough received the following letter from his former, ever-modest captain in 1873.

December 3, 1873

My dear Friend and Shipmate:

I believe there are but three of us left; at least I know of no more. I saw Henry Ferguson last summer. He had almost finished his study for the ministry. He inquired after you. Cox is dead. We certainly had a wonderful and providential escape, and nothing but God's grace sustained us — not a particle of credit is due to me. I only did what any other man must have done under the circumstances. It was the long, constant watchfulness that broke me down more than all the rest.

(S) J. A. Mitchell

It was reported that Clough's mother had been so upset when she read in some account of the voyage that "the castaways had intended to devour one another," she made her son promise never to speak of the dreadful events again while she was living. After she died, however, and no longer under a promise of silence to his aged parent, Clough's belated account of the trip as written by Legh H. Irvine appeared in *Wide World Magazine* in the September 1900 issue.

Shortly before his own death in 1917, Henry Ferguson heard rumors that his former shipmate Clough — by then a San Francisco waterfront courtesy "captain" — had fallen on hard times. Although he had not laid eyes on Clough for half a century, the Trinity professor promptly arranged for a Hartford insurance company to pay out a small annuity to Clough for the rest of his life. It is reported* that the company's San Francisco office had difficulties locating him as he drifted among the city's shabby rooming houses, but that he was ultimately found and the quarterly payments duly made.

Henry Ferguson had been dead nine years when, at length, on July 14, 1926, Clough was found dying in a house in Kearney Street, near San Francisco's notorious Barbary Coast. A story in the *Call and Post*, quoted by George Bragdon, carried the "Captain's" picture with the announcement that: "Old cronies of the mariner, smoking their pipes in the sun in front of Billy Lyons' bail bond shop in Merchant Street, learned he was dead at Central Emergency Hospital."

Apparently Frederick Clough was the very last of the fifteen men who had defied death for 43 days during the *Hornet* longboat's epic 4,000 mile voyage, sixty years earlier.

* *By George W. Bragdon, "43 Days in Open Boat Epic of HORNET'S Men." The Hartford TIMES, Monday, November 27, 1939.*

San Francisco as it looked when the Hornet survivors arrived August 13, 1866. From a lithograph courtesy the Mariners Museum

DISASTER VOYAGES

DISASTER VOYAGES — A PARTIAL ROSTER

In staking a claim for the *Hornet's* longboat the distinction of being one of, if not the most remarkable open boat voyage ever chronicled, we are well aware that many such feats of endurance, bravery and skill have taken place from the very beginnings of recorded maritime history.

The famous voyage of the *Bounty* launch in 1789,[1] previously cited in the Forword, is generally used as the grim yardstick against which all other such ventures are compared. Indeed, in both distance covered and time spent under unique privations, together with lives spared, it justly deserves the highest rating. But, though the *Hornet's* boat traveled farther — 4,000 to 3,618 miles — and the time spent afloat was longer — 43 to 41 days without stopping on the way — Captain Mitchell in 1866 knew that if he so much as came in sight of inhabited land he would receive every assistance. Captain Bligh, fearing slaughter by unfriendly natives, deliverately steered away from inhabited islands in the Pacific he might easily have reached until he knew he could make a friendly port in far-distant Timor without risking a second disaster. This, of course, increased the bitterness of his venture.

Such feats of navigation hardly stand any form of comparison, however, for how may human suffering, privation and desperation be compared? Certainly some voyages of shorter duration might seem even more unbelievable of success when one realizes the odds to be overcome — particularly on those which occurred in polar seas like that, for example, of doughty Dutch explorer William Barents who escaped ice-bound Nova Zemblya in the Arctic Ocean in his boats during the summer of 1597 and sailed back to Holland.[2]

However, we do not plan to consider here the numerous small boat voyages voluntarily undertaken — some for the sheer pleasure of it, some to be able to chalk up a record for the smallest, the farthest sailed, and some to prove something to themselves, or other reasons. Remarkable as are these ventures — like rowing across the Atlantic or sailing around the world without stopping any place — and as necessary as they might have been to the people who undertook them, those who intentionally go to sea to risk their lives are hardly in the same league as those who go to sea to save them. Captains Bligh, Mitchell, et al., set out in desperate haste in the wake of a catastrophy and without the luxury of advance planning and provisioning their craft before they started. Historically, all too frequently lifeboats have been tragically ill-equipped and unseaworthy.

And yet, there are even degrees of the compelling necessity to use the boats. Many noteworthy voyages have been made after the shipwreck of the parent ship on a desert island where the castaways were afforded sufficient time and resources to rebuild or strengthen a surviving small craft, if not wholly to construct a brand new vessel out of wreckage from ship or shore.

One such voyage occurred in the early days of American history.[3] Captain Christopher Newport's flagship of a major expedition to Virginia, the *Sea Venture*, was bringing future settlers and provisions for the Jamestown colony when she was wrecked on Bermuda reefs on July 28, 1609 following a terrible storm. Providentially, all hands made it ashore and they were able to salvage a large quantity of supplies as well.

Soon afterwards, the ship's longboat was sent out with an eight-man crew in charge of the mate to try to reach the mainland to summon help. Alas, she never made it and her fate is unknown. In due course, however, employing wreckage salvaged from the *Sea Venture*, plus native Bermuda cedar wood, two seaworthy pinnaces were constructed by the castaways. Named the *Deliverance* and the *Patience*, they successfully brought the entire ship's company on to Jamestown in safety, landing May 23 the following year.

In 1938, Victor Slocum, son of the redoubtable Captain Joshua who sailed his famous little sloop, the *Spray*, first singlehanded around the world in 1895 - 1898, compiled an interesting book of such voyages entitled *Castaway Boats*.[4] He offers a baker's dozen true stories ranging in time from the disorderly trip of the *Wager's* rebuilt longboat in 1741, to Sir Ernest Shackleton's 1916 escape from sub-Antarctic seas.

His Majesty's Store Ship *Wager* was a member of Commodore Anson's squadron which left England on a voyage of Pacific exploration in September 1740.[5] The ill-managed *Wager* had already lost a mast when she struck a sunken rock off the desolate shores of Patagonia and was ultimately beached, the captain being the first man to abandon ship. After some four months work, her longboat was converted to a 40-foot schooner by cutting it in half and building in a new 'midships section — an early example of the "jumboizing" process, so named and developed by the Newport News Shipbuilding and Dry Dock Company after World War II as a means of lengthening tankers.

Following her launching October 12, 1741, the newly christened schooner *Speedwell* set off with many of the crew, in defiance of the incompetent captain's order, and ultimately completed a successful voyage through Magellan Straits, thence 1500 miles up the east coast of South America to the Rio Grande. There were thirty survivors of the original sixty embarked.

Another voyage mentioned by Victor Slocum was that of the gig of the U.S.S. *Saginaw* in 1870.[6] The *Saginaw* was an auxiliary steam brig built for the U.S. Navy in 1859. While returning from Midway Island bound for San Francisco with a large company of construction workers on board, she was so unfortunate as to run on a coral reef at uninhabited Ocean Island at 3 A.M. on October 30, 1870. Though all hands got ashore with a fair amount of supplies and equipment, the crew undoubtedly would have starved to death on the bleak atoll unless succor could soon be obtained.

Accordingly, the 22-foot gig was decked over and, rigged as a little schooner, she set sail heading eastward for Hawaii. On board was a four-man crew in charge of the executive officer, Lieutenant J. C. Talbot, USN. After a 31-day, 1800 mile voyage, the gig arrived off Kauai Island December 29, 1870. But all except one man, Coxwain William Halford, were drowned in getting ashore when the gig capsized and was rolled over on a fringing reef. Properly alerted by brave Halford who struggled to land, the government immediately dispatched an expedition to rescue the castaways, arriving at Ocean Island some 46 days after the little gig had taken her departure on this errand of mercy. The gig, once preserved at the United States Naval Academy Museum at Annapolis, now reposes in a museum at Saginaw, Michigan.

The final voyage of this type, that of British polar explorer Sir Ernest Shackleton,[7] took place following the destruction of the former auxiliary whaling bark *Endurance*, chartered by the Admiralty for Antarctic exploration. This was reminiscent of the dreadful 500-mile voyage of the three boats of the Arctic expedition ship *Jeanette* in 1881. Caught in the ice and crushed, the *Endurance* sank on November 21, 1915. Following this, the men dragged their sleds, boats and equipment over the ice floes to the dubious haven of uninhabited Elephant Island in the South Shetlands. But they could go no further and a slow death obviously awaited all hands unless help could be summoned. Their 20-foot whaler was in fair condition and it was equipped as best they could for an ocean voyage to the island of South Georgia where a whaling station was located.

The rebuilt lifeboat was duly named the *James Caird* and Shackleton and five men embarked in her, leaving twenty-two of their companions behind. The 800-mile trip was a nightmare lasting 16 terrible days while their little craft was beset by breaking seas and Antarctic blizzards. But they made it to land and ultimately, after further privations, crossed the mountainous crest of the island to reach the whaling station on the other side whence help was sent.

To bear comparison with the *Bounty* and *Hornet*, however, survival craft would have to be those used exactly as they were when tragedy struck. On the spur of the moment Bligh and his men — 19 in all — were herded into the 23-foot *Bounty* launch at gunpoint and what supplies the mutineers felt they needed to make nearby islands were thrown in after them and they were then set adrift. Similarly with the *Hornet*, once the fire started there was only the briefest time left in which to gather stores before they must pull away from the inferno. Two *Hornet* boats were damaged in their haste to embark.

One such truly comparable adventure befell the whaleboats of the Nantucket whaleship *Essex*,[8] already described in a footnote in connection with mention of Henderson Island in the journals for May 4, 1866. This curious little island lies in the South Pacific, but had also been incorrectly located in the northern hemisphere on charts available in the *Hornet's* day.

As stated in the note, on November 20, 1820, the *Essex* was rammed and sunk by an enraged whale. Hastily provisioned, the three whaleboats contrived to reach Henderson Island after sailing some 1500 miles from the spot where the *Essex* went down. Three of the crew elected to remain on Henderson despite the very good chance they might starve to death. After a week ashore at that desolate place, the others proceeded on in the boats. One disappeared at sea, but the other two, having covered no less than 4,500 miles, were picked up within a few days of each other near the coast of Chile after being adrift for more than three desperate months. Captain Pollard's 95-day voyage, as far as we can determine, made some sort of a grim record. Eight survived out of the original twenty aboard the whaler, but the luster of this attainment was dimmed by the fact that some of the men resorted to cannibalism, the cabin boy being expressly shot for the others to eat.

Another remarkable boat voyage — in that there were no casualties — followed the burning of the British East Indiaman *Lord Eldon*[9] in the middle of the Indian Ocean in 1834 on a voyage back home from Bombay. As with the *Hornet*, the ship's company hastily took to the three boats when spontaneous combustion ignited the Indiaman's cargo of baled cotton. After a few days sailing southward in company, the mate's boat split her seams and its ten occupants had to be quickly taken into the already well-filled longboat. This, with 36 people then embarked, had only eight inches of freeboard and might easily swamp at any moment. The two surviving boats were extremely fortunate to be able to cover the thousand-mile distance to Rodriguez Island in 14 days with constant bailing but without further serious mishap. Perhaps the most remarkable thing was that in the longboat with Captain Theaker were four women, a four-months-old baby and two invalid men. But the weather remained good and the wind reasonably steady for the entire trip, else they would surely never have made it.

Many other nineteenth century castaway voyages could be cited in the era before steamships, accurate navigation and wireless telegraphy replaced sailing vessels, dead reckoning and visual messaging. But even these changes in man's ways of seafaring have not completely eliminated the call for skill and daring in small boat seamanship and some equally remarkable voyages have been made in comparatively modern times.

One began on June 4, 1923 following the foundering during heavy gales in the Indian Ocean of the venerable British cargo steamship *Trevessa*.[10] Though wireless messages were sent out describing their plight, by the time rescue vessels could search the region where the *Trevessa* sank, her lifeboats had apparently vanished. Actually, Captain Cecil Foster, exercising splendid judgment and seamanship, despite the stormy weather, had safely embarked his entire crew of 44 in two of the ship's 26-foot clinker-built wooden lifeboats. Equipped with dipping lug sails, they headed westward with the prevailing monsoon urging them along.

Though they kept in sight of each other at the beginning, the two boats later separated. The captain's boat reached land in 23 days at Rodriguez Island — incidentally the same haven reached by the *Lord Eldon's* boats, just mentioned — having covered 1700 miles. The other boat, in charge of Chief Officer J.C.S. Smith, missed Rodriguez and sailed on by, but made port two days later a couple of hundred miles farther on at Mauritius. Eleven men lost their lives by reason of exposure and exhaustion, though drinking sea water on the sly was also contributory.

Coming down to even more modern times, World War II was responsible for three small craft voyages detailed in this brief review.

The British tramp steamer *Anglo-Saxon*,[11] with a crew of 40 men, was transporting a cargo of coal from Newport, England, to South America. On August 21, 1940, in 26° 10′ north latitude by 34° 09′ west longtitude, the unfortunate ship was attacked "with homicidal fury" by the Nazi surface raider *Weser*, a converted 9,000-ton German motor cargo liner. Though virtually all officers and crew of the *Anglo-Saxon* who survived the initial shelling and the resultant explosion of the boilers were mercilessly machine-gunned when they attempted to abandon ship, one boat — the 18-foot, bitterly mislabeled "jolly boat" — managed to sneak away with eight men on board.

Some of the men, badly wounded, soon died. But for others, like courageous Chief Mate C.B. Denny, who kept a journal in which he made carefully considered recommendations on how lifeboats might better be equipped, the period of suffering was far longer.

At length, after an incredible seventy days, the jolly boat with two sailors, Robert Tapscott, 19, and Wilbert Widdicombe, 21, emaciated skeletons but still miraculously alive even though they had had neither water nor nourishment for the final week, came ashore on the island of Eleuthera in the Bahamas. They had drifted some 3,000 miles from the point where the *Anglo-Saxon* went down.

After careful attendance at Eleuthera, at length the pair of survivors was well enough to go on to the United States. Widdicombe was the first to leave to return to England. But he lost his life when the British steamer *Siamese Prince* was torpedoed by a Nazi U-boat on February 18, 1941, and sank with all hands — so compounding an already all-too-grim tragedy!

Another lengthy World War II disaster voyage came about with the ditching of a lost U.S. Army Air Corps Flying Fortress.[12] The bomber with eight on board was en route Hickham Field, Honolulu, on October 18, 1942, following an intelligence gathering mission in the central Pacific. The plane missed its bearings in bad weather, radio contact was lost and, running out of fuel, it was forced to come down in the ocean eastward of the Gilbert Islands.

In addition to the regular crew, the Flying Fortress carried an illustrious passenger — World War I flying ace Eddie Rickenbacker. As their plane sank, all embarked in tiny inflatable rubber rafts and somehow managed to survive 21 days of merciless heat by day and chilling cold by night. Though one man succumbed, at length the others were spotted by a U.S. Navy plane and help was soon at hand.

Though no reliable navigational data could be kept, Rickenbacker estimated that the rafts had drifted in the neighborhood of five hundred miles during the three-week period. It was truly a miraculous feat of survival.

Another truly remarkable World War II open-boat voyage occurred in the wake of the torpedoing in the South Atlantic of the American Liberty Ship *Roger B. Taney*, commanded by Captain Tom Potter.[13] On the night of February 9, 1943, the unfortunate *Taney* was pursued by a surfaced German submarine, the *U-160*, which, after chasing the 12-knot freighter for an hour, contrived to put a torpedo in her engine room, sending her to the bottom.

All hands, save three on watch below who lost their lives in the explosion, boarded two lifeboats and elected to strike out for the southeast trade winds and the coast of Brazil. Soon separated by rough weather, the first mate's boat was fortunate to be picked up 21 days later. Captain Potter's boat, however, had a far longer ordeal. After 42 grueling days at sea, experiencing everything from flat calm to gales of hurricane force, the lifeboat was spotted near the coast of Brazil by a passenger ship which hastened to bring aid. Safe at last after this 42-day ordeal, the captain estimated that they had sailed more than 2,600 miles from the point where his ship went down.

Of all the near-incredible feats of courage and seamanship recounted in this section apparently none, perhaps, can compare with the two most recent ones to have occurred. Both of these closely parallel the *Hornet* longboat's voyage in significant respects, the most notable of which is that they took place in almost the very same waters in which the *Hornet's* men were suddenly cast adrift. Also like the *Hornet*, an almost preternatural determination to survive on their own resources, come what may, galvanized these recent castaways to defy the elements and to accept the fact that they must make it completely by themselves. This followed the crushing disappointments of coming within plain sight of ill-watched vessels that failed to heed their distress signals and sailed obliviously right on by. Captain Mitchell's men must have experienced the same desperate grief when they passed directly over the non-existent mythical isles of the American Group, a thousand miles east of Hawaii.

In 1972 this great feat of seamanship and endurance was recorded by a Scots family of five — the father, 48-year-old Dougal Robertson, a former British merchant mariner, his wife Lyn, their twin twelve-year-old sons, their 18-year-old older brother and a 22-year-old student friend. The family was engaged in a leisurely 'round the world educational cruise on board a 43-foot, 50-year-old wooden schooner yacht, the *Lucette*.

Having crossed the Atlantic and traversed the Panama Canal, they had left the Galapagos Islands some 200 miles behind en route to the Marquesas, when, at 10 A.M. on June 15, 1972, their schooner was rammed by a school of killer whales. With the bottom torn out, the *Lucette* went down in less than a minute, barely giving Robertson time to cast off their nine-foot plywood dinghy and an inflatable rubber raft and for all hands to squeeze aboard.

Taking stock of their provisions and water, Robertson estimated that at best they would last only six days. It would, then, be fruitless to expect they could continue on their present course to islands weeks ahead, despite the prevailing trades. Ironically, the weather would be too good, for without squalls to replenish their water, they all must surely die.

Accordingly, they headed north for the very same doldrums that the *Hornet's* men sought. Their destination, hopefully, would be the coast of Costa Rica, a thousand miles distant. At first all hands rode the inflatable raft which had a canvas awning, while the dinghy, untended but rigged with a crude square-sail, provided the motive power. They soon became adept at catching fish and turtles and began to live entirely off what they could wrest from their alien environment. Robertson proved himself skillful at making do as the famous Swiss castaway of the same name.

Sooner or later, though, the badly chaffed rubber raft must give out. This it did on the seventeenth day. Undaunted, all hands then moved into the dinghy, now down to a mere six-inch freeboard and in constant danger of capsizing. But they made out well and, at length, on the thirty-eighth day, when their tiny craft was sighted by a Japanese tuna boat with a proper lookout, the Robertsons still had the determination and resources to continue.

Dougal Robertson estimated that they had sailed more than 750 miles from the time their schooner sank and, with land less than three hundred miles away, he was certain that they would have been able to make it to shore. His unassuming narrative of this voyage must surely rate one of the recent classics of the sea.[14]

Finally comes the publication of a remarkable book which may well chronicle the most incredible voyage of survival of all time. By an unusual coincidence, it so closely parallels the story of the Dougal Robertson family as to be almost uncanny. It, too, recounts the voyage of an English family who had decided to pull up stakes and sail for the Antipodes to start new lives.

The husband and wife team of Maurice and Maralyn Bailey purchased a 31-foot ketch and, like the Robertsons, had successfully crossed the Atlantic west-bound, transited the Panama Canal and were well out in the Pacific when their craft, too, was fatally disabled by a denizen of the deep — in their case a single huge sperm whale which surfaced under the ketch and stove a lethal hole in the venerable *Auralyn*.

The Baileys contrived to board their rubber life raft and then, for a virtually unbelievable 117 days — some four months (a world's record by anybody's count) — they managed to wrest their existance from the sea, alternately threatened by crashing waves and blistered by a relentless Doldrums sun. At length, buoyed only by their sheer determination to survive, they were sighted and picked up by a Korean fishing vessel on June 30, 1973. A total of seven other vessels had passed them by!

Their book, too, is a remarkable testament of faith and love for each other.[15]

These, then, are some of the more remarkable examples of seamanship and bravery which, as with the *Hornet* longboat, made it possible to snatch victory from the jaws of disaster. It is a proud record and those who made it were men indeed, for, as redoubtable Captain John Smith well expressed it in his *Seamen's Grammar* — as timely today as when written in 1627 — "there is no dallying nor excuses with stormes, gusts, overgrowne Seas and lee-shores."

Yet all accounts of survivors of small-boat voyages agree that there is in addition to good leadership and good luck, a further ingredient for success to gain the victory. Captain Mitchell was not alone in gladly confessing that though their escape was "wonderful and providential" in the end "nothing but God's grace sustained us."

The *Hornet's* company threw themselves on His mercy and He upheld them through their travail. Many other fortunate mariners experienced the same salvation.

A.C.B.

1. *Captain Bligh's own account is best: A VOYAGE TO THE SOUTH SEA . . . IN H. M. SHIP THE BOUNTY . . . London, 1792. This was reprinted in A BOOK OF THE BOUNTY, edited by George Mackaness. Everyman Library No. 950, London, 1938.*

2. *THE THREE VOYAGES OF WILLIAM BARENTS TO THE ARCTIC REGIONS (1594, 5, 6), by Garrit de Veer. Translation for the Hakluyt Society. London, 1876.*

3. *HAKLUYTUS POSTHUMUS OR PURCHAS HIS PILGRIMES, by Samuel Purchas. Reprinted in 20 volumes, Glasgow, 1906. Vol. 19 gives the full text of William Strachey's contemporary "Letter to an Unknown Lady" (pp. 5 - 44) describing the wreck of the SEA VENTURE and her company's subsequent two-month enforced stay on the island of Bermuda. The story was retold in a modern version in BEYOND HORIZONS, VOYAGES OF ADVENTURE AND DISCOVERY, by Carleton Mitchell. New York, 1953, in Chapter 7, "An Enchanted Shore - Shipwreck on Bermuda" (pp. 175 - 191).*

4. *New York: Lee Furman, Inc., 1938.*

5. *A VOYAGE TO THE SOUTH SEAS IN HIS MAJESTY'S SHIP THE WAGER IN THE YEARS 1740 - 1741, by John Bulkeley and John Cummins. London, 1743. (New edition London: Harrap, 1927). Retold by Victor Slocum: Chapter 11, "Voyage of the Wager Longboat" (pp. 204 - 244).*

6. *"Narrative of William Halford, Only Survivor of the Cruise of the Gig of the SAGINAW," by Hanson W. Baldwin. United States Naval Institute PROCEEDINGS (Volume 61, Number 391), September 1935 (pp. 156 - 178).*

7. *SOUTH: THE STORY OF SHACKLETON'S LAST EXPEDITION, 1914 - 1917, by Sir Ernest Shackleton, New York, 1920. Retold by Victor Slocum: Chapter 10, "Shackleton's Boat Voyage" (pp. 190 - 203).*

8. *NARRATIVE OF THE MOST EXTRAORDINARY AND DISTRESSING SHIPWRECK OF THE WHALE SHIP ESSEX OF NANTUCKET, by Owen Chase. New York, 1821. (The narrative of Mate Owen Chase, together with that of Thomas Chappel, first published in 1830 and notes by Herman Melville, was reprinted New York: Corinth Books, Inc., 1963). The story has been retold on many occasions. Victor Slocum has Chapter 4, "The Essex Castaways" (pp. 79 - 102).*

9. *Retold by Victor Slocum: Chapter 5, "The Lord Eldon's Boats" (pp. 103 - 109).*

10. *1700 MILES IN OPEN BOATS: THE STORY OF THE LOSS OF S.S. TREVESSA . . . by Capt. Cecil Foster. London, 1924.*

11. *TWO SURVIVED: THE STORY OF TAPSCOTT AND WIDDICOMBE, WHO WERE TORPEDOED IN MID-ATLANTIC AND SURVIVED 70 DAYS IN AN OPEN BOAT,* as narrated to Guy Pearce Jones. London, 1941.

12. *SEVEN CAME THROUGH: RICKENBACKER'S FULL STORY,* by Edward V. Rickenbacker. Garden City, 1943. Also, *WE THOUGHT WE HEARD THE ANGELS SING . . .* by Lieut. James C. Whittaker. New York, 1943.

13. *LIBERTY SHIPS: THE UGLY DUCKLINGS OF WORLD WAR II,* by John Gorley Bunker. Annapolis, Md., 1972 (pp. 103 - 105).

14. *SURVIVE THE SAVAGE SEA,* by Dougal Robertson. New York, 1973.

15. *STAYING ALIVE,* by Maurice and Maralyn Bailey. New York, 1974.

Note: *A United Press International news release of August 30, 1974, received as we go to press, relates that two U.S. Naval Reserve pilots recently undertook a lengthy ocean voyage voluntarily in a 16-foot raft as a means of testing survival gear. The men, George Sigler, 29, and Charles Gore, 27, both of Alameda, California, left San Francisco on July 4, 1974 and were picked up by a U.S. Coast Guard helicopter almost two months later, some 120 miles from their planned landfall on the Hawaiian island of Kauai, and were taken to Honolulu. They had sailed 2,600 miles in 56 days.*

The voyage was intended to prove that two people, starting out without food or water, but with simple survival gear, could wrest a living from the sea and contrive to find their way across the ocean. Each man lost 40 pounds on the voyage and they reported that their principal diversion was talking about food.

Since the two pilots elected to take this trip, it could hardly qualify as a "disaster voyage." But we are glad to include it here since the experience of the pilots obviously parallels that of the several involuntary raft voyages already cited in this section.

BIBLIOGRAPHY

BIBLIOGRAPHY

MANUSCRIPT SOURCES

JOURNAL OF CAPT. JOSIAH A. MITCHELL, Freeport, Maine

POCKET DIARY FOR 1866, published annually by Bailey and Noyes, Portland.

Date entries of eight lines each are printed three to a 3¼ by 5½ - inch page. A monthly calendar is printed in the front of the book and space for memoranda, cash accounts, and so forth, is provided in the back.
Captain Mitchell wrote an entry for virtually every day in the entire year 1866 and also filled up the back with notes, letters, expense accounts and memoranda. The original is in possession of the descendants of the captain's daughter. The complete diary was privately printed in Hartford in 1927.

JOURNAL OF HENRY FERGUSON, Stamford, Connecticut

DAILY MEMORANDUM BOOK FOR 1866 . . . published annually by Francis & Loutrel, New York.

Date entries of twenty lines each are printed one to a page measuring 3¼ inches by 5½ inches. Space for miscellaneous entries is given at the end.
Henry Ferguson contributed an entry for practically every day from January to August, 1866. He made pencil drawings of the HORNET burning, the two quarter boats and a map of the Hawaiian Islands which appear in the back. The original is in the possession of descendants of Henry Ferguson's son Samuel Ferguson [II] of Hartford. The greater part of Henry Ferguson's journal was privately printed in Hartford in 1924. The book also includes extracts from Sanuel Ferguson's journal.

JOURNAL OF SAMUEL FERGUSON, Stamford, Connecticut

DAILY MEMORANDUM BOOK FOR 1866 . . . published annually by Francis & Loutrel, New York.

An identical memorandum book.
Samuel Ferguson wrote more fully than his younger brother Henry, but omitted quite a number of days toward the end and no entries are recorded after July 21, 1866. The original is in the possession of the descendants of Henry L. Ferguson of Fishers Island, New York, a descendant of Henry Ferguson. The privately printed version of Henry Ferguson's journal includes only that part of Sanuel Ferguson's journal covering the longboat voyage and arrival at Hawaii, i.e. May 3 to June 25, 1866.

PRINTED SOURCES — THE JOURNALS

Mitchell, Josiah A. THE DIARY OF CAPTAIN JOSIAH A. MITCHELL, Hartford: Privately printed, c. 1927.

Captain Mitchell's pocket diary, January 2, 1866 to December 31, 1866, memoranda, accounts, clippings, etc. as described above.

Ferguson, Henry. THE JOURNAL OF HENRY FERGUSON, JANUARY TO AUGUST 1866. Hartford: Privately printed by the Case, Lockwood & Brainard Co. for Samuel Ferguson [II], 1924.

Henry Ferguson's journal, January 1 to August 13. Letters written from Hawaii June 18, 1866. Newspaper account from the Stamford ADVOCATE of August 17, 1866, taken from the Sacramento DAILY UNION. Samuel Ferguson's journal, May 3 to June 25, 1866, as described above.

Brown, Alexander Crosby. "The HORNET Journals." THE AMERICAN NEPTUNE (Vol I, No. 2), April 1941, pp. 164-165.

PRINTED SOURCES — THE SHIP

Clark, Arthur H. THE CLIPPER SHIP ERA. New York: Putnam's 1910.

Cutler, Carl C. GREYHOUNDS OF THE SEA: THE STORY OF THE AMERICAN CLIPPER SHIP, with a Foreword by Charles Francis Adams, Secretary of the Navy, 1929-1933. New York: G.P. Putnam's Sons, 1930. Reprinted Annapolis: United States Naval Institute, 1961.

Records of the California passages of the HORNET, 1851-1866, pp. 184, 193, 236, 253, 254, 255, 276, 333, 368, 416, 462, 481, 490, 496, 501, 514, 518.

Forbes, Allan, and Eastman, Ralph M. OTHER YANKEE SHIP SAILING CARDS: PRESENTING THE COLORFUL CARDS ANNOUNCING SHIP SAILINGS . . . Boston: State Street Trust Company, 1949.

The HORNET, pp. 48 - 52.

Howe, Octavius T., M.D., and Matthews, Frederick C. AMERICAN CLIPPER SHIPS. Salem: Marine Research Society, Publication No. 13, 1926.

The HORNET, Vol. I, pp. 268 - 272.

PRINTED SOURCES — REPORTING THE EVENT, NEWSPAPERS AND MAGAZINE ARTICLES

PACIFIC COMMERCIAL ADVERTISER, Honolulu, Hawaii
June 23, 1866. "Ship Burned at Sea."
June 29, 1866. "Loss of the HORNET" — Captain Mitchell's letter dated June 18 to the U.S. Consul, Honolulu, from Laupahoehoe, Hawaii.
June 30, 1866. "Burning of the American Ship HORNET." First detailed account of the disaster, from the testimony of Third Mate Thomas and Seaman Clough.

SACRAMENTO DAILY UNION, Sacramento, California
July 16, 1866. Postscript to Mark Twain's Letter No. 14, dated Honolulu, June 22, 1866, announcing the disaster.
July 19, 1866. "Letter from Honolulu. Burning of the Clipper Ship HORNET at Sea. Detailed Account of the Sufferings of Officers and Crew, as given by the Third Officer and Members of the Crew." Mark Twain's Letter No. 15, dated Honolulu, June 25, 1866.

Mark Twain's letters to the SACRAMENTO DAILY UNION are reprinted in John W. Vandercock, LETTERS FROM HONOLULU. Honolulu: Thomas Nickerson, 1939; A. Grove Day, MARK TWAIN'S LETTERS FROM HAWAII, New York: Appleton-Century, 1966.

STAMFORD ADVOCATE, Stamford, Connecticut
August 17, 1866. "The SACRAMENTO DAILY UNION publishes a letter from Honolulu. . ."

Reprint of Mark Twain's Letter No. 15 of June 25, 1866. Reprinted in JOURNAL OF HENRY FERGUSON. Hartford: Privately Printed, 1924, pp. 145-159.

HARPER'S WEEKLY, New York, N.Y.
September 29, 1866. "Burning of the Clipper HORNET." (Vol. 10, No. 509, pp. 614, 616).

An account based on the SACRAMENTO DAILY UNION report of July 19, 1866, from the testimony of Third Mate Thomas and Seaman Clough, plus a full page woodcut view of the burning ship. Reprinted in THE RUDDER MAGAZINE (Vol. 23), 1910, p. 392.

HARPER'S NEW MONTHLY MAGAZINE, New York, N.Y.
   December 1866 (Vol. 34), pp. 104 - 113. "Forty-Three Days in an Open Boat. Compiled from Personal Diaries," by Mark Swain.

   Mark Twain's account (mislabeled Swain) dated Honolulu, Sandwich Islands, July 2, 1866, based on the journals of Captain Mitchell and the Ferguson Brothers which he copied on the ship bringing them from Honolulu to San Francisco. Rewritten by Mark Twain for Century Magazine, November 1899 (Vol. 59, No. 1) pp. 76-88: "My Début as a Literary Person."

PRINTED SOURCES — MARK TWAIN'S SUBSEQUENT ACCOUNTS AND COLLECTED WORKS

Mark Twain, "My Début as a Literary Person." CENTURY MAGAZINE (Vol. 59, No. 1), November 1899, pp. 76 - 88.

   Mark Twain re-wrote his HARPER'S MONTHLY, December 1866, article based on the journals of Captain Mitchell and the Ferguson Brothers. This article appears in his Collected Works in the volume entitled THE MAN THAT CORRUPTED HADLEYBURG AND OTHER STORIES AND ESSAYS. New York: Harper & Brothers, Publishers, 1901.

Howells, William Dean, and Perry, Thomas Sergeant. LIBRARY OF UNIVERSAL ADVENTURE BY SEA AND LAND, compiled and edited by Howells and Perry. New York: Harper & Brothers, 1893.

   By "S. L. Clemens, Honolulu, Sandwich Islands, July 2, 1866." pp. 965 - 980. Reprint of the HARPER'S MONTHLY, December 1866 article.

Mark Twain. THE MAN THAT CORRUPTED HADLEYBURG AND OTHER STORIES AND ESSAYS. New York: Harper & Brothers, publishers, 1901.

   "My Debut as a Literary Person." pp. 84 - 127. Reprinted from the CENTURY MAGAZINE, November 1899 article.

Paine, Alfred Bigelow. MARK TWAIN'S LETTERS. Arranged, with Comment. New York: Harper & Brothers. Two vols. 1917.

   HORNET correspondence, pp. 108, 109, 112, 114, 115, 116.

Vandercook, John W. LETTERS FROM HONOLULU, WRITTEN FOR THE SACRAMENTO UNION BY MARK TWAIN. Introduction by Vandercook, Honolulu: Thomas Nickerson, 1939.

   I. "The Burning of the Clipper Hornet."

Day, A. Grove. MARK TWAIN'S LETTERS FROM HAWAII. Edited and with an Introduction by A. Grove Day. New York: Appleton-Century, 1966, pp. 135-160.

   "Burning of the Clipper Ship HORNET at Sea: Detailed Account of the Sufferings of Officers and Crew, as Given by the Third Officer and Members of the Crew." Honolulu, June 25, 1866. Mark Twain's "scoop" from the SACRAMENTO DAILY UNION, July 19, 1866, page 1.

PRINTED SOURCES — SECONDARY ACCOUNTS (ARRANGED CHRONOLOGICALLY)

Irvine, Legh H. "The Lone Cruise of the HORNET Men: The Personal Narrative of Frederick Clough." THE WIDE WORLD MAGAZINE, London (Vol. 5, No. 30), September 1900, pp. 571 - 577.

Waldo, Harold. "Yankee Captain and Southern Pilot." OVERLAND MONTHLY AND OUT WEST MAGA-ZINE, May 1924, pp. 199, 200, 201, 233.

Biographical sketch of Captain Mitchell and Mark Twain's connection with the disaster.

Rowe, William Hutchinson. SHIPBUILDING DAYS ON CASCO BAY, 1727-1890. Yarmouth, Maine, 1929.

Chapter XIV, pp. 197 - 198: "Forty-Three Days in an Open Boat."

Hall, James Norman. THE TALE OF A SHIPWRECK. Boston and New York: Houghton Mifflin Company, 1934.

A letter to Hall from Marian Mitchell, a granddaughter of Captain Mitchell, relating the story of the HORNET'S longboat voyage, is printed pp. 128 - 133. It is significant to note that when the three volumes comprising THE BOUNTY TRILOGY were published (Boston: Little, Brown and Company, 1936), Hall and Nordhoff dedicated the second volume, MEN AGAINST THE SEA, describing Captain Bligh's famous voyage in the BOUNTY launch, "To the Memory of Captain Josiah Mitchell of the Clipper Ship HORNET..."

Macdonald, Alexander. "The Sea Spared Fifteen." Honolulu ADVERTISER. Magazine section, November 29, December 6, 1936.

A fictional account.

Bragdon, George W. "Epic of the HORNET'S Men: 43 days in an open boat." The Hartford TIMES, Monday, November 27, 1939.

THE LOOKOUT, Seamen's Church Institute of New York. "The Clipper Ship HORNET" (Vol. 30, No. 9), September 1939, pp. 4 - 6.

THE LOOKOUT. "Seventy Days in an Open Boat." December 1940, pp. 12, 13

Comparison of the voyage of the lifeboat of the steamship ANGLO-SAXON, 1940, with the HORNET'S longboat, 1866.

Parmenter, Charles. "Clipper Ship HORNET." THE LOOKOUT, New York. (Vol. 31, No. 9), September 1940, pp. 3 - 5.

Reprinted from an article in THE NEW YORK TIMES, July 7, 1940. The cover of THE LOOKOUT reproduces an oil portrait of the HORNET as recently restored for the Seamen's Church Institute of New York.

Thurston, Florence G., and Cross, Harmon S. THREE CENTURIES OF FREEPORT, MAINE. Freeport: 1940, pp. 93 - 123.

Chapter XX, Capt. Josiah A. Mitchell.

Roos, William. THE HORNET'S LONGBOAT. Boston: Houghton Mifflin Co., 1940.

This book presents a fictional treatment of the voyage principally based on the journal of Captain Mitchell, who is the narrator of the story.

William, S. Barnitz, editor "The Hornet's 21-foot longboat . . . sailed 4000 miles in 43 days. Her captain was Josiah Angier Mitchell, an Alumnus of Hebron Academy." HEBRON SEMESTER, Hebron, Maine (Vol. 2, No. 2) Spring 1956, pp. 20 - 24.

Crane, J. R. "They Rowed Four Thousand Miles." THE LOOKOUT (Vol. 61, No. 6), July - August 1970, pp. 11 - 13.

Note: The Nineteenth Century Woodcuts of sea birds, fishes, etc. used as decorations in the text have been taken from the following sources:

BALLOU'S PICTORIAL DRAWING ROOM COMPANION, Oct. 6, 1855, "Voyage of an American Clipper Ship."

P. H. GROSSE, The Ocean, PHILADELPHIA, 1856.

THE REV. H. MARTYN HART, TRANSLATOR, The World of The Sea. (ORIGINALLY Le Monde de la Mer, BY MONS. MOQUIN TANDON) LONDON, CASSELL, 1882.

SIR WILLIAM JARDINE, EDITOR, The Naturalists Library - Mamalia. VOL. VI, EDINBURGH, 1837.

DAVID STARR JORDAN AND BARTON WARREN EVERMANN, The Shore Fishes of Hawaii. RE-PRINT OF Bulletin of the U.S. Fish Commission FOR 1903 (VOL. 23) RUTLAND AND TOKYO, 1973.

JOHN STERLING KINGSLEY, EDITOR, The Riverside Natural History. VOL. V, MAMMALS, BOSTON 1884.

The Monsters of the Deep and Curiosities of Ocean Life. LONDON, 1875.

GENIO C. SCOTT, Fishing in American Waters, NEW YORK, HARPER, 1869.

INDEX

Index Of Ships

*NOTE: Illustrations are indicated *

Index Of People, Places And Marine Life

NOTE: Illustrations are indicated *